Re-Envisioning the Publi Research University

This volume explores the numerous and competing demands that face America's public research universities and considers how institutions and their leaders can best navigate this challenge to ensure longevity, relevance, and success on the local, national, and global stage.

Today's public research universities have the unique challenge of responding to new societal pressures and policies, while remaining true to their core educational missions and values. Highlighting the multiple roles that universities must now fulfill—as institutions of higher learning, as research bodies, as institutions with global reputations, and as organizations that serve the public—the volume asks how they can best evolve in the rapidly changing education landscape. Tackling subjects such as faculty culture, the role of technology, financial sustainability, institutional identity, diversity, and organizational development, chapters identify innovative and transformative mechanisms for acclimatizing the public research university to current educational, academic, and societal needs.

This text will benefit researchers, academics, and educators with an interest in higher education, educational reform and policy, and the sociology of education more broadly.

Andrew Furco is Associate Vice President for Public Engagement and Professor of Higher Education in the Department of Organizational Leadership Policy and Development at the University of Minnesota, USA.

Robert H. Bruininks is President Emeritus and Professor Emeritus of the University of Minnesota, USA.

Robert J. Jones is Chancellor at the University of Illinois at Urbana-Champaign, USA.

Kateryna Kent is Assistant Director of Public Engagement Research and Assessment in the Office for Public Engagement at the University of Minnesota, USA.

Routledge Research in Higher Education

Higher Education in the Gulf
Quality Drivers
Edited by Reynaldo Gacho Segumpan and John McAlaney

Establishing an Experimental Community College in the United States
Challenges, Successes, and Implications for Higher Education
Chet Jordan

Research Methods in English Medium Instruction
Edited by Jack K.H. Pun and Samantha M. Curle

Understanding Individual Experiences of COVID-19 to Inform Policy and Practice in Higher Education
Helping Students, Staff, and Faculty to Thrive in Times of Crisis
Edited by Amy Aldous Bergerson and Shawn R. Coon

Re-Envisioning the Public Research University
Navigating Competing Demands in an Era of Rapid Change
Edited by Andrew Furco, Robert Bruininks, Robert J. Jones, and Kateryna Kent

Campus Service Workers Supporting First-Generation Students
Informal Mentorship and Culturally Relevant Support as Key to Student Retention and Success
Edited by Georgina Guzmán, La'Tonya Rease Miles, and Stephanie Santos Youngblood

For more information about this series, please visit: www.routledge.com/Routledge-Research-in-Higher-Education/book-series/RRHE

Re-Envisioning the Public Research University

Navigating Competing Demands in an Era of Rapid Change

Edited by Andrew Furco, Robert H. Bruininks, Robert J. Jones, and Kateryna Kent

NEW YORK AND LONDON

First published 2022
by Routledge
605 Third Avenue, New York, NY 10158

and by Routledge
2 Park Square, Milton Park, Abingdon, Oxon, OX14 4RN

Routledge is an imprint of the Taylor & Francis Group, an informa business

Library of Congress Cataloging-in-Publication Data
Names: Furco, Andrew, editor.
Title: Re-envisioning the public research university : navigating competing demands in an era of rapid change / [edited by] Andrew Furco, Robert H. Bruininks, Robert J. Jones, and Kateryna Kent.
Description: New York, NY : Routledge, 2022. | Series: Routledge research in higher education | Includes bibliographical references and index.
Identifiers: LCCN 2021028834 | ISBN 9781032150888 (hardback) | ISBN 9781032145730 (paperback) | ISBN 9781315110523 (ebook)
Subjects: LCSH: Public universities and colleges--United States--Administration. | Education, Higher--United States--Planning. | Education, Higher--Aims and objectives--United States. | Higher education and state--United States.
Classification: LCC LB2341 .R37 2022 | DDC 378/.050973--dc23
LC record available at https://lccn.loc.gov/2021028834

ISBN: 978-1-032-15088-8 (hbk)
ISBN: 978-1-032-14573-0 (pbk)
ISBN: 978-1-315-11052-3 (ebk)

DOI: 10.4324/9781315110523

Typeset in Garamond
by KnowledgeWorks Global Ltd.

Contents

Tables

Figures

Contributors

Heidi Lasley Barajas is Associate Professor and former Chair of the Department of Organizational Leadership, Policy, and Development in the College of Education and Human Development at the University of Minnesota. Her primary research and teaching focus on the transformation of educational institutions through the contexts of diversity, engagement, and leadership.

Burton A. Bargerstock is Executive of the Office of Public Engagement and Scholarship, Director of Communication and Information Technology, and Special Adviser to the Associate Provost for University Outreach and Engagement at Michigan State University. His work focuses on institutional research, culture, and communication related to community-engaged scholarship and university outreach.

Karen Brown is Director of the Interdisciplinary Center for the Study of Global Change at the University of Minnesota. Her work focuses on fostering interdisciplinary and global education and research related to global social justice. Her research interests center on gender and international policy.

Robert H. Bruininks is President Emeritus and Professor Emeritus of the University of Minnesota. His primary research and related interests focus upon civic leadership, development of human capital from early childhood through postsecondary education, policy and reform of education, developmental assessment, and advancing opportunity for people with disabilities.

Diane D. Craig is a Research/Data Analyst at the University of Florida and Research Associate at the Center for Measuring University Performance, University of Massachusetts Amherst and Arizona State University. Her primary interest is using reliable institutional data to measure performance, show impact, and support improvement.

Laurie Van Egeren is Interim Associate Provost for University Outreach and Engagement at Michigan State University. She studies applied development and evaluates intervention programs.

Hiram E. Fitzgerald is University Distinguished Professor in the Department of Psychology and the former Associate Provost for University Outreach and Engagement at Michigan State University. His primary research interests focus on the etiology of alcohol use disorders, fathers and boys at risk, and university-community partnerships focused on systems change.

Andrew Furco is Associate Vice President for Public Engagement and Professor in the Department of Organizational Leadership Policy and Development at the University of Minnesota. His primary research and teaching interests focus on educational reform, experiential learning, and the role of community engagement in primary, secondary, and higher education.

Ann Hill Duin, former Vice Provost and Associate Vice President for Information Technology, serves as Professor of Writing Studies at the University of Minnesota. Her commitment to shared leadership has resulted in collective vision and action: a virtual university, business intelligence/academic analytics initiatives, and numerous inter-institutional partnerships.

Karri A. Holley is Professor of Higher Education Administration and Coordinator of the Higher Education Program at The University of Alabama. Her research interests include graduate and doctoral education, interdisciplinarity, and qualitative inquiry.

Robert J. Jones is the Chancellor at the University of Illinois at Urbana-Champaign. Jones, and Former President of the University at Albany, SUNY. He spent 34 years as a faculty member and senior administrator at the University of Minnesota. He is also an internationally respected authority on plant physiology.

Kateryna Kent is Assistant Director of Public Engagement Research and Assessment in the Office for Public Engagement at the University of Minnesota. Her primary research interests are interdisciplinary engagement collaborations and effective assessments of university-wide engagement.

Erin Konkle is the Director of Civic Engagement at Wellesley College in Massachusetts. Erin's research focuses on assets based community and organizational change. Her practice focuses on the intersection of civic engagement and career development, designing programs that map civic responsibility for social change to every career community and path.

John V. Lombardi is Professor of History and Director of the Center for Measuring University Performance at UMass Amherst and Arizona State University. He works on using reliable data to understand the competitive performance of research universities.

Bruce Maas is Emeritus Vice Provost for IT and Chief Information at the University of Wisconsin-Madison. He is presently serving as Innovation Fellow for Internet2, Partnerships Evangelist for IMS Global, and Honorary Fellow at the University of Wisconsin-Madison School of Information. He has served as a past Board Chair and Faculty Director of the Leadership Institute at EDUCAUSE.

Caryn McTighe Musil, Former Senior Vice President of the office of diversity, equity, and global initiatives at the Association of American Colleges and Universities, is Senior Scholar and Director of Civic Learning. A national speaker, writer, and consultant, she has directed more than two dozen national higher education projects.

John Saltmarsh is Professor of higher education in the Department of Leadership in Education, College of Education and Human Development at the University of Massachusetts, Boston. His primary research interests are the institutionalization of community engagement in higher education and re-theorizing the public good in higher education in an age of neoliberalism.

Lorilee R. Sandmann is Professor Emerita in the College of Education at the University of Georgia and former editor of the *Journal of Higher Education Outreach and Engagement*. Her research, teaching, and consulting focus on leadership and organizational change in higher education with an emphasis on the institutionalization of community engagement and community-engaged scholarship.

Jayne K. Sommers is an Assistant Professor at the University of St. Thomas in St. Paul, Minnesota.

Nichole Sorenson is Dean of Institutional Research, Planning, and Grants at Saint Paul College. Previously, she served as a research and policy analyst with the Minnesota Office of Higher Education, where she was responsible for student health and safety reporting as well as research on persistence, completion, equity, and transitions into and out of postsecondary education.

Jim Thorp served for several years as Communications Officer and Editorial Assistant to former University of Minnesota President Robert H. Bruininks. Today he works as a freelance writer, editor, and speaker, primarily on topics related to his Catholic faith.

Mary Walshok has been an Associate Vice Chancellor, Dean of Extension and Adjunct Professor of Sociology at UC San Diego, one of the nation's top five universities in terms of research funding, for four decades. She has led a number of regional initiatives focused on economic and talent development. She is also an active researcher and author on topics related to the role of research institutions in technology based economic growth and the shifting talent needs of regions authoring more than 100 articles, book chapters and reports as well as six books, most notably Knowledge Without Boundaries, the topic of her chapter.

David Weerts is Professor in the Department of Organizational Leadership Policy and Development at the University of Minnesota. He also serves as Faculty Director for Academic Planning and Programs in the University's Office for Public Engagement. His research and teaching interests lie at the intersection of state-university relations, community engagement, alumni giving, volunteerism, and advocacy.

Brad Wheeler is James H. Rudy Professor of Information Systems in the Kelley School of Business and the former Vice President for Information Technology & CIO at Indiana University. He has led university-wide IT services for Indiana University's eight campuses.

Wim Wiewel is the President of Lewis and Clark College in Portland, Oregon. Previously he was the President of Portland State University. He has written extensively on university real estate development and university-city/community relations.

Nancy L. Zimpher served as the twelfth Chancellor of The State University of New York, the largest comprehensive public university system in the nation, from 2009 to 2017. She is a senior fellow at the Rockefeller Institute of Government and Founder of the Center for Education and Social Systems Change.

Acknowledgments

This volume would not be possible without passion and dedication of countless individuals who assisted us in completing this publication. We extend our gratitude to Abdul Omari who assisted us with the early stages of the volume in organizing some of the main themes that appear in the volume. We feel very privileged to have worked with all the authors and contributors to the volume who dedicated their time, expertise, and a lot of patience. We thank Jessica Neidle for her invaluable insights and contribution to the volume. We are very grateful to Heather Jarrow for her initial review and for guiding us in shaping the volume to align with Research in Higher Education series. We would like to thank the reviewers of the initial manuscript for providing substantive feedback. We thank Karen Adler, Katherine Tsamplantis, Matthew Friberg, AnnaMary Goodall, and Elsbeth Wright for their guidance in shepherding the publication through the editorial process.

Introduction

A Call for Renewal and Transformation

Andrew Furco, Robert H. Bruininks, Robert J. Jones, and Kateryna Kent

When we started working on this manuscript the world looked very different from what it is now. Our initial context was *the public research university in transition* as funding models and demographic shifts were taking hold. We sought to focus on the internal policies, structures, and culture of public research universities and the ways in which these institutions are responding to (or should respond to) these changing societal conditions. It is true that America's public research universities have evolved over the decades to become some of the world's most highly recognizable and sought-after institutions of higher learning. They are consistently listed among the most prominent universities, and they continue to operate some of the most prestigious and most highly regarded academic programs. Originally designed to serve the needs of the respective states that fund them, these universities must now play on the global stage to remain relevant and successful. In addition, whereas these institutions emphasized advanced specialization in traditional academic disciplines, they increasingly are called to provide multidisciplinary strategies to address solutions to society's complex problems while preparing students for a changing workforce. When compared to other types of post-secondary institutions, today's public research universities hold a unique status within the higher education landscape.

However, while on the one hand public research universities are highly revered and are viewed by other higher education institutions as aspirants, they are on the other hand criticized for being overly bureaucratic, unable to adapt easily to new modes of work, and too detached from the everyday needs and issues of the public they are supposed to serve. If there is any doubt that the public is losing confidence in the value or relevance of these institutions, one only needs to point to the steady and precipitous drop over the last two decades in the overall percentage of funding that states allocate to their respective public research universities. Despite ongoing calls for these institutions to transform and adapt more fully to societal changes, public research universities (with a few exceptions) have not been quick to respond.

Across the higher education landscape (and across many other sectors), the arrival of the COVID-19 global pandemic and heightened attention

DOI: 10.4324/9781315110523-1

to issues of systemic racism precipitated by the murder of George Floyd raised the stakes for change and transformation. These cataclysmic events upended the status quo creating a new societal normal that no institution of higher education could ignore. For public research universities in particular, which by definition are situated within the public domain, these and other societal realities tested their genuine commitment and resolve to respond to and adapt to the rapidly changing needs of society. It also tested the extent to which the deep inequalities entrenched in our society, which COVID-19 and Mr. Floyd's murder only further exposed, would be met with real and substantive institutional transformation. In addition to bringing profound changes to how the work of public research universities is conducted and delivered, these crises have engaged those who work in these institutions in critical introspection regarding what the roles, identity, purposes, and values of public research universities are, and what they should be.

Although much of this volume was completed prior to these impactful and sobering events, the changes and path forward proposed in the chapters resonate now more than ever as public research universities face the realities of post-pandemic work, racial reckoning, new forms of social connectedness, community rebuilding, and innovative uses of ever-advancing technologies. Public research universities will need to attend to these and other newly emerging challenges while managing decreased public funding, the diversification of student and faculty populations, the balancing of local and global priorities, and an increased responsibility to ensure educational quality, access, and affordability. To this end, this monograph analyzes the ways in which various key tensions within these institutions are playing out as they search for ways to respond to pressures to adopt new educational practices and institutional priorities while remaining true to the core educational philosophy, mission, and practices that have propelled these universities to the top of the ranks.

The implications of these tensions and competing purposes for contemporary public research universities are many. As large, multi-faceted, complex institutions, they are asked to fill a tall order as *institutions of higher learning* that educate undergraduate and graduate students, as *research universities* that are to compete for limited dollars to conduct significant research that benefits society, as *highly ranked institutions with global reputations* that must maintain high standards and selectivity, as *public institutions* that are to provide great access and openness to the public, as *comprehensive institutions* that are to incorporate a broad range of disciplines within the academy, and in many cases, and as *land-grant institutions* that were established primarily to serve the needs of the state. The multiple identities that public research universities must assume put to the test these institutions' ability to adapt and evolve in nimble and transformative ways that can continue make them relevant and influential in the rapidly changing education landscape. Overlaid on this complexity is the need to adapt and incorporate across these identities several contemporary higher education reform efforts, such as interdisciplinarity, campus-community partnerships, urban-focused development, technological advancement, student diversity, new funding models, and for-profit competition.

In addition to providing an analysis of these various tensions, the monograph offers a futuristic look at how public research universities can best position themselves for continued success in the education landscape. Each chapter identifies a critical institutional issue that today's public research universities face, and the main tensions that undergird the issue. Each chapter is intentionally co-authored, both to provide diverse perspectives on the root causes for the issue's tension(s) and to secure a broad range of recommendations for resolving the tensions. The first two chapters offer a backdrop of how today's public research universities are in transition as they must respond to evolving social, cultural, and financial realities. The subsequent chapters take an in-depth look at how these institutions are reshaping their practices and systems to address specific tensions.

As described throughout the volume, the tensions and demands that public research universities are grappling with are not new. What is new is the need for public research universities to be more nimble and more adaptive as we continue to face an intense pace of rapid change and a redesigned work environment in a post-COVID-19 society, which will require institutional commitments, leadership, and advocates dedicated to fight against structural racism and systemic inequalities. In order to develop these qualities, the volume stresses the need for organizational change that emphasizes novel approaches, such as incentivizing collaborative and interdisciplinary spaces and inviting students, faculty, and community partners to work together to foster entrepreneurship and innovation. Complex problems, such as climate change, racial disparities, and deepened economic inequalities that have been exacerbated in the past couple of decades cannot be solved by siloed disciplines. Addressing these issues calls for interdisciplinary approaches and partnerships not only within public research universities, but also between universities, private and public organizations, and local and global communities.

In addition to re-envisioning disciplinary boundaries in favor of interdisciplinarity, this volume calls for the re-evaluation of traditional academic epistemology in favor of epistemologies that value community engagement and multiple ways of knowing. Even though universities historically have been seen as knowledge holders and places of knowledge production, they need to make space to accommodate a new, diverse cadre of faculty who place emphasis on the scholarship of engagement. This requires integrating community-held knowledge with that of the university, and shifting the focus from research output to research process and societal impact. Moreover, the growing diversification of the student population is placing increased pressure on public research universities to provide learning opportunities that reflect students' cultural, racial, and ethnic experiences and perspectives. Students are no longer passive recipients, but rather active co-creators of knowledge.

During the COVID-19 pandemic, technological advances in higher education took center stage, providing mechanisms for conducting not only teaching and research, but also the broad array of university functions. Holding events in virtual formats helped universities reach a record number of stakeholders, many of whom would not have been able to participate had the events been offered only through an in-person modality. As public research universities chart their paths forward into a post-pandemic future and look for a tangible balance between virtual and in-person operations, this volume offers insights on the impact that changing technologies are having on higher education.

Overall, this volume offers a set of strategies, frameworks, and recommendations that can guide leaders and other professionals situated in public research universities to address these challenges and to guide their institutions to becoming even stronger pillars of higher education. As the authors of the volume suggest, the qualities that need to come to the fore are collaboration, invention, shared knowledge, diversity, interdisciplinarity, and most importantly, commitment to the public good.

As highly regarded, prestigious institutions with an imperative to serve society, public research universities have played and continue to play a unique and important role in higher education. Over the years, America's public research universities have weathered many storms and have persevered through various tumultuous times in our nation's history. Evolution is often slow for these large, iconic institutions. It remains to be seen to what degree they will ultimately heed the current call for renewal and transformation. But no matter where they are in their process of change, one constant should always remain—an unfaltering commitment to the betterment of society as their primary driver.

1 The Multiversity Revisited

The Quest for Institutional Identity in an Era of Rapid Change

Andrew Furco and Kateryna Kent

The Multiversity

Clark Kerr in his treatise, *Uses of the University,* captured the decentralized, multifaceted nature of America's universities with the term "multiversity" (1965, p. 14). Kerr sought to characterize the complex nature of universities that had come into being by the middle of the 20th century. According to Kerr, the multiversity is an internally inconsistent university that seeks to achieve multiple purposes, serve multiple stakeholders, and balance multiple power centers. In essence, the multiversity is a confederation of loosely coupled academic units (i.e., disciplines) bound by institution-wide policies and procedures, but which operate under their own established ways of knowing, academic standards, and scholarly priorities. A consequence of this structure, as Kerr suggests, is that "the university is so many things to so many different people that it must, of necessity, be partially at war with itself" (1965, p. 7).

In recent years, higher education reform efforts have sought to address the multiversity issue and strengthen institutional cohesiveness by promoting cross-unit and interdisciplinary collaborations, centralizing administrative policies, and developing institutional branding initiatives (Martin, 2016). Despite such efforts, the inherently decentralized structure of universities—that is, entities that are organized by academic disciplines rather than by functions—has kept universities operating as multiversities. This is perhaps most evident among today's public research universities, whose missions are being diffused by increasing pressure to fulfill a broader array of purposes, educate a larger percentage of students, respond to the needs and interests of a more diverse group of external stakeholders, while maintaining their prestige and prowess as leading institutions of higher education (Morphew, Fumasoli, & Stensaker, 2018).

Over the last five decades, there has been a global expansion of research universities as the demand for more advanced credentials has increased worldwide (Frank & Meyer, 2007). The increased number of research universities has created greater competition for a shrinking pool of student and faculty talent and research dollars (National Research Council, 2012).

DOI: 10.4324/9781315110523-2

Within public research universities, this competition has catalyzed a seemingly never-ending parade of institutional reforms designed to establish a leading edge over institutional peers. For example, to attract a more diverse student body and to ensure that its educational interests are met, leaders of public research universities have overhauled their curricula and have instituted new majors and innovative instructional practices. To demonstrate that the new knowledge and discoveries are relevant and directly beneficial to society, these leaders are initiating bold interdisciplinary research initiatives designed to address large-scale societal challenges, such as global pandemics, climate change, and systemic social injustices. Other reform efforts have focused on programs that can prepare students better for the changing global workforce, on educational access to a broader array of students, on diversifying the faculty body, on incorporating the latest technologies, on instituting operational and administrative efficiencies, and the list goes on. With an ever-expanding roster of external and internal stakeholders, purposes, and goals to satisfy, today's public research institutions have grown into what Frank and Meyer (2007) characterize as "much enlarged organizations" devoid of a centrality of purpose or identity (p. 22).

Faced with less public funding, shifting legislative priorities, and additional competition with resource-rich private research universities, leaders of public research universities find themselves at crossroads as they struggle to find the right balance between promoting and advancing a core institutional brand and identity, and being attentive and responsive to an ever-expanding list of new demands and expectations from an increasingly diverse group of stakeholders (Morphew et al., 2018). This balancing act requires leaders of public research universities to engage their campuses in the delivery of a wide range of services, which, if not kept in check, can weaken an institution's overall core mission and turn internal systems into fractious "organized anarchies" (Maassen & Stensaker, 2019, p. 457).

In this chapter, we examine how Kerr's concept of the multiversity is playing out in today's public research universities and the different identities public research universities must adopt as they strive to meet increased demands and expectations from internal and external stakeholders. We posit that these demands and expectations have only deepened these universities' status as multiversities, and that the current trend to centralize and consolidate institutional priorities might not be the best strategy for securing the future success of public research universities.

Mission and Identity Diffusion

The persistent multiversity culture of public research universities has taken its toll, not only on these universities' effectiveness and efficiency, but on their overall institutional identity (Henkel, 2016). As Henkel suggests, the presence of a multiplicity of reform priorities obscures institutional direction and purpose. She characterizes this mission diffusion as follows: "The defining characteristic of the 'new multiversities' is diversity … and the concept can still be seen as centered in paradoxes, conflicts, constant interaction, and flux" (p. 207). Disciplinary silos, duplication of efforts and services, lack of shared resources, and absence of a concentrated mission hinder institutional progress (Kezar, 2009). Layered over these challenges are high levels of administrative turnover, situational societal crises, and political divisions. Such disruptions can produce dramatic and abrupt shifts in political winds and institutional priorities that, if mismanaged or not kept in check, can create internal discord, institutional splintering, and mission drift (Weerts, Freed, & Morphew, 2014).

Maassen and Stensaker (2019) found in their research that when managing the challenge of mission and identity diffusion, leaders of public research universities search for ways to build greater institutional cohesiveness that can translate into a recognizable, widely understood institutional identity. To accomplish this, these leaders tend to put in place hierarchical governance and financial structures, branding initiatives, and other administrative policies that elevate institution-wide priorities over the more disparate and specialized interests of individual units. These centralization efforts are sometimes applied explicitly to subdue or even quell the internal warring that Kerr (1965) suggests is an inherent characteristic of multiversities. To demonstrate institutional coordination and centrality of purpose, these efforts are typically accompanied by institutional priority statements or slogans designed to capture, encapsulate, and articulate the institution's core mission and values (Morphew & Hartley, 2006).

However, attempts to centralize operations and policies, especially when presented as a means to simultaneously enhance coordination, optimize efficiency, and advance individual units' goals, can stoke internal skepticism and mistrust. Lucas (2006) reminds us that such sentiments manifest when members of particular departments or academic units perceive such centralization efforts as disempowering or disruptive. In complex systems like those that operate within public research universities, efforts to centralize a broad suite of processes for the sake of organizational efficiency are often not effective in capturing a sufficient scale or scope of the institution's diverse operations (Maassen & Stensaker, 2019). Consequently, various sectors of the institution will ultimately feel excluded, and in turn, these institutional priorities, which are designed to reflect the work of the collective, run the risk of being internally perceived as rhetoric rather than reality (Morphew & Hartley, 2006). Even worse, resentment, lack of buy-in, and disassociation can manifest when espoused institutional priorities lack resonance and relevance among key and influential stakeholders (Kezar, 2009).

To this end, any attempt to encapsulate the true essence of the broad, deep, and layered scope of the multiversity in a few words, a statement, or a logo is likely misguided, if not futile. Rather than extracting and naming a few institutional priorities to describe their institutions' identity or brand, leaders of public research universities instead should embrace and invest in the full suite of identities and missions that characterize and define the complex and multifaceted nature of their multiversities. In other words, the status of public research universities as multiversities is not something that should be suppressed. Rather, it is a defining feature of the public research university of the future, and therefore, it should be leveraged, promoted, and celebrated.

Embracing Competing Missions

Congress defines public research universities as "research intensive, doctorate-granting institutions that receive a share of funding from state and local appropriations and serve as a critical component of the overall higher education landscape". (National Science Board, 2012, p. 2). This group of approximately 200 academic institutions comprise 4.2 percent of America's postsecondary institutions. They include some of the most highly regarded and recognizable universities in the world, such as Berkeley, UCLA, Michigan, University of North Carolina-Chapel Hill, the Ohio State University, just to name a few. They make education accessible to the world's best and brightest students, promote regional and local economic development, produce new research discoveries, and help develop the nation's future workforce (American Academy of Arts and Sciences, 2015). These institutions' long histories of influence have cemented their prominence in American society, playing a crucial role in advancing the nation's educational, social, and cultural agendas. Their faculties include many of the world's most distinguished scholars and scientists, and their alumni include world-renowned inventors, entrepreneurs, political leaders, and celebrities. They also boast athletic prowess through high performing sport teams that attract large number of fans who promote and advance the institutions' brand.

However, public research universities also face much external criticism, as they are often perceived as ivory towers that are disconnected from the needs and issues of everyday society (Lucas, 2006). For example, business leaders lament that graduates of public research universities, in general, do not possess the skills necessary to succeed in a rapidly changing global workforce, and in turn, businesses must spend much money to train newly hired graduates (National Research Council, 2012). Parents express concerns over high tuition costs and lack of affordability. Other stakeholders express concerns over declining academic standards, administrative bloat, and increased commercialization. A consequence of these persistent criticisms has been the steady decline of the public's confidence in and respect for American higher education overall (Bok, 2013; Hersh & Merrow, 2005).

For public research universities in particular, the loss of public confidence may explain why funding for public research universities has been on a precipitous decline over the last 30 years (American Academy of Arts and Sciences, 2015). Since 2001, most states have cut funding for higher education, allocating a lesser portion of the overall state budget to public colleges and universities. Whereas 14.6 percent of the states' general fund spending was allocated to higher education in 1990, the portion of general fund spending for higher education fell to 9.4 percent in 2014 (American Academy of Arts and Sciences, 2015). For public research universities, the cuts have been especially severe. In 1987, on average, 51 percent of public research universities' overall revenues came from state allocations (Chronicle of Higher Education, 2014). By 2001, state allocations had dropped to 30 percent of public research universities' overall revenue. By 2012, the percentage had dropped to 17 percent (American Academy of Arts and Sciences, 2015).

In response, leaders of public research universities have sought to regain the public's confidence and support, primarily through the fallback approach of reaffirming commitments to a core institutional mission and set of priorities (Morphew & Hartley, 2006). Such reaffirmations serve as a way of demonstrating attentiveness to quality assurance, operational efficiency, and fiscal transparency, as well as responsiveness to the needs, expectations, and interests of the broad array of external stakeholders.

Herein lies the struggle that leaders of public research universities face. In attempting to establish a core institutional identity, they must decide on which purpose(s) or institutional goal(s) they forefront and highlight. On the one hand, they must embrace their institutions' identity as public, state-funded entities that need to be responsive to the taxpayers who support them. On the other hand, they need to maintain selectivity, a global footprint, and a competitive research profile brand as highly ranked national and global institutions. In this attempt to codify a core institutional identity, it is unlikely that a diverse cadre of internal and external stakeholders can arrive at a consensus regarding the institution's core purposes, goals, and priorities. If Kerr's characterization of the multiversity as an institution with disparate and competing priorities is true, then efforts to establish a core, central institutional identity that reflects the institution's actual work may prove to be difficult, if not impossible, to accomplish. As Kissel (2011) reminds us, "... the university's mission may say one thing, but its practices all too often demonstrate something else". (p. 434). Therefore, rather than attempting to encapsulate the institution's core purposes and identity into a single slogan or set of priorities, efforts should focus on embracing and articulating the public research university's status as a multiversity—a complex, multifaceted institution that is intentionally and uniquely designed to fulfill a broad and varied set of purposes.

The Centrality of Prestige

Perhaps the most complicating factor for institutional leaders who wish to embrace the multiversity framework is the strong and influential role that prestige plays within public research universities. Public research universities are distinguished by the fact that they "enroll the best students in every state: 87 percent of entering first year students at these institutions are from the top half of their graduating class" (American Academy of Arts and Sciences, 2016, p. 8). Public research universities also offer opportunities for these students to earn the most advanced academic and professional degrees. These purposes contribute to these institutions' sense of importance, prominence, and prestige. Indeed, maintaining high academic prestige and a strong reputation of excellence is especially important for those who lead and work at public research universities. Is it not uncommon to find superlatives such as "largest", "best", "flagship", "top-ranked", and "top-rated" prominently and proudly displayed on public research universities' websites. Comparisons to private, elite universities, such as Harvard and Stanford, are common.

Public research universities' quest for prominence and prestige has long been criticized for measuring institutional success based on ranking systems and research grant funding rather than on the quality of instruction and the societal impact of the research produced (Tuchman, 2009). Critics suggest that the quest for prestige based on rankings stifles innovation. They claim that ranking systems are not strong measures of institution success because they rely on traditional and sometimes arcane institutional metrics rather than on more contemporary, innovative, and transformational practices (i.e., diversity and equity initiatives, community-engaged scholarship, interdisciplinary research) that represent new and expanding areas of work in and across the disciplines (Amsler & Bolsmann, 2012). They also claim that a focus on climbing the rankings downplays the importance of many key and central features that distinguish public research universities from their private peers (Brewer, Gates, & Goldman, 2001).

For example, student selectivity (as measured by the percentage of student applicants accepted for admission) is a common measure used in rankings to measure institutional prestige. The more selective the institution, the higher it is ranked on that measure. Herein lies the challenge for leaders of public research universities, as a balance must be struck between securing prestige (i.e., being highly selective) and ensuring students' access to these publicly funded institutions. Similarly, as taxpayer-supported institutions, public research universities must maintain a local focus and be responsive to the priorities of their state. Yet to maintain their high rank and prestige, they also must demonstrate a robust global prominence and presence. Managing and balancing seemingly diametrical pursuits perpetuate mission diffusion and bring to the fore the challenge of establishing a recognizable, core institutional identity.

In this regard, with a broad range of contemporary tensions and demands before them, leaders of public research universities should move away from settling on a limited set of institutional priorities and purposes to establish institutional focus. Instead, they should embrace and promote the comprehensive and multifaceted character of their institutions. A multiversity's identity should not be tilted in one direction or centered on a limited set of purposes. Rather, multiversities will flourish and succeed when there is capacity and intentionality to meet the broad range of demands and expectations that are upon them. In essence, the distinguishing feature, brand, and identity of the public research university is its multidimensionality. Given the complex and diverse expectations that public research universities must respond to, their status as multiversities should be viewed not as a dysfunction or weakness, but rather should be leveraged to meet ever-increasing and ever-changing internal and external demands and expectations.

The Public Research Multiversity

The multidimensionality of the public research multiversity is held up and supported by a series of foundational pillars, each of which contributes to the institution's overall identity and each of which keeps the institution rooted in a set of purposes. (see Figure 1.1). For a multiversity to thrive, the work within each pillar must be valued, nurtured, invested in, and celebrated (Henkel, 2016). Each pillar supports a distinct set of critical and

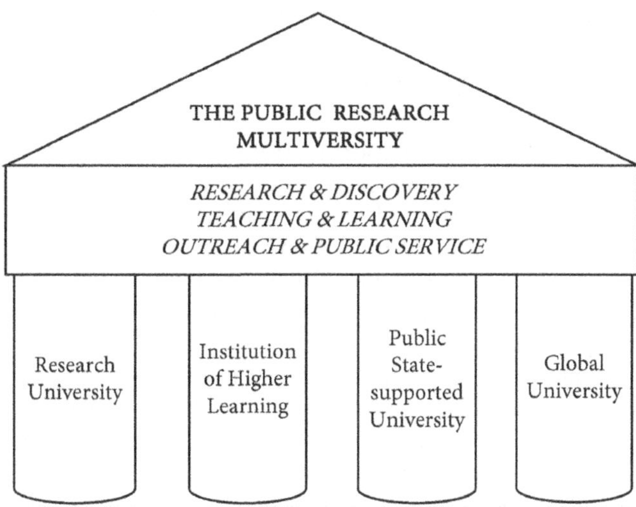

Figure 1.1 The Pillars of the Public Research Multiversity

important goals and expectations that contribute to the institution's overall success. When the multiversity is challenged by high levels of mission diffusion, the pillars serve as anchors that not only ground the institution to its foundation but can serve as guideposts that remind us of the institution's inherent multidimensionality of purpose.

Associated with each pillar are various areas of work that are conducted through particular departments and disciplines, that involve particular stakeholder groups (internal and external), that operate under particular norms of practice, and that have particular measures of success. What is most important is that each pillar is viewed to be an equally important contributor to the viability of the multiversity. Lack of success in one pillar weakens the institution's overall stability and strength. Therefore, attentiveness to each facet of the multiversity's identity is essential for ensuring the multiversity's overall success.

The Public Research Multiversity as a Research University

Public research universities are distinguished from other public institutions of higher education by their emphasis on the production and advancement of research. The production of research and the external revenue procured play a significant role in determining the success, ranking, and prestige of research universities. They have a bearing on an institution's rankings and whether a university is eligible for membership in the elite and exclusive Association of American Universities (AAU), which according to AAU's website are 66 research universities "on the leading edge of innovation, scholarship, and solutions that contribute to scientific progress, economic development, security, and well-being". (Association of American Universities, 2017).

The ways in which faculty deliver their work is also shaped by the institution's identity as a research university. When compared with faculty at other types of higher education institutions, faculty at research universities generally have higher expectations to produce research, garner grants, publish in peer-reviewed journals, and educate graduate students. They also tend to be rewarded more for their research activities than their teaching or outreach efforts (Bok, 2013). At institutions with a strong research identity, research priorities tend to take precedence over other institutional priorities.

For the public research multiversity, the research identity is pervasive, strong, and permeates the institution. Rarely does the public research multiversity turn away or divert from its research focus. As a centerpiece of the institution's work, the research pillar must remain strong if the institution is to maintain its prominence and reputation. This pillar also provides opportunities to leverage needed support for the other institutional pillars. For example, in their study of more than 59,000 students enrolled in 22 universities, Kim, Rhoades, and Woddard (2003) found a positive correlation between the universities' sponsored research expenditures and undergraduate students' graduation (i.e., support for the higher learning pillar).

The Public Research Multiversity as an Institution of Higher Learning

Public research multiversity's role is to not only educate the most talented and brightest undergraduate students in the state, but also to confer terminal academic degrees and certifications. Recent studies reveal public research multiversities award 60 percent of all doctoral degrees, including 72 percent of all doctoral degrees in science and engineering (American Academy of Arts and Science, 2015; Bound, Burga, Khanna, & Turner, 2019). These institutions are also responsible for preparing the lion's share of states' teachers, doctors, lawyers, and other licensed professionals.

The ways in which academic curricula, degree programs, and student support systems are organized and delivered at a public research multiversity influence both the nature of the student body and the type and quality of students' overall academic experience. Some scholars have argued that public research multiversities' emphasis on graduate studies has hampered both the success of undergraduate students and the institutions' capacity to achieve their full potential as institutions of higher learning (Lucas, 2006). A heavy focus on graduate education has long been associated with public research universities that are concerned with prominence and prestige (Brewer et al., 2001). As Brewer and colleagues (2001) note, graduate programs prepare future scholars and professors who can, in turn, bring future prestige and notoriety to the institution.

Websites are good barometers of the image that institutions wish to portray. In coming to terms with their status as multiversities and realizing the importance of having a strong pillar of higher learning, leaders of public research universities are recasting their website content to focus less on research discoveries and more on issues that speak directly to current and prospective students. Interestingly, even when attention is paid to the higher learning pillar, the image-conscious nature of public research multiversities is evident. In their analysis of a broad range of university websites, Saichaie and Morphew (2014) found that to compete in the marketplace, university websites are increasingly targeting prospective undergraduate students with content focused on six themes: academics; campus aesthetics (i.e., campus lawns, architecture); fine arts; intercollegiate athletics; student life; and value (i.e., cost, financial aid, rankings). Questioning the reality of the image portrayed and messages sent by this content, Saichaie and Morphew (2014) write, "Across the sample, students were portrayed as active, attractive, and welcoming. No instances of obese, overweight, or unhappy students appeared in the sample" (p. 519).

In the midst of a global decline in student enrollments, public research multiversities could lose their competitive edge in attracting talented students if there is insufficient attention paid to their important role as student-oriented institutions expected to provide access to quality higher learning. Therefore, multiversity leaders must be strategic in how they balance a focus on research prowess with the advancement of educational access and student success.

The Public Research Multiversity as a Public State-Supported University

As state-funded entities, public research multiversities must adhere to and operate within a set of legislative parameters that define particular areas of academic work funded through taxpayer dollars. Heavily influenced by state-wide political, economic, and cultural shifts, these institutions require nimbleness to respond to the crises and critical issues of the day. The internal clash of purposes inherent in the structure and character of public research multiversities is perhaps most obvious when reconciling the needs and expectations of the state with the passions and nuanced interests of faculty and students. As the American Academic of Arts and Sciences (2015) notes, incompatibilities between faculty members' scholarly interests and the state's research and education priorities frustrate legislators and external stakeholders who seek accountability for the taxpayer dollars that public research universities consume. Therefore, leaders of public research multiversities must be attentive to and place high value on their institutions' status as state-funded entities. This requires investments, commitments, and policies that demonstrate that this pillar is not only valued and championed, but it is as important and critical as the other institutional pillars.

State support for public research universities continues to decline. In turn, institutional leaders question whether this institutional pillar has been irreparably weakened (National Science Board, 2012). Some contend that the decline of state support for public research universities (including land-grant universities) is a response to these institutions' lack of genuine commitment to serve the needs of the state and the broader public (Lucas, 2006). Morphew and Eckel (2009) suggest that as a result of less state support, there is a trend toward the privatization of public universities as these institutions' budgets are increasingly reliant on extramural funding and tuition dollar. Given that state support is at an all-time low and given that there are many other purposes and areas of work that the institutions must attend to, one could argue that leaders of public research multiversities should instead place more emphasis and attention on the other pillars. However, in most cases, states still hold much dominance and power over public universities in that they provide essential funding for salaries, benefits, and buildings, and influence who serves on the institutions' governing boards. Not attending the needs and demands of the state, despite the weak state of this pillar, can jeopardize essential funding that the institution is not likely to secure elsewhere.

As state-funded institutions, public research multiversities have an inherent public mission. While they often stand apart from their local communities with defined campus boundaries, they are in many ways an integral part of the neighborhoods, communities, and regions that surround them. As anchor institutions, public research multiversities shape surrounding communities, influencing everything from housing costs to traffic flows to the availability of cultural opportunities. When compared to private universities, public institutions of higher education are also expected to have broader public engagement, such as offering the public access to their libraries, museums, theater productions, and educational opportunities (Lucas, 2006).

Commitment to the public state-funded university pillar requires ongoing programming and support that may not necessarily be core to the academic mission of the university. With a long history of focusing on research, academic prowess, and selectivity, offering and providing greater institutional access can be a risky prospect for highly ranked public research universities. Not only might it place the institution's reputation at risk, but it might also have financial costs. As O'Meara (2007) explains, student admission selectivity provides economic benefits to an institution as it favors students from upper- and middle-income families who likely require less grant aids than applicants from lower income backgrounds. However, such practices make these universities less affordable and thus less accessible to students from lower income families (O'Meara, 2007). Therefore, leaders of public research multiversities must be proactive in dedicating resources and attention to their institutions' foundation as public, state-funded entities in order to succeed in having their institutions meet the needs of the broad range of external stakeholders they are expected to serve.

The Public Research Multiversity as a Global University

Despite being publicly funded and needing to focus on the needs of the state, public research multiversities must also maintain a global reputation if their prestige and high rankings are to be maintained (Mohrman, Ma, & Baker, 2008). Mohrman and colleagues (2008) suggest that the most highly ranked universities in the world have in place a global mission, are research intensive, engage in worldwide recruitment, and have global collaborations with peer institutions.

Having global visibility and a globally respected brand expands public research multiversities' opportunities to attract the best talent and funding in ways that help maintain the institutions' prominence. Global issues (i.e., climate change, hunger, poverty) can be incorporated into and applied to the priorities of all of the pillars, allowing for the integration of work across the pillars. Indeed, efforts and initiatives that can be applied to and used to advance the work of all the pillars are useful in mitigating mission diffusion and promoting a more coordinated and aligned institutional culture.

The Future of the Public Research Multiversity

Clark Kerr's (1965) idea of the multiversity offers a lens through which we can characterize the expanding, multifaceted roles that public research universities must play to stay relevant, prominent, and financially viable. Although Kerr applied this term to describe the universities of his day, the term continues to have resonance for today's public research universities. As Henkel (2016) reminds us, diversity is at the core of the new multiversity. This diversity is rooted in multiplicity of purposes, visions, expectations, and priorities that are not only varied in scope, but are often incompatible. This diversity has bred mission diffusion and a lack of understanding regarding what public research universities stand for and whom they serve (Henkel, 2016). In response, leaders of public research multiversities have sought to rein in the multiplicity of purposes by developing institution-wide identity statements and by instituting centralized policies and branding initiatives. However, such attempts have been met with skepticism, especially among internal stakeholders, who often view those efforts as rhetoric rather than a depiction of the reality.

Today's public research universities are called to adopt and embrace multiple identities. Such institutions will, at times, be cast as research universities focused on producing new discoveries. At other times, they will be considered institutions of higher learning that promote undergraduate and graduate education programs that educate the populace for productive citizenship and employment. Yet, at other times, they will be viewed as public, state-funded institutions that must provide educational and public access and be responsive to the needs of the state. Then, when needed and when convenient, they will be cast as institutions that have international prominence and attend to global issues.

Looking to the future, the public research multiversity is here to stay. As the educational environment continues to see profound shifts in student bodies, faculty roles, epistemologies, pedagogical practices, and technologies, the public research multiversity will need to adapt to new ways of doing business in order to remain relevant, prominent, and viable. Therefore, rather than working to rein in these changes and expanding purposes, leaders should embrace these new ways of thinking and doing, and incorporate them into the established institutional pillars that define public research universities. To this end, the multiversity concept offers leaders a framework for anchoring the complex work found in today's public research universities. It also provides a means for tackling and responding to the complex higher education changes that public research university leaders are likely to face in the years to come.

References

American Academy of Arts and Sciences (2015). *Public research universities: Changes in state funding. A publication of the Lincoln project: Excellence and access in public higher education.* Cambridge, MA: American Academy of Arts and Sciences.

American Academy of Arts and Sciences (2016). Public research universities: Recommitting to Lincoln's Vision: An educational compact for the 21st century. *A publication of the Lincoln project: Excellence and access in public higher education.* Cambridge, MA: American Academy of Arts and Sciences.

Amsler, S., & Bolsmann, C. (2012). University ranking as social exclusion. *British Journal of Sociology of Education*, 33(2), 283-301.

Association of American Universities (2017, January 9). Main website. Retrieved from https://www.aau.edu/who-we-are/our-members

Bok, D. (2013). *Higher education in America* (Revised ed.). Princeton: Princeton University Press.

Bound, J., Burga, B., Khanna, G., & Turner, S. (2019). *Public universities: The supply side of building a skilled workforce.* Cambridge: National Bureau of Economic Research, 44 pages.

Brewer, D. J., Gates, S. M., & Goldman, C. A. (2001). *In pursuit of prestige: Strategy and competition in U.S. higher education.* New Brunswick: Transition Publishers.

Chronicle of Higher Education (2014). Retrieved March 5, 2016 from https://www.chronicle.com/interactives/statesupport

Frank, D. J., & Meyer, J. W. (2007). Worldwide expansion and change in the university. In G. Krucken, A. Kosmutzky, & M. Torka (Eds.), *Towards a multiversity?: Universities between global trends and national traditions* (pp. 19–44). Transcript Verlag.

Henkel, M. (2016). Multiversities and academic identities: Change, continuities, and complexities. In L. Leišytė, & U. Wilkesmann (Eds.), *Organizing academic work in higher education* (pp. 205–222). London: Routledge.

Hersh, R. H., & Merrow, J. (2005). *Declining by degrees: Higher education at risk.* New York: Palgrave Macmillan.

Kezar, A. (2009). Change in higher education: Not enough, or too much? *Change: The Magazine of Higher Learning, 41*(6), 18–23.

Kim, M. M., Rhoades, G., & Woddard, D. B. (2003). Sponsored research versus graduating students? Intervening variables and unanticipated findings in public research universities. *Research in Higher Education, 44*(1), 51–81.

Kissel, A. (2011). Will universities rediscover their core mission as they shrink? *Academic Questions, 24*(4), 429–437.

Lucas, C. J. (2006). *American higher education: A history* (2nd ed.). New York: Palgrave Macmillan.

Maassen, P., & Stensaker, B. (2019). From organized anarchy to de-coupled bureaucracy: The transformation of university organization. *Higher Education Quarterly, 73*, 456–468.

Martin, B. R. (2016). What's happening to our universities. *Prometheus, 34*(1), 7–24.
Mohrman, K., Ma, W., & Baker, D. (2008). The research university in transition: The emerging global model. *Higher Education Policy, 21*(1), 5–27.
Morphew, C. C., & Eckel, P. D. (Eds.). (2009). *Privatizing the public university: Perspectives from across the academy.* Baltimore: Johns Hopkins University Press.
Morphew, C. C., Fumasoli, T., & Stensaker, B. (2018). Changing missions? How the strategic plans of research-intensive universities in Northern Europe and North America balance competing identities. *Studies in Higher Education, 43*(6), 1074–1088.
Morphew, C. C., & Hartley, M. (2006). Mission statements: A thematic analysis of rhetoric across institutional type. *The Journal of Higher Education, 77*(3), 456–471.
National Research Council (2012). *Research universities and the future of America: Ten breakthrough actions vital to our nation's prosperity and security.* Washington, DC: National Academies Press.
National Science Board (2012). *Diminishing funding and rising expectations: Trends and challenges for public research universities.* Washington, DC: National Science Board.
O'Meara, K. (2007). Striving for what? Exploring the pursuit of prestige. In J. C. Smart (Ed.), *Higher education: Handbook of theory and research* (pp. 121–180). Dordrecht: Springer.
Saichaie, K., & Morphew, C. C. (2014). What college and university websites reveal about the purposes of higher education. *Journal of Higher Education, 85*(4), 499–530.
Tuchman, G. (2009). *Wannabe U: Inside the corporate university.* University of Chicago Press.
Weerts, D. J., Freed, G. H., & Morphew, C. C. (2014). Organizational identity in higher education: Conceptual and empirical perspectives. In M. B. Paulsen (Ed.), *Higher education: Handbook of theory and research* (pp. 229–278). Dordrecht: Springer.

2 Addressing the Gathering Storm of External Forces

Erin A. Konkle, Jayne K. Sommers, Robert H. Bruininks, and Jim Thorp

Until relatively recent times, the public value of higher education has been largely undisputed. The nation's founders saw the value of education for society: colonial governments oversaw primary public education for the masses (Yudof & Callaghan, 2012), and the nation's earliest universities educated clergy for societal benefit (Cole, 2010). Many public universities were established even before territories achieved statehood. Nowhere is this commitment to the value of higher education more obvious than in the nation's public research universities.

The Morrill Act of 1862 became law during the height of the Civil War highlighting a conscious shift in policy toward advancing explicit public purposes in higher education. It provided land and funding to establish state "land grant" colleges and universities throughout the United States. It also expanded higher education as a means of promoting economic development, research with public application, and broader student access. Nevins (1960) suggested that Congress had "a vision of hundreds of thousands of lawyers, doctors, engineers, farm experts, and other professional men scattering fruitfully over the land" (p. 208). While proposed changes to the Morrill Act appear in the Congressional Record as early as 1872, Congress would not redress the Act until the second Morrill Act of 1890 passed. The second Act included funding for Historically Black Colleges and Universities, presaging the Supreme Court decision in *Plessy v. Ferguson* in 1896 endorsing separate but equal education, which was later reversed by the Supreme Court in the landmark case of *Brown v. Board of Education*. This legislation and subsequent laws in the late 19th century influenced the future of higher education in the United States and globally, especially in advancing research and innovation, support and infrastructure, educational opportunity, and public engagement.

In the decades between World Wars I and II, public research universities enjoyed immense growth, expanding educational opportunities for a broader range of citizens. In 1945, as World War II was winding down and American servicemen returned to a saturated job market, Congress passed the Serviceman's Readjustment Act, or G.I. Bill. Intended as a short-term fix for the flooded job market, the G.I. Bill provided funding

DOI: 10.4324/9781315110523-3

for veterans to enroll in postsecondary education. In the years directly following the war, more than two million veterans—approximately one in every eight—enrolled in college (Bound & Turner, 2002). Congress anticipated neither the popularity nor the implications that the Act would have on education (Thelin, 2004), setting a precedent for a significant investment in future federal student aid.

The Morrill Act of 1862 and subsequent legislation signaled a national investment strategy in promoting higher education to advance economic development and the public good. This approach was further codified in legislation and programs that included the National Defense Education Act of 1958 (NDEA), the Higher Education Act of 1965, the establishment of the National Science Foundation (NSF) and the strengthening of the National Institutes of Health (NIH) in the 1950s and 1960s, and the creation of Pell grants, subsidized loans, and tax benefits for students and their families. During the last century, these federal actions were accompanied by significant state investments in higher education as well.

These legislative initiatives expanded access and strengthened the connection between universities and the economy, our democracy, and national advancement, creating an undeniable place for higher education in the public sphere. These policies stimulated a national partnership between government, universities, and the private sector that has elevated U.S. universities to global preeminence. The resulting *multiversity* was not universally embraced (Cole, 2010); however, its impact is evident. In the 2013 Academic Ranking of World Universities, U.S. Institutions were 35 of the top 50 universities in the world—including 17 public research institutions (Academic Ranking of World Universities, 2013). The centrality of universities to U.S. economic growth and quality of life led economist Richard Florida (2004) to assert "the presence of a major research university is a basic infrastructure component of the Creative Economy…and a huge potential source of competitive advantage" (p. 291–292).

This chapter focuses on the dilemmas facing American public research universities, and a re-envisioned future. While this chapter focuses on public research universities, all public universities share a collective responsibility for public value and education. We offer no fervent defense of these institutions, but rather highlight their current tensions and future realities. Finally, we suggest specific ways to strategically lead public universities forward and to leverage their public value and impact for long-term sustainability.

Growing Tensions in Preserving and Renewing Public Research Universities

More recently, society has begun to question the perceived value of higher education. The Pew Research Center (2011) noted that 57 percent of U.S. adults surveyed believe that college is *not* a good value for the money spent, and 75 percent believe that college is too expensive for the average American. Even in the face of increasing calls for job creation, greater innovation, economic development and educated workers, state legislators continue to reduce public funding for public universities. Demands for more accountability and better results often accompany criticism that "greatness" is too costly.

In 2009, the global economic downturn accelerated the new realities facing U.S. higher education (Bruininks, Keeney, & Thorp, 2010), including:

Declining Educational Leadership, Public Funding, and Competitive Advantage

Within the past 30 years, the U.S. has declined in global educational leadership from preK through higher education (Tucker, 2011). This decline has been accompanied by sharp reductions in support of public higher education, particularly in the last decade, producing increased tuition costs and significant growth in student debt (Quinterno, 2012). State appropriations for higher education in the United States should be at least 20 percent higher than current levels had appropriations kept pace with inflation and maintained the same ratio to personal income as in 1977 (Orszag & Kane, 2003). As public funding decreases and tuition costs increase, more is demanded from colleges and universities in terms of service, efficiency and accountability, often increasing the staff and budget required to ensure improved student support, and research compliance (Zemsky, 2010).

Additionally, higher education faces new realities because of its own choices and evolution. Technological advances and institutional inertia have resulted in a proliferation of new higher education providers, leading to mission creep as public, private, and for-profit institutions expand competing programs to attract people and resources.

Changing Demographics

An aging population means future workforce shortages and a growing demand for costly entitlements and services (Peck, 2011), as well as growing financial pressures to shift resources from programs benefiting youth, including higher education, to health care and related needs. These fiscal pressures are a growing threat to our nation's investment in education, economic growth, and quality of life. Future costs of retirement pensions and health care alone are projected to consume 17 percent of U.S. GDP by 2037 (*The America that works,* 2013). At the same time, U.S. schools are serving more students of diverse nationalities and lower income backgrounds who are often less likely to consider—and less prepared for—our schools and higher education (Gillaspy, 2011). The growing achievement gap between less economically advantaged students, combined with inadequate performance of the U.S. preK-12 grade system, poses a real threat to the nation's future economic leadership (Bruininks et al., 2014).

The Changing Labor Market

The United States has evolved from its initial reliance on the natural resource base to industrialized manufacturing to technological innovation for economic growth and development. As a result, in the last several decades the U.S. employment structure has changed dramatically toward more technical and service occupations. This trend toward more technically oriented jobs places a premium upon more advanced and specialized levels of postsecondary education and training. James (1996) has referred to this trend as "smart work", in which "80 percent of the jobs available in the United States …will be cerebral and only 20 percent manual, the exact opposite of the ratio in 1920" (p. 19). The trend toward more technically oriented jobs has been greatly accelerated by the great recession of 2008–2009, and the disruptive effects of technology in selected occupations that eliminated vast numbers of middle management positions (Peck, 2011).

Recent studies show that investing in a college degree yields a high rate of return in terms of employment and lifetime earnings (Pew Charitable Trust, 2012; Toutkoushian et al., 2013). These labor market trends have created increased challenges for recent college graduates, especially in degree programs outside of the sciences, mathematics, health care, technology, and other technically oriented, high-demand positions. Fewer college students are electing liberal arts majors, and more students, parents, and critics are questioning the value of even pursuing higher education. As universities begin to examine the efficiency and effectiveness of what they do, some have begun to question longstanding values, such as academic freedom, equity and diversity, tenure, shared governance, liberal education, public purposes, and even basic research.

Growing Costs and Increasing Debt

Reduced public funding, intense competition, and growing reliance on private-sector support mean universities are operating more like businesses—reducing costs and risk, and increasing efficiency and productivity. Historically, state level support has acted as a subsidy which defrayed costs that would otherwise fall upon students and their families. A recent analysis showed, "the total state revenues have declined due to both recessionary shortfalls and the failure of states to modernize their revenue systems to collect the resources needed to finance the services demanded by the public" (Quinterno, 2012, p. 18). State funding of higher education declined 26.1 percent from 1990 to 2010. For many universities, it is difficult to raise tuition enough to offset cuts in state support, as "a given percentage reduction in state appropriations requires a much larger percentage increase in tuition, since state appropriations continue to represent a much larger share of public university revenue than tuition" (Quinterno, 2012, p. 22).

To bridge the gap between rising cost and available financial aid, students borrow higher amounts from federal loan programs and private sources. Outstanding student loan debt has grown by a factor of 4.5 since 1999 (Quinterno, 2012). In 2007–2008, 25 percent of public four-year university students who maxed out their Stafford Loan eligibility took out private loans, while 18 percent relied on additional borrowing on the part of their parents (p. 28). More students come from low- and moderate-income families, the groups most affected by these factors. Financial motivations also exist for enrolling on a part-time basis to create more time for work. This decreases chances of graduation and often increases higher education costs, and debt, as students are less committed to the experience and less likely to fully value the benefits of timely completion of degrees.

The Disruptive Impact of Technology

Technology has redefined university cost structures, requiring creative funding strategies as state support declines; but it also creates important opportunities for higher education to expand and innovate in its reach and impact. These opportunities create new dilemmas related to leveraging opportunities in learning processes and credentialing, and shifts in costs and revenues. Broadly speaking, roughly 80 percent of universities' expenditures relate to four main cost drivers—human resources, facilities, information technology (IT), and financial aid—all of which impact an institution's ability to deliver on its academic mission.

Higher education has experienced an unprecedented increase in the use of IT in the past three decades; largely because of the IT revolution, which, between 1978 and 2008, put a computer on every desk. Public higher education must not only find creative ways to effectively use these emerging technologies, but also creative ways to fund them. The impact of technological innovation and research on teaching and learning will also permit the expansion and distribution of content and experience beyond institutional affiliations, greatly expanding learning opportunities while also further fueling competition.

Public Engagement

Public research universities are unique among institutions in their missions and expressed public value. Within research universities, land-grants were especially intended to be learning centers, accessible to all in the state, from which students would return to their communities of origin to share their knowledge for the good of the whole (Gee, 2012). As the world becomes increasingly "flat" (Friedman, 2005) and connected, research universities have expanded to include a global perspective (Schulenburger, 2012). The Kellogg Commission on the Future of State and Land-grant Universities (2000) describes what they call a *covenant* between research universities, including land-grant institutions, and society at large, positing that these institutions hold an almost sacred and irreplaceable position to enhance the public good. However, recent decreases in funding for most public research universities suggest the need for a strengthened dialogue about the new realities of higher education (Kezar, Chambers, & Burkhardt, 2015).

Public research universities have *inherent public value*: a research university exists to preserve, advance, distribute, and apply knowledge to improve the human condition. Public universities served 7.7 million students in 2009 and awarded nearly two-thirds of all bachelor's degrees in the United States—significantly more than U.S. private universities and for-profit providers (National Center for Education Statistics, 2011a). Universities contribute more to society than an educated populace. They also change the way individuals perceive and experience society (Meynhardt, 2009), and they convey other public and private, social and economic benefits (Habley et al, 2012).

The six new realities above create tensions, but also suggest creative ways to reduce costs and increase the public value and impact of higher education. Vast opportunities are emerging to extend and improve learning opportunities, and advances in science and technology are creating deeper connections among fields of study that hold great promise for resolving some of society's most vexing challenges. These dilemmas and opportunities are magnified by emerging global trends in higher education, including increased investment in higher education and research abroad, new funding and student aid models, and increased U.S. regulation of international student and scholar visas. These trends suggest that U.S. universities must act with purpose to maintain and strengthen their quality, affordability and global leadership, so much a part of the Nation's past comparative advantage in an increasingly global economy.

Strengthening Commitment to Public Purposes and Enhancing Global Leadership

Public research universities preserve and strengthen public value through their commitment to addressing challenging questions and problems. This responsibility is more difficult in turbulent economic times, when budgetary and political pressures constrain discretionary resources and push universities to reconsider activities that yield public value but are viewed as less central or economically viable. Unless the creation of public value is a key priority of institutions of higher education, their engagement agenda is often less strategic and episodic, further reducing public commitment, public support, and public understanding.

While several universities have pushed for a resurgence of the public engagement mission of U.S. higher education, the act of guiding such resurgence poses significant challenges to institutional leaders. Votruba (2005) argues that for engagement to influence institutional culture, leadership must tie engagement directly to the institutional mission statement, and use *level of engagement* as a criterion for evaluating high-level leadership personnel. He argues for campus guides that implement specific policies and procedures (e.g., faculty tenure decisions) that promote, support, and reward engagement initiatives.

The public looks to higher education to address significant challenges facing society at large, including the strengthening of human capital and a culture of innovation. Academic freedom, one of higher education's most cherished values, provides a unique space for addressing contentious global problems, ranging from the social to the scientific. Cole (2010) notes the many profoundly important university discoveries that have significantly advanced U.S. economic development and quality of life. This evolution in the U.S. of research universities that advance knowledge, innovation, and educational opportunity is the highest aspiration and realization of the Morrill Land Grant Act.

Cole also makes clear the value of academic freedom by imagining a world in which it does not exist: "If we threaten academic freedom and free inquiry, we threaten the ability of universities to make great discoveries, and we potentially sacrifice the fruits of both the transmission of knowledge and the creation of new knowledge—knowledge on which our society greatly depends" (p. 347). Institutional leaders must cultivate key stakeholders as allies for public engagement. In advancing ideas and important solutions to our society's most vexing challenges, policy-makers, legislators, and lobbyists need to provide substantial support to engagement programs and engaged institutions (Gilliland, 2005). The National Academies report (Augustine, 2007) and the subsequent signing of the American COMPETES Act by President Obama are promising steps in this direction (Holdren, 2011), promoting research, technology transfer, and advancement of human capital for a more competitive, global economy. Additional support from professional associations, to which faculty turn for recognition and validation in their respective disciplines, can also help establish public engagement as a valued and valid research practice (Gilliland, 2005).

Access and Affordability

For more than 150 years, U.S. public universities have provided exceptionally broad access to higher education for students from all socioeconomic backgrounds, becoming the nation's most productive source for the development of human capital. Goldin and Katz (2007) suggest that *universal* access to postsecondary education will be key to keeping the U.S. competitive in the global economy of the 21st century; at the same time, our population of prospective college students is shifting to cultural and socioeconomic groups who have traditionally been less prepared for the rigors of higher education (Bowen, Chingos, & McPherson, 2009). Our national and global long-term success will increasingly depend upon the ability to shepherd more (and more diverse) students through our higher education systems than ever before. While potential students and their families debate whether college is "worth it", most agree that a postsecondary degree will enhance economic progress and improve quality of life (Baum & Payea, 2011). Given the new economic realities of higher unemployment rates, family incomes failing to keep up with inflation, eroding investments, and rising college costs, an examination of student financial aid is of vital importance to sustaining the future of public research universities. While potential students and their families debate whether college is "worth it", most agree that a postsecondary degree will improve quality of life (Baum &Payea, 2011).

Many strategies can help resolve the issues of affordability in public higher education. As state funding for public universities has diminished, many institutions have begun to depend more than ever on tuition revenue, shifting to a higher tuition, higher aid financial model that depends more heavily on the availability of state and federal financial aid as well as institutional grants and scholarships to preserve broad access. The tension between the need to grow tuition as a university's most predictable and flexible source of revenue and the need to provide affordable access requires creative resolution. Charging higher tuition not only requires higher aid for students with financial need, but also requires universities to demonstrate higher value to students and their families. This can be accomplished by improving the quality of education and academic support, raising completion rates, reducing time to degree, and better managing the total net cost of education for students. These efforts, in turn, require a careful reexamination of college preparation and admission standards, academic advising and intervention, student service, and more.

Helping students graduate in four years (or even less) increases institutional capacity, enabling universities to serve a higher volume of students over time with the same faculty, staff, and space to better address issues of developmental disparities, the achievement gap, and college readiness. By addressing issues of P-20 articulation and progression through additional graduate/professional education—along with issues of affordability, student debt, and time to degree—public higher education can help create a higher capacity P-20 pipeline producing a well-educated, highly skilled, diverse, and employable workforce that will attract economic investment.

The increasing level of student debt now totals more than $1 trillion (Hechinger & Lorin, 2012), and has led to high loan default rates by students—currently one in ten. It is obvious that the government must continue to encourage increased long-term savings by families to reduce higher education debt levels. If significant numbers of students default on their loans, the economy is unable to replenish capital at a healthy rate, and opportunities for others to access higher education are mortgaged. It is obvious that the government must continue to encourage increased long-term savings by families to reduce higher education debt levels. But public higher education must be also more vigilant in reducing waste and in encouraging affordability and timely degree completion, not only because of the economic impact, but also because of the ethical and opportunity costs for future students and society. It is also incumbent upon government and our institutions to reduce excessive loan default trends in particular institutions.

To improve the public value of U.S. higher education, it may be time for the federal government and our states to strengthen the connection of tuition, financial aid, and loan repayment more closely to long-term earnings or the specific field or career a student pursues. In Australia, for example, students repay loans via a supplementary tax calculated from their level of taxable income and only when the student has adequate income to do so (Jones, 2011). The "Pay as You Earn" plan recently implemented by President Obama makes strides toward addressing the issue of student loan payment relative to income (Federal Student Aid, 2012). The federal government and the states also must demand greater accountability from higher education including more reasonable net costs and loan repayment. The issues of college readiness, costs and debt are shared responsibilities of students and families, higher education providers, and the government. Programs of this nature will not only reduce indebtedness and default rates, but could also be modified to provide incentives for students to pursue degrees and careers in higher demand fields, such as family medical practice, with less regard to expected income.

Net Costs and Financial Aid

To alleviate the growing challenge of access and affordability, some public research universities have joined states and private institutions to expand internal financial assistance to students. While need-based aid continues as the dominant form of financial assistance, universities are increasingly seeking to improve their academic profiles by focusing on merit-based aid and scholarships, and many states have also begun a shift toward merit-based financial aid programs. This trend often restricts opportunity by rewarding talented students who have access to good schools and stronger academic, community and family support at the expense of talented students who do not. In 1984, for example, 90 percent of state-based aid was awarded based on need; by 2005, this proportion had dropped to 80 percent (Doyle, 2010). Dynarski (2003) and Heller (2002) argued that the creation of large merit-based programs reveal a shift in priority for states, away from improving access, particularly for the middle class. Public research universities have an especially important role in addressing this challenge, since they educate most U.S. students and an affordable four-year degree is one of the best strategies to promote economic mobility (Pew Charitiable Trusts, 2012).

Public concern about the rising cost of higher education has increased substantially in recent decades (Akers et al, 2015; Pew Charitable Trusts, 2012). The rise in student debt is real, but the level of discussion among political leaders and in the popular press is often distorted in relationship to the facts. Nearly half of the reported debt is attributable to the rising debt loads of students who have pursued graduate and professional education for careers that are related to higher postgraduate earnings. Furthermore, the debt load and loan repayments represent a relatively modest impact upon living expenses compared to primary living costs for most students (Akers et al, 2015). There are clear challenges in student debt, particularly for students from modest economic circumstances who do not actually complete requirements and graduate, and those students whose debt has been incurred through private loans with higher market rates and without favorable repayment provisions.

A wake-up call came in 2003, when the state of Minnesota cut $185 million for the following biennium to the University of Minnesota—the deepest single budget reduction in history. In the next several years, the university experienced two more deep state cuts, reducing state support from approximately 30 percent to approximately 16 percent of the University's overall annual operating budget within the decade (2001–2011). These reductions, adjusted for inflation, reduced state support for the University in 2011 to 1998 levels.

Beginning in 2003, the university made scholarship support its top fundraising priority, launching the Promise of Tomorrow Scholarship Drive, establishing a matching funds strategy to encourage giving and multiply the impact of scholarship gifts, and inaugurating the U Promise (Need-based) Scholarship by reallocating internal resources to ensure that low- to moderate-income Minnesota students could afford a University of Minnesota education (now up to an adjusted annual family income of $125,000). As of 2011, the Promise of Tomorrow Scholarship Drive had raised about $350 million in private support for scholarship endowments, with rates of giving seven to ten times higher than previous averages. The university even leveraged the football stadium campaign to grow student funding: every major fundraising "ask" included a request for academic support, garnering about $70 million in additional contributions to support scholarships and other academic priorities. The TCF Bank stadium naming agreement also included a provision to generate at least $25 million in additional student support over 25 years.

The Promise Scholarship Campaign created a strong sense of urgency among donors to support the institutional goal of maintaining affordable access across all campuses of the University of Minnesota System. The goal of increased affordability was further strengthened by establishing the Promise Scholarship from internal university resources. This need-based scholarship, first provided to students with family incomes of up to $100,000 per year, is combined with Pell and Minnesota state grant programs, producing the lowest net tuition price for moderate income families across higher education institutions in Minnesota. Through these strategies, private scholarship support and need-based internal aid increased nearly ten-fold over a 10-year period. Public institutions must make need-based financial aid a continuing priority and strive to maintain net cost increases modest, especially for students from low to moderate income families.

Leveraging Technological Transformation

Technology has had a transformative impact on higher education over the last 20 years, and continues to change the face of teaching, learning, and research at an astounding rate. While these shifts can be disruptive (Christensen, 2002), they cannot be avoided. Instead, through strategic actions, U.S. public higher education must leverage these changes to improve the public value of higher education. Given the realities of their lives prior to college, today's students expect higher education systems to be customer-service-oriented and technology-enabled. Students want access to their educational experience—including coursework, services, and other resources—anytime, anywhere. Higher education must nimbly respond to these changing needs to ensure continuing student success.

Other technological developments, such as private online courses, flipped classrooms (in which the typical order of lecture then homework is reversed) and digital badging (digital tokens that appear as icons or logos on a webpage or other online venue) (Educause, 2012a, 2012b), have the potential to reform many practices within higher education. As higher education leaders think strategically about the future, they have a responsibility to engage these technological advances productively to improve and expand learning (Brown, Roediger, & McDaniel, 2014), and the quality and productivity of public universities.

As students and faculty move increasingly toward the facilitation of learning via portal-based software such as Moodle and Blackboard, so too must our assessment of the effectiveness of such models. A recent report published by Educause (Brown et al., 2015) argues that the future of learning involves "digital learning environments", in which individual components, from analytics to competency-based education, "fit together like Lego bricks" (p. 7). Perhaps most innovatively, the report recommends that higher education abandon the "walled garden" approach, which assumes that courses must be either public or private.

Elite research institutions such as Harvard, Duke, and Georgia and Massachusetts Institutes of Technology have begun work toward "flexible" curriculums that will be delivered through a combination of face-to-face instruction, distance education, and blended courses (Straumsheim, 2015). According a report published by MIT in 2013, "Achieving [the goal of flexibility] will require a commitment to adopting new models of blended learning—again emphasizing the flexibility to use different pedagogies in different settings—and an investment in a diverse and flexible range of spaces that cater different formats of learning" (Straumsheim, 2015, p. 29).

Interdisciplinary Collaboration

Boyer (1990) argued that "[T]he work of the professoriate might be thought of as having four separate, yet overlapping, functions. These are: the scholarship of *discovery*; the scholarship of *integration*; the scholarship of *application*; and the scholarship of *teaching*" (p. 16). Increasingly, if faculties are to embrace these responsibilities, they must work across disciplinary and organizational boundaries. Locally and globally, the most challenging problems in our future cross boundaries between traditional academic disciplines and between the values of liberal education and the demands of careers. Complex problems demand strong academic disciplines and well-educated, flexible, and collaborative problem solvers who work across fields of study. Institutions of higher education have not only the expertise and capacity to seek solutions to these vexing problems, but also the historic responsibility to do in deepening the public value and impact of higher education. Thus, the 21st century vision for public universities must strongly embrace *interdisciplinary or cross-boundary collaboration.*

The breadth and depth of public university expertise, coupled with strategic investment in areas of emerging challenges or opportunities, can burgeon into multidisciplinary centers of excellence with the financial resources to truly make a difference. New knowledge, ideas, and modes of expression are of limited public value unless they are developed and applied. To this end, research universities must provide greater incentives to expand partnerships and collaboration, streamline and improve technology commercialization, reform their approaches to intellectual property and risk management, and strengthen central support for research and other mission-related public responsibilities.

Many examples illustrate the growing importance of interdisciplinary collaboration. Already, federal funding agencies have begun to reward expanded interdisciplinary, inter-institutional, international, and public–private research efforts to tackle national and global problems such as mapping the human brain, preventing global infectious diseases, preserving water quality and the environment, expanding renewable energy sources, and providing expanded nutrition and food safety. The Imagine America Foundation created under the APSCU (Association of Private Sector Colleges and Universities) provides scholarships to two million students each year. This program serves as a leading example of collaboration across institutions of various types and sizes. The STRIVE Partnership in Cincinnati provides services and funding to children "from cradle to career" (Worth, 2013) and brings together resources from the education, nonprofit, community, civic, and philanthropic sectors to improve academic growth of preK-12 students. Inspired by practices in Germany, many business and higher education sectors are collaborating to offer apprenticeship programs in increasing numbers (Labi, 2012). As these examples illustrate, interdisciplinary collaboration is transforming access to higher education and increasing its public value.

Universities have little choice but to embrace public–private–government partnerships to achieve their full impact. Demonstrating, documenting, and communicating the results of these efforts in a way that conveys real public value, however, is difficult, which contributes to the challenge of assessing performance.

Performance Assessment

Successful organizations measure what they value, and asserting *public value* without relevant standards or metrics is meaningless. The complexity of public universities, the abundance of (often conflicting) data available to higher education's stakeholders, and the rise of multiple alternative providers mean leaders of public universities cannot ignore calls for increased transparency and accountability. To maintain the public trust and earn public investment, universities must clearly demonstrate that they are delivering on the public mission and communicate public value in ways stakeholders can easily understand. Universities must take responsibility for measuring such essential aspects of their mission as student outcomes, the changing net cost of education, faculty productivity, and public return on investment and impact on society.

Many public research universities now produce regular, annual accountability reports. Starting in the late 1990s, for example, the University of Minnesota sought legislative approval to consolidate several annual reports to the Minnesota legislature into a combined University Plan, Performance, and Accountability Report. This report has been prepared and has been submitted annually for 15 years to the broader University community, the Minnesota Legislature, and the Board of Regents. This public report (University of Minnesota, 2013) provides information on approximately 100 measures for the university system and each campus, with appropriate trend analyses and peer group comparisons. It is also a convenient place to summarize information from special studies, for example, on the University's economic impact (or return on public investment), and on its progress in addressing issues of longer term efficiently and productivity.

Addressing current shortcomings in this area must begin at the institutional level, establishing, with the consent of governing boards, a performance framework that includes key measures and processes not limited to inputs or end results, but including those leading indicators that warn us of concerns before they become problems. Media portrayals of the cost of education provide an example of the need for clearer measures. Most media reports disconnect this discussion from measures of net price after financial aid, the role of the nation's low savings rate (e.g., on student debt), tax benefits for college savings, costs, impact, and productivity of institutions, and trends in need versus merit aid, in favor of simplified articles that report increases in nominal tuition, "sticker price" and aggregate debt levels regardless of educational attainment.

Without clearer policy-oriented measures, it is difficult to address urgent reforms needed in policy and practice. Metrics strategies no doubt need to be aligned with national, state, and institutional goals and resources; coherent and relevant to policy-makers and the public; and comparable in meaningful ways across peer institutions. They must also incorporate long-term planning processes, continuous feedback mechanisms, and regular internal and external reporting.

Comprehensive evaluation strategies are essential to strengthening public trust and making the case for the public value of higher education. They may also serve as an antidote to narrowly focused reports or inquiries that question the stewardship of resources and the ultimate value of public investment in higher education (Bruininks, 2011). In short, comprehensive evaluation and reporting strategies can serve all interests; moreover, demonstrating value should help restore what ideally is a covenant between public universities and the states and nation.

Road to Innovation and Renewal: The Essential Importance of Long-term Strategic Vision and Positioning

Given these tensions facing higher education, *public universities must embrace a culture of planned change and performance management* that is longer-term, analytical, self-critical, principled, sustainable, and above all, strategic, to discern the public good and strengthen public value. While emerging opportunities provide new context for universities' historical mission and responsibilities, the needs and circumstances of society are constantly changing, and higher education must evolve, too.

Confronting the many challenges in higher education today will require more disciplined ways of thinking and more coordinated actions to shape the longer term future of public research universities. Initiating and guiding strategic planning and positioning in higher education are a daunting undertaking, but these processes are essential today to ensure continuing relevance and renewal. The processes start with building broad consensus on the contextual influences that are likely to shape the future, or "thinking in the future tense" (James, 1996), and the aspirations of our institutions.

Fortunately, methods to promote and facilitate change exist, even for organizations as vast, diverse, and complex as public research universities. Bryson (2011) defines strategic positioning as a "deliberative, disciplined approach to producing fundamental decisions and actions that shape and guide what an organization (or other entity) is, what it does, and why it does it" (p. xii), with the fundamental goal of promoting strategic thinking, acting, and learning. This basic goal leads to other outcomes that directly contribute to a university's ability to create public value, including improved, experience-based decision making; enhanced organizational effectiveness, responsiveness, and resilience; enhanced organizational legitimacy; enhanced effectiveness of broader societal systems with which the university interacts; and direct and indirect benefits accrued to the people involved (Bryson, 2011). In addition, organizations with strong strategic plans whether economic storms better than those without them (Fain, 2009).

The process of strategic planning and positioning obviously must be adapted to the culture, history and circumstances of every college or university, but there are several lessons from research and successful practice that merit consideration (Bruininks, 2010; 2011; Bryson, 2011; Kotter, 1996; Kotter, 2014):

- Prepare and make the case for change, thoughtfully recognizing environmental trends, mission, culture, resources, and other salient factors, with attention to both internal and external audiences.
- Charter the process with relevant constituencies, including the institution's governing board, faculty and staff leadership groups, administrative leadership, alumni, and important external organizations and groups.
- Establish strong, visible leadership at all levels of the institution to drive the planning and change process.
- Address the most critical long-term academic operational and administrative university priorities, since they support and sustain academic excellence.
- Provide ample opportunity for engagement and consultation from the university and broader community to insure transparency and improved strategies.
- Communicate the long-term vision and recommended actions broadly, both inside and outside the institution, and be prepared to defend them vigorously.

- Develop an implementation plan and strategies as part of the process—many strategic planning efforts fail due to inadequate attention to these issues—and move quickly to implementation.
- Implement an assessment and public accountability system to track and revise strategies to ensure progress and renewal over the long run.

These strategies for promoting longer term transformational change emphasize creating a longer term view and vision for sustainable improvement (James,1996), identifying the most critical areas of focus (Delp, Thesen, Motiwalla, & Seshardi, 1977, p. 241–251), broad engagement of relevant communities, effective, and frequent communication, a clear plan and strategies for managing the change process, and sound practices and shared information to assess progress, revise strategies, and renew the plan (Bryson, 2011; Kotter, 1996).

The strengthening of U.S. public research institutions will likely require the federal government, states, and institutions to renew their long-term visions, using more longer term, comprehensive strategic positioning strategies that balance competing tensions while maximizing both public and private value across colleges and universities. In leveraging strategic planning to address the new realities and trends faced by higher education, at least five major challenges must be considered: (1) strengthening the commitment to public purposes, (2) increasing access and affordability, (3) leveraging benefits of technology, (4) expanding interdisciplinary collaborations, and (5) improving performance assessment and productivity.

The immediate future is filled with challenges and opportunities for the nation's public research universities. Thus, these institutions must work cooperatively to sharpen their distinctive missions, avoid mission creep and redundancy, expand internal and external collaboration, improve productivity, and develop transparent measures of accountability. If public universities act with urgency—seek honest answers to the tough questions about their public purposes and responsibilities and pursue them with vigor—they may outpace the gathering storm and begin again to set the standard for public higher education, as universities, as states, and as a nation.

References

Academic Ranking of World Universities, ARWU (2013). Retrieved from www.shanghairanking.com/ARWU2011.html

Akers, E., Chingos, M. M., & Henriques, A. M. (2015). Understanding changes in the distribution of student loan debt over time. In Hershbein, B. & Hollenbeck, K. *Student loans and the dynamics of debt.* W.E. Upjohn Institute for Employment Research.

Augustine, N. R. (2007) *Is America falling off the flat Earth.* Retrieved on January 18, 2013, from National Academy of Science website: http://www.nap.edu/catalog.php?record_id=12021

Baum, S., & Payea, K. (2011). Trends in For-Profit Postsecondary Education: Enrollment, Prices, Student Aid and Outcomes. Trends in Higher Education Series. *College Board Advocacy & Policy Center.*

Bowen, W. G., Chingos, M. M., & McPherson, M. S. (2009). *Crossing the finish line: Completing college at America's public universities.* Princeton University Press.

Bound, J., & Turner, S. (2002). Going to war and going to college: Did World War II and the GI bill increase educational attainment for returning veterans? *Journal of Labor Economics, 20*(4), 784–815.

Boyer, E. L. (1990). *Scholarship reconsidered: Priorities of the professoriate.* Princeton, NJ: The Carnegie Foundation for the Advancement of Teaching.

Brown, M., Dehoney, J., & Millichap, N. (2015). The next generation digital learning environment. *A Report on Research. ELI Paper. Louisville, CO: Educause April, 5*(1), 1-13.

Brown, P. C., Roediger, H. L., & McDaniel, M. A. (2014). *Make it stick: The science of successful learning.* Cambridge: Mass.

Bruininks, R. H., Furco, A., Jones, R., Sommers, J. K., & Konkle, E. A. (2014). Institutionalizing civic engagement at the University of Minnesota. In H. Boyte (Ed.), *Democracy's education: Public work, citizenship, and the future of colleges and universities* (pp. 80–90). Nashville, TN: Vanderbilt University Press.

Bruininks, R. H., Keeney, B., & Thorp, J. (2010, January 27) Transforming America's universities to compete in the "new normal." *Innovative higher education.* Retrieved from springerlink.com/content/w628653494687221/

Bruininks, R. H. (2011, November). Public Good: Road to Renewal for American Higher Education. Retrieved from blog.lib.umn.edu/cil/myblog/2011McBeeRemarks_PUBLIC.pdf

Bryson, J. M. (2011). *Strategic planning for public and nonprofit organizations: A guide to strengthening and sustaining organizational achievement.* Vol. 1. Jossey-Bass.

Cole, J. R. (2010). *The great American university: Its rise to preeminence, its indispensable national role, why it must be protected.* PublicAffairs.

Doyle, W. R. (2010). Does merit-based aid "crowd out" need-based aid?. *Research in Higher Education, 51*(5), 397-415.

Dynarski, S. M. (2003). Does aid matter? Measuring the effect of student aid on college attendance and completion. *American Economic Review, 93*(1), 279-288.

Educause (2012a). *Things you should know about flipped classrooms* [Brochure].

Educause (2012b). *What campus leaders need to know about MOOCs* [Brochure].

Fain, P. A. U. L. (2009). Financial crisis could give jolt to strategic planning on campuses. *The Chronicle of Higher Education.* Retrieved from chronicle.com/article/Financial-Crisis-Could-Give/1246/

Federal Student Aid. Income-based plan. (2012). Retrieved from http://studentaid.ed.gov/repay-loans/understand/plans/income-based

Florida, R. (2004). The Rise of the Creative Class (and How It's Transforming Work, Leisure, Community and Everyday Life)..

Fogel, D. M., & Malson-Huddle, E. (Eds.). (2012). *Precipice or crossroads?: Where America's great public universities stand and where they are going midway through their second century.* Albany: State University of New York Press.

Friedman, T. L. (2005). *The world is flat: A brief history of the twenty-first century.* New York: Farrar, Straus and Giroux.

Gee, E. G. (2012) The modern public university: Its land-grant heritage, its land-grant horizon. In D. M. Fogel & E. Malson-Huddle. *Precipice or crossroads? Where America's great public universities stand the where they are going midway through their second century*. Albany: State University of New York Press.

Gillaspy, T. (2011, January). Minnesota and the new normal. Retrieved from amsd.org/docs/2011 winter conference/Gillaspy Stinson ppt.pdf

Gilliland, M. W. (2005). Presidential leadership for the public good. In A. J. Kezar, T. C. Chambers, & J. Burkhardt (Eds.), *Higher education for the public good: Emerging voices from a national movement*. San Francisco: Jossey-Bass.

Habley, W. R., Bloom, J. L., & Robbins, Steve, R. (2012). *Increasing persistence: Research-based strategies for college student success*. San Francisco: Jossey-Bass.

Heller, D. E. (Ed.). (2002). *Condition of access: Higher education for lower income students*. Westport, Conn.: American Council on Education/Praeger.

Hechinger, J., & Lorin, J. (2012, September 29). Student loan defaults rise as government scrutiny grows. Retrieved from http://www.businessweek.com/news/2012-09-28/student-loan-defaults-soar-as-government-scrutiny-grow

Holdren, J. P. (2011). America COMPETES Act keeps America's leadership on target. Retrieved from http://www.whitehouse.gov/blog/2011/01/06/america-competes-act-keeps-americas-leadership-target

Imagine America Foundation. (2012). About Imagine America Foundation. Retrieved from http://www.imagine-america.org/history-mission

James, J. (1996), "Thinking in the future tense", *Industrial and Commercial Training*, 28(7), 28-32.

Jones, D. A. (2011, November). Does Australia have the answer? *The Chronicle of Higher Education* (online only). Retrieved from chronicle.com/blogs/brainstorm/does-australia-have-the-answer/41015

Goldin, C., & Katz, L. F. (2007). *The race between education and technology: The evolution of US educational wage differentials, 1890 to 2005. No. w12984*. National Bureau of Economic Research.

Kellogg Commission on the Future of State and Land-grant Universities (2000). *"Renewing the Covenant: Learning, Discovery, and Engagement in a New Age and Different World". March 2000 Report*. Washington D.C.: National Association of State Universities and Land-grant Colleges

Kezar, A., Chambers, A. C., & Burkhardt, J. C. (Eds.). (2015). *Higher education for the public good: Emerging voices from a national movement*. Hoboken, NJ: John Wiley & Sons.

Kotter, J. P. (1996). *Leading change*. Boston: Harvard Business Press.

Kotter, J. P. (2014). *Accelerate: Building strategic agility for a faster-moving world*. Boston: Harvard Business Review Press.

Labi, A. (2012, November 26). Apprenticeships make a comeback in the United States. *Chronicle of Higher Education* (online only). Retrieved from http://chronicle.com/article/Apprenticeships-Make-a/135914/?cid=at&utm_source=at&utm_medium=en

Meynhardt, T. (2009). Public value inside: What is public value creation?. *International Journal of Public Administration*, *32*(3-4), 192-219

National Center for Education Statistics. (2011, May). The Condition of Education 2011. Retrieved from http://nces.ed.gov/pubsearch/pubsinfo.asp?pubid=2011033

Nevins, A. (1960). *The War for the Union*. Vol. 8. Scribner. p. 208

Orszag, P. R. & Kane, T.J. (2003). Higher education spending: The role of Medicaid and the business cycle. *Brookings Policy Brief Series.*

Peck, D. (2011). *Pinched: How the great recession has narrowed our futures and what we can do about it.* New York: Crown Publishers.

Pew Charitable Trusts (2012). *Pursuing the American dream: Economic mobility across generations. July 2012 Report.* Washington D.C.: Pew Charitable Trusts.

Pew Research Center. (2011, May 15). Is college worth it? College presidents, public assess value, quality and mission of higher education. Retrieved from pewsocialtrends.org/2011/05/15/is-college-worth-it/

Quinterno, J. (2012). The great cost shift. How higher education cuts undermine the future middle class. *Demos.* Retrieved from http://www.demos.org/sites/default/files/publications/TheGreatCostShift_Demos.pdf

Schulenburger, D. E. (2012). Challenges to viability and sustainability: Public funding, tuition, college costs, and affordability. In D. M. Fogel, & E. Malson-Huddle (Eds.), *Precipice or crossroads? Where America's great public universities stand the where they are going midway through their second century.* Albany: State University of New York Press.

STRIVE Foundation. The partnership. (2012). Retrieved from http://www.strivetogether.org/about-the-partnership

The America that works. (2013, March 16). *The Economist,* 13. Retrieved from https://www.economist.com/weeklyedition/2013-03-16

Thelin, J. R. (2004). *A history of higher education.* Baltimore: Johns Hopkins

Thelin, J. R., & Gassman, M. (2003). Historical overview of American higher education. *Student services: A handbook for the profession, 4,* 3–22.

Toutkoushian, R. K., Shafiq, M. N., & Trivette, M. J. (2013). Accounting for risk of non-completion in private and social rates of return to higher education. *Journal of education finance, 39*(1), 73–95.

Tucker, M. (2011). *Standing on the shoulders of giants: An American agenda for education reform.* Washington, DC: National Center on Education and the Economy.

Votruba, J. (2005). Leading the engaged institution. *Higher education for the public good: Emerging voices from a national movement.* 263–271.

Worth, M. J. (2013). *Case 8.2: Strive.* In *Nonprofit management: Principles and practice* (3rd ed., pp. 207–208). Los Angeles: SAGE Publications

Yudof, M. G., & Callaghan, C. (2012). Commitments: Enhancing the public purposes and outcomes of public higher education. In D. M. Fogel, & E. Malson-Huddle (Eds.), *Precipice or crossroads? Where America's great public universities stand the where they are going midway through their second century.* Albany: State University of New York Press.

Zemsky, R. (2010). *Making reform work: The case for transforming American higher education.* New Brunswick, NJ: Rutgers University Press.

3 The Nature of Innovation and Change at Public Research Universities

Erin A. Konkle, Jayne K. Sommers, Nichole Sorenson, and David J. Weerts

Research in the fields of organizational development and education clearly agree on one issue: change is a complex process, even under the most ideal and planned circumstances. This is particularly true of public research institutions that have complex organizational structures, deeply rooted cultures, and multitudes of stakeholders. These institutions are often thought of as stagnant enclaves deeply rooted in tradition, all the while situated within a rapidly changing context of "irreversible change" in American higher education (Ward, 2013, p. 14).

Western higher education, particularly in the United States, has enjoyed a long period of relatively little competition. However, this status is shifting. Developing countries are catching up, creating higher education systems that are more adaptable and that emphasize science and technology over the liberal arts (Bui & Baruch, 2010; Christensen & Eyring, 2011). Higher education faces a constantly evolving job market that is increasingly global and technology-based, but something else is changing as well. A growing body of "pop-culture psychology" has questioned what we know about the very structure and value of education (Khan, 2012; Seligman et al., 2009; Tucker, 2012). From flipped teaching methods to new understandings of motivation for degree attainment, higher educations' lecture halls and ivory towers are increasingly being challenged as outdated.

Adding to these challenges are concerns about public support for higher education. Public spending on higher education over the last three decades has not kept pace with escalating costs, and some argue that tuition levels are nearing their peak (Rawlings, 2012; Ward, 2013). In an era of scarce public resources, institutions of all types are increasingly driven by their pursuit of prestige and desire to enhance their market position. New degrees, larger and more competitive incoming classes, and state of the art buildings are all part of the institutional arms race in a market where "the quality of the product is hard to measure" (Christensen & Eyring, 2011, p. 47).

There is also a growing tension between long-standing values and traditions that have guided public research universities and the public's view

DOI: 10.4324/9781315110523-4

about the value and purposes of college. Historically, these institutions have been viewed as unique places where the pursuit of knowledge, innovation, creativity, and change can thrive. However, the public's view of higher education today focuses primarily on the role of undergraduate education in preparing students for jobs (Gallup, 2013). In this context, new providers have entered the market and have changed the competitive landscape. For example, for-profit institutions and job training companies offer alternatives to traditional public research universities through certificate and other career programs. The presence of these new providers has required these traditional institutions to rethink strategies that have guided them for over a century (Garrity, Garrison, & Fiedler, 2010; Hentschke, Lechuga, & Tierney, 2010; Wilson, 2010).

The preceding paragraphs provide a glimpse into the increasingly complex landscape of American higher education, particularly public research universities. This chapter aims to explore opportunities and challenges for public research universities as they respond to these new realities. The central premise of this chapter is that such institutions must be more adaptive, nimble and open to change to thrive in an uncertain future. This chapter is organized into three sections. First, we discuss readiness and resistance to change at the individual and organizational level, and the role of leaders in preparing their institutions for change. Second, we introduce literature articulating traditional approaches to planned change within an institution. Third, we offer the concept of *innovation* as a way to reframe the way leaders think about institutional change. In closing the chapter, we provide an example of innovative practices that support change efforts in public research universities.

Change Readiness and Resistance in the Public Research University: Leadership and Culture

Change is constant and occurs in organizations and individuals alike. Change is often unplanned and unexamined. This chapter focuses on the notion of planned change, or organizational development, defined as a long-range and intentional change (Cummings & Worley, 2014). Planned change in the context of public research universities takes the form of processes entered by choice, with an intended outcome and a system-wide lens. In any planned change process, readiness, and resistance from both the organization as a whole and individuals within the organization must be incorporated. Individuals within an organization have the ability, and often the power, to undermine any change effort toward which they feel resistance. Scholars agree that leadership and culture are central elements in successful planned change (Bolman & Deal, 2008; Kotter, 1998). Leadership and culture emerge to create a dynamic pair that helps organizations to move into a state of change readiness. Strong leadership rooted in an understanding of the existing culture and a clear vision of the critical path forward has been vetted in research in organizational development and business fields. Understanding leadership and culture as key elements that undergird change readiness helps to frame the change strategies within the research university context.

Leadership

Leadership is a key element of any change process. Leaders are tasked with envisioning, articulating, implementing, and maintaining the mission and vision of an organization. They serve as guides to help the change process flow with the organization's goals and values and adjust both when warranted. A leader's style must match with the culture of the organization as well as the needs of a particular situation. Therefore, frames of leadership serve as an important way to understand style and direction. Successful leaders know themselves and their organizations well enough to adapt to the situation as necessary (Collins & Hansen, 2008).

Bolman and Deal (2013) assert the existence of four "images", or frames, for viewing institutional leadership and the need to understand each in order to propel meaningful change: structural, human resources, political, and symbolic. *Structural leaders* focus on designing and building an organization. Bolman and Deal (2013) refer to structural leaders as "analysts" and "architects". *Human resources* leaders are facilitators and catalysts; they are there to motivate and empower others. Human resources leaders are sensitive to followers' needs. *Political leaders* know how to network and work the system and to get individuals and groups to "buy in". *Symbolic leaders* inspire their charges to act by effective communication and by capturing our attention (Bolman & Deal, 2013).

Bolman and Deal's (2013) frames can be uniquely interpreted within the research university setting. Leaders of research universities lead in anarchical settings (Cohen et al, 1972), which are characterized by a community of autonomous actors with different values, interests and degrees of authority (Birnbaum, 1988). In these institutions, goals are primarily understood as a loose set of ideas. Furthermore, participation is fluid in enacting these ideas. A number of differing agendas and points of view regularly pass through committees and other institutional structures, making decision making unpredictable (Birnbaum, 1988; Cohen et al, 1972). Another key distinction lies in the fact that faculty at public research universities have been categorized as "cosmopolitan" in nature rather than "local" (Birnbaum, 1988; p. 19), referring to the notion that their academic colleagues are more likely to be peers around the world who share their scholarly interests, rather than their own campus colleagues.

In this complex context, public research university leaders have limits in directly influencing the direction of their campuses, and typically can only attend to some key important matters. According to Birnbaum (1988), a central role among research university leaders is to shape the values, symbols, and emotions that affect how others interpret changes at the institution. Through this lens, leaders of research universities may primarily rely on Bolman and Deal's (2013) symbolic frame to help to create meaning of change and how people react to it at the institution. In addition to shepherding the change message on their own campuses, public research institution leaders are often charged with guiding the "innovation eco-system" in regional, state, and sometimes global contexts, leading to greater scrutiny (Butler & Gibson, 2013). Planned changed at research universities, then, includes a significant investment in a communication strategy to successfully position ideas relating to planned change.

Research university leaders do well to recognize that stakeholders are invested in some way to all outcomes of a planned change process. In this way, all leadership might be viewed as collective. The W.K. Kellogg Foundation (2007) defines collective leadership as occurring when "the members of a group, motivated by a common purpose, begin to build relationships with each other that are genuinely respectful enough to allow them to co-construct their shared purpose and work" (p. 3). Collective leadership intentionally includes all stakeholders, values differing perspectives, and fosters transparency and knowledge transfer (Bloom, Hutson, He, & Konkle, 2013). This notion reflects Bolman and Gallos's (2011) notion of a leadership epistemology, which centers on the leader's role in making sense of complex circumstances and helping organizational members, interpret events and move forward with action strategies.

Organizational Culture

Developing an organizational culture responsive to change may be among the most important tasks for 21st century research university leaders. Leaders must leverage their dynamic environments to create a culture that is responsive to changes from within and outside the system. For example, colleges and universities continually assimilate new student populations and are therefore frequently afforded the opportunity to develop their cultures with changes in the student body. In order to successfully develop or change an institutional culture, individuals within that institution must have a firm grasp of current cultural nuances (Kezar, 2013). The process of change is not a universal or uniform process. It varies significantly from institution to institution and often even within a single institution.

Public research university leaders must also be cognizant of the notion that multiple sub-cultures exist within a larger institutional culture. Bergquist and Pawlak's (2008) scholarship on academic cultures is especially germane to understanding the various subcultures that exist within the complex research institution. Among the six academic cultures, the *collegial culture* is tied closely to research universities where academic freedom and the pursuit of knowledge in academic disciplines are strongly valued (Bergquist & Pawlak, 2008). Meanwhile, *managerial cultures* are frequently found at state system institutions that rely heavily on public funding, which encourages efficiency and accountability (Bergquist & Pawlak, 2008). The *developmental culture* provides a contrast to the collegial culture, acknowledging that learning occurs outside of the classroom, which encourages student development and professional development for faculty and staff (Bergquist & Pawlak, 2008). The *advocacy culture*, which encourages collective action and activism, is strongly tied to the rising prevalence of faculty and staff unions (Bergquist & Pawlak, 2008). *Virtual cultures* are relatively new and incorporate rapidly evolving technology, which have permeated most institutions in ways ranging from instructional delivery models to student support services (Bergquist & Pawlak, 2008). Finally, *tangible cultures* are those that have stable roots that provide grounding despite fluctuations in innovation, technology, and mission creep (Bergquist & Pawlak, 2008). Having an understanding of these subcultures is critical for leaders of research universities not because they provide steps to follow for successful change, but rather because they provide an understanding of the existing contexts within which institutional leaders must work to produce successful change.

Institutional leaders must also pay attention to the ways that organizational actors relate to one another and participate in the life of the community. Doing so ensures the development of a civil culture in which change can occur in a productive manner. Leaders must also consider who can make change outside of those with positional leadership. Kezar (2013) uses the language of "change agents" rather than leaders to clarify that it is not just those in traditional positions of power. In many instances change is championed by those not afforded positional leadership (Kezar & Lester, 2011). Social norms and practices within campus cultures guide behaviors of individuals within the community (Braskamp, Trautvetter, & Ward, 2008). These social norms create an emotional connection between the individuals and their institution (Kezar, 2007). In developing the character of their institutions, leaders must help their campuses consider their collective vision for the future (Braskamp, Trautvetter, & Ward, 2008). As with values, campus leaders must ask if their institutional character supports the institution's vision. Campus cultures can be sustained, developed, or changed. To develop a positive and strong campus culture, "educators must tend to their institution's ethos on an ongoing basis and consistently work to align policies and practices with it" (Kezar, 2007, p. 14). Importantly, leaders must give thoughtful attention to how students are involved in creating a strong and positive culture. Berger (2001), drawing upon the previous work of Bolman and Deal (1991), suggested that institutions can leverage their own cultures, allowing for student participation in decision-making, clear processes, open communication, student advocates, and an environment of fairness among other ideas to help positively influence student outcomes.

Evaluating, or even understanding, a particular campus' unique culture is difficult at best. Not only does campus culture constantly evolve, but it may not always be consistent within a single institution (Colby, Ehrlich, Beaumont, & Stephens, 2003). Individuals who come to an institution having had different life experiences as well as having varied relationships to the institution, understand their campus culture in different ways (Colby et al., 2003). For this reason, universities must be clear in defining their culture through mission and values, and must work to ensure that both are continuously incorporated into every aspect of the institution (Kuh, Kinzie, Schuh, & Whitt, 2005).

Kuh et al. (2005) differentiated between an *espoused mission*—what one might find on an institution's website—and an *enacted mission*—the principles that guide the day to day work of faculty, staff, and students. The authors noted that the enacted mission:

> is arguably more important to student success than the espoused mission because it guides the daily action of those in regular contact with students—in classrooms, residence halls, and on playing fields—as well as those who set institutional policy, make strategic plans and decisions, and allocate resources.
>
> (Kuh et al., 2005, p. 26)

Institutions with strong enacted missions find that their mission "lives" on campus and provides vision and value to the work of their employees (Kuh et al., 2005).

In order to create institutions that are ready to change, leaders need to develop cultures that encourage change and are nimble in adapting to change as it happens. The presence of an existing culture that encourages change does not necessarily mean that change will occur or that the effects will be long lasting. Institutions must recognize the strengths of their own cultures to most effectively align a strategy for change. Change is most effective when it is culturally respectful and responsive.

One way that public research university leaders can influence this process is by inviting outside perspectives to inform and challenge institutional practices. Kezar and Eckel (2002) suggest that

> strategies for achieving this outside perspective...include working with a network of institutions, using outside consultants, presenting at and attending conferences where they publicly explore their assumptions, bringing in new leadership, and participating in exchange programs to broaden the horizons of personnel.
>
> (p. 32)

The use of one or more of these strategies provides ways to conceptualize change and its relationship to culture, highlighting culture as the modifying element in the change process rather than the element to be changed (Kezar & Eckel, 2002).

Finally, management scholars have emphasized the importance of transparency in creating organizational cultures that are open to change. Within an organizational context, *transparency* is primarily defined as the free flow of accurate information between appropriate internal and external stakeholders (Bennis et al., 2008). Transparency has the effect of boosting individual accountability by making clear where responsibility is delegated. Bennis et al. (2008) argues that transparency also increases the probability of organizational success because it aids in accurate, unbiased decision-making. This suggests that organizations must work to create a *culture of candor*—one in which individuals feel comfortable exchanging information openly (Bennis et al., 2008).

In sum, both leadership and culture influence an institution's readiness for change. The public research university context consists of autonomous actors where decision-making and consensus building are difficult due to individual agendas and viewpoints. This environment leads to unique challenges for leaders at research universities interested in championing institutional change. Additionally, organizational culture impacts change processes. Leaders must be aware of the culture of their particular research university and the multiple subcultures within the institution that may impact any change initiative. Part of the role of leaders in public research universities is understanding this complex environment and developing strategies that may be successful given the institution's unique culture and circumstances. The following sections outline traditional change strategies as well as contemporary change and innovation strategies for leading public research universities in the future.

Strategies for Planned Change

The previous section provided insights on creating readiness for change within the public research university context. We now turn our attention to change processes that provide a framework for leading change efforts within complex research institutions. A significant amount of literature explores the process of change in complex organizations. Many of these studies use higher education settings as their subjects and case analyses, from leadership studies on college presidents to change models of outlier institutions (Bastedo, 2012).

In navigating these models, we articulate four paradigms of change, which inform ways in which higher education leaders might make sense of leading change in the public research university context. These four paradigms include linear change strategies (Lewin, 1947), systemic change strategies (Bryson, 2011; Kotter, 1996), positive change strategies (Cooperrider & Srivastva, 1987; Cummings & Worley, 2014; Senge, 2006; Cameron & Quinn, 2011), and innovation (Martinez, 2013).

Linear Change Strategies

Lewin (1947) provides one of the earliest and most simplistic models for a planned change process. Lewin presented a three-step change process: unfreezing, movement, and refreezing. Lewin based his model on the idea that when the forces that kept an organization in the status quo became less rigid, the organization would naturally "unfreeze", a change would occur, and then the status quo forces would again assert themselves to cause a refreezing around the new change.

Ely and Atkinson (1976) first introduced the *Conditions for Change* model, which theorized that change, either planned or organic, was inevitable in an organization and the success of change would be predicated on the acceptance or rejection by the organization itself. Ely introduced a five step-model that followed the path that knowledge (step 1) leads to persuasion (step 2), or change attitude, of those in positions of power. Then a decision (step 3) is made to pursue change. The change is accepted or rejected (step 4) by the organization and the process is confirmed complete (step 5).

While Lewin and Ely and Atkinson conducted their research in different arenas, businesses and universities libraries respectively, both provide useful information when considering linear change in the research university. While sometimes hierarchical, research universities are places with robust structures that are responsive to outside forces, the same conditions described by Lewin and Ely. Additionally, university leadership, while often charged with guiding change, frequently have little control over the external forces that result in reactionary change.

Linear Change Models in the Public Research University Context

Linear change models were useful in their early stages to conceptualize the process of organizational change because at the time, no such models existed. However, as the field of organizational development has evolved and more is understood about planned change, these models have been deemed overly simplistic for most organizational contexts today, including the ever-complex structures and cultures of public research universities. Linear change models are also quite hierarchical and assume that planned change will naturally occur with little direction. The linear models also fail to account for the loosely coupled organizational structures at public research universities (Fumasoli & Stensaker, 2013).

Systemic Change Strategies

System change models differ from linear models in important ways. First, system change models are cyclical and grounded in the belief that organizations are in a constant state of planned change. Second, they tend to be more collaborative and less hierarchical than linear models. Finally, system change models stress data gathering and understanding. Several scholars have outlined strategic change models, including Poister and Streib (1999), Bryson (2011), and Kotter (1996).

Strategic Planning

Poister and Streib (1999) assert that public and nonprofit strategic planning should be concerned with identifying and responding to the most fundamental issues facing an organization. The authors assert that effective strategic planning addresses the most subjective question of purpose and the often competing values that influence mission and strategies. Emphasis is also placed on the importance of external trends and forces and the ways in which they can influence an organization's mission. Organizations need also to be responsive to internal and external stakeholders and actively involve all stakeholders in the strategic planning process where possible. Strategic planning needs to address mission critical issues, be action-oriented, and stress the importance of developing a plan. Finally, decisions should always have a long-term focus in order to best position the institution for the future.

The work of Bryson (2011) and his colleagues provides an ambitious strategic positioning plan. His *Strategy Change Cycle* provides an iterative approach to strategic change that enables an organization to begin anywhere in the cycle and is flexible enough to recognize and incorporate institutional and political complexities (Bryson, 2011). Although the stages of the cycle are not necessarily sequential for every institution, Bryson presents them in numerical order. Bryson suggests a ten step process to strategic planning: (1) initiate and agree on a strategic planning process; (2) identify organizational mandates; (3) clarify organizational mission and values; (4) assess the external and internal environments to identify strengths, weaknesses, opportunities, and threats; (5) identify the strategic issues facing the organization; (6) formulate strategies to manage the issues; (7) review and adopt the strategic plan or plans; (8) establish an effective organizational vision; (9) redevelop an effective implementation process; and 10) reassess strategies and the strategic planning process.

These steps require a painstaking review of values, purposes, and expectations that balances internal aspirations and external demands, different notions and measures of success, and competing priorities and responsibilities. Later steps address strategies, measures, and timeframe. Bryson's *Strategy Change Cycle* (2011) places great emphasis on the groundwork for change; it is not until Step nine of ten that implementation is addressed, followed by step 10, which reassesses all that has come before. Implementation and evaluation should be an integral and ongoing part of the process, not just something included at the end.

Kotter's Eight Stages

Kotter (1996) challenged the notion that major change "is not possible without carnage" (p. 17). Kotter suggested an eight-step change process that can be employed to help institutions avoid extensive damage to morale and create a more welcoming environment for moving through needed change.

Kotter's first four steps argue for actions that encourage readiness for change: (1) establishing a sense of urgency; (2) creating the guiding coalition; (3) developing a vision and strategy; and (4) communicating the change vision. These steps acknowledge that institutions are often steeped in history and culture, and that these realities may necessitate a period of preparation for change.

Steps five, six, and seven in Kotter's (1996) model—empowering broad-based action, generating short-term wins, and consolidating gains and producing more change—focus upon the actual change itself. Many public research universities that experience a failed change process find that they focused too heavily on these three steps while neglecting the earlier steps in the process. Kotter (1996) argues strongly that sequence is not just important, but actually paramount in creating successful change. Readiness to accept change must be assessed and established before change can actually be made. Likewise, successful change must be navigated before efforts to sustain it begin.

Kotter's (1996) final step involves anchoring new approaches in the culture, which addresses the sustained nature of successful change. Kotter notes that if change is to be successful and sustained, it has to become an embedded part of an institution's culture. Acculturation aims at shifting existing cultural norms to include the change, and encourages harnessing the momentum that builds during the previous seven stages among individuals as well as the institution.

System Change Models in the Public Research University Context

Research has clearly demonstrated that change processes can be used successfully to help public agencies, governments, nonprofit organizations, and entire communities navigate a change process. The public research university often falls in with many of these constructs because of its size and purview. It makes sense, then, to use these strategies to construct change processes at public research universities. System change models are the dominant approaches to planned change (Cummings & Worley, 2014) and have guided the strategic positioning committees at many public research universities.

Kezar and Lester (2009) suggest that collaboration is key to systemic changes in higher education. Using a collaborative model, especially in a large public research institution, where each college is intended to operate as a discipline-specific silo can be challenging. Though, collaboration between all stakeholders at public research institution—faculty, administration, students, government, and public and private sector communities—becomes more and more necessary to sustain these institutions (Kezar & Lester, 2009).

Positive Change Strategies

Positive change models differ from linear and system change models in a number of important ways. First, while they share an understanding of the cyclical nature of the change process with the systems models, they are not focused on identifying a problem within the organization. Rather, positive change models suggest that rather than attempting to change what is *wrong* with an organization, it is more advantageous to try to build more of *what already works*. This idea of reframing the change mindset from fixing what is wrong to building on what works has shown some promise, discussed below. Research on the concepts of appreciative inquiry (AI), learning organizations, and virtuous organizations contribute to this scholarship.

Appreciative Inquiry

Cooperrider and Srivastva (1987) proposed that most organizations have an inherently positive core and that if they effectively tap into that core, organizations can use the positive effect to generate success (Cooperrider, 1997; Cooperrider & Srivastva, 1987; Whitney & Trosten-Bloom, 2010). These advances can spur organizations to identify solutions previously not considered or imagined, and because solutions are internally generated, this process can provide an intrinsic motivation for implementation. Cooperrider's theory strayed from the idea of a single right answer and offered that for any given problem the "range of cognitive heuristics that may be employed in solving problems is an adaptation limited only by the human imagination" (Cooperrider & Srivastva, 1987, p. 133). Cooperrider (1987) asserted that the positive assets that organizations already possess, often through the individuals that comprise the organization, provide the best solutions to the problems faced by an organization.

AI has proven to be a powerful approach for creating positive change in businesses, nonprofit organizations, and most recently, educational institutions (Whitney & Trosten-Bloom, 2010). Cooperrider proposed a four-phase cyclical structure for using AI to spur organizational development. These phases are commonly referred to as the "Four Ds"—Discover, Dream, Design, and Destiny/Deliver (Cooperrider & Srivastva, 1987). AI provides a platform for individuals to become positively engaged in the change process, and as strengths are developed in one area, other areas naturally improve, and weaknesses become less important.

Learning Organizations

Senge (2006) developed the theoretical framework that underpins the understanding of learning organizations. Learning organizations can be defined as multi-faceted and requiring learning within individual members as well as learning as a group. Linked to quality improvement and strategic positioning, learning organizations encourage change as a part of the development and improvement processes (Bak, 2012). Senge (1999) posed five characteristics that define the learning organization: personal mastery, team learning, building a shared value, systems thinking, and use of mental models. Higher education is not always quick to change because of deeply rooted culture and complex structure, as outlined above. In particular, when it comes to cultivating a learning organization, the structure and political influences in higher education pose real challenges (Bak, 2012). Institutions tend to operate in silos across campus in administration and academic departments, making systems thinking and team learning challenging characteristics to adopt (Bak, 2012).

Bui and Baruch (2010) offered a number of *antecedents* to help higher education become more adaptive learning organizations: values, motivation, individual learning, vision, and development and training. In many ways, higher education institutions are comprised of individualistic, self-motivated academics charged with creating and disseminating knowledge. As a result, an institutional culture can work against the creation of a learning organization when the focus is not on the group or organization. However, higher education institutions could be particularly well-suited to become model learning organizations because they already support an environment that encourages questioning, risk-taking, and knowledge creation, which are often "the precursors to innovation and creation" (Bui & Baruch, 2010, p. 231).

Virtuous Organizations

The concept of virtuousness developed from the fields of positive psychology and organizational development (Cameron, Bright, & Caza, 2004). Virtuousness is defined as "what organizations and individuals aspire to be when they are at their best" (Cameron et al., 2004, p. 767). Virtuousness leads to flourishing conditions that can be developed and enabled in organizations (Cameron et al., 2004; Cameron, Dutton, & Quinn, 2003).

Cameron et al. (2004) explored the relationship between virtuousness and organizational performance. The researchers found that "when virtuous behavior is displayed by organization members and enabled by organizational systems and processes, the organization achieves higher levels of desired outcomes" (p. 25). Their results showed a relationship between an organization's reported virtuousness and both the perceived and objective outcomes, including innovation, customer retention, turnover, quality, profitability, and financial outcomes. In the domain of higher education, Cameron and Smart (1998) found that university downsizing during the 1992 recession did not lead to organizational ineffectiveness if administrators prioritized employee morale and commitment and avoided the "dirty dozen". The dirty dozen refers to negative attributes such as loss of trust and lack of teamwork that can lead to organizational decline. This study provides additional evidence suggesting that a focus on organizational virtue can help sustain institutions in difficult times.

Positive Change Models in the Public Research University Context

Positive change models offer a new way to approach planned changed in the research university. Their focus on collaboration and maximizing existing strengths works well with the complex nature of the public research universities. Positive models craft the change message in from the outset and encourage buy-in from all stakeholders by including them in all stages of the process.

Innovation Change Strategies

The first three theories of change discussed here largely focus a long-term, macro view of moving an organization toward a preferred state. Alternatively, innovation is more tactical, process-oriented approach to change, and can be defined as anything that "substantially alters the way in which the work of management is carried out, or significantly modifies customary organizational forms, and by so doing, advances organizational goals" (Hamel, 2007, p. 19). Thus, the key difference is that innovation is a tactical strategy for organizations to approach the change processes. Like scholars focusing on change, scholars in the area of innovation have categorized this work in various ways.

Martinez's Stages of Innovation

Martinez (2013) outlines three stages of innovation–invention, innovation, and adoption—which situates Hamel's (2007) concepts of operational, product, and strategy innovation. The *invention* stage occurs from the individual to inter-organizational scale. At the individual level, simple creativity often serves as the impetus of invention.

Martinez (2013) notes that both relational and technical factors need consideration during the invention stage at the inter-organizational level. Attention to relational factors involve bringing the right people together and removing personal barriers that could inhibit individuals' ability to collaborate, and include: sense of belonging, cohesion, time, status, and others. At the public research university, this might mean creating forums for collaborative work that foster creative thinking and risk-taking around processes that may improve outcomes related to student learning and cost containment. Meanwhile, technical factors address that the innovation process involves than simply having the right people at the table, including space, purpose, tools, and more. Specifically, technical factors refer to the notion that those people at the table have unique sets of skills, knowledge and competencies that complement one another. As Martinez (2013) notes, "effective design-driven invention includes cultural and technological viewpoints—both the poet and scientist are necessary parts of the equation" (p. 9). The invention stage is often exciting and exhilarating, but participants can struggle to materialize the concepts without managing both the technical and relational aspects.

Design Thinking

The growing movement around "design thinking" provides a compelling example of how inventions may emerge within a context of inter-organizational collaboration. Briefly summarized, design thinking is an emerging field that applies tools and processes from the design disciplines (architecture, landscape architecture, interior design, graphic design, product design, apparel design and others) to complex, system-wide problems. The design thinking process involves problem definition, field research, idea generating, storyboarding, frequent prototyping and narrative as a method for engaging participants and motivating action (Weerts, Rasmussen, & Singh, 2015).

In the early 1990s, Buchanan (1992) argued that design thinking should be considered a new liberal art of technical culture that could be used to "address the concrete needs and values of human beings in diverse circumstances" (p. 21). Guided by this rationale, design thinking has been leveraged in a wide variety of sectors to foster creativity and innovation within complex organizations and organizational change processes. The method emphasizes a human-centered approach that draws on the knowledge and understanding of the individuals and groups using the system and requires empathy for their experiences and perspective. Furthermore, the method promotes a "bias toward action". calling for rapid experimentation and prototyping to find the flaws in the initial prototype and make improvements. These processes promote engagement and inventive thinking, which may lead to new products, processes, or business models.

Innovation Change Strategies in the Public Research University Context

An example of design thinking being applied in public research universities can be seen in the Higher Ed Redesign Initiative, a collaborative venture of the University of Minnesota and the Midwestern Higher Education Compact. In 2013–2014, a pilot program brought together mid-career professionals in higher education, the creative industries (e.g., arts, theatre, design), and the nonprofit sector to address a design challenge related to improving college access and affordability in Minnesota. Upon completion of the program, participants developed three unique prototypes that they shared with higher education leaders and policymakers for potential implementation in state-wide systems of higher education. Among its outcomes, the pilot project expanded leadership capacity to address educational attainment and workforce development in the state. In addition, it yielded unique prototypes for testing in state-wide settings (Weerts et al., 2015).

Conclusion

Traditional approaches to organizational change, including linear change models and system change models, provide a foundation of understanding for leaders of research universities. However, these traditional approaches are not sufficient to respond to the rapidly changing realities facing public research institutions today. This chapter has invited a shift in thinking from a focus on eliminating unsuccessful programs and waste to a commitment to building on existing strengths and implementing innovative practices in order to meet the changing needs of students and communities.

Positive organizational development and innovation theory provide additional processes leaders might use to transform research universities to remain competitive and relevant in a changing higher education landscape. Their focus on collaboration and stakeholder involvement not only informs the outcomes but also encourages buy-in and builds institutional readiness for change. This culture of readiness for innovative change influences how widely innovative practices are adopted and the ultimate impact of innovation.

The innovative public research university employs methods such as design thinking to encourage creative thinking and novel responses to fast changing realities. Public research universities might also borrow some ideas from private college colleagues. Institutions like Standford and MIT have design labs and makers spaces to allow for collaborative and interdisciplinary innovation and entrepreneurship to thrive. They incentivize creative approaches through funding and other administrative support. They also open these spaces to those beyond faculty and administrative roles. They invite students and community collaborators to join them in developing new ways to approach challenges. Innovative practices must take into account unique institutional cultures, and stakeholder involvement can help institutional leaders understand how culture will impact adoption and diffusion of innovative ideas and practices throughout the organization and beyond. Further, at an innovative research university, individuals who create innovation at any level are rewarded and recognized by leadership.

This chapter provides an understanding of how leaders of public research universities can build on organizational change frameworks to create the innovative institutions needed to face the challenges of the 21st century. Given the realities facing higher education in the future and the unique role of public research institutions, a commitment to innovation is only logical. Change is not enough anymore—only truly innovative transformation in the public research university will carry us into the future.

References

Bak, O. (2012). Universities: Can they be considered as learning organizations?: A preliminary micro-level perspective. *The Learning Organization, 19*(2), 163–172.

Bastedo, M. N. (Ed.). (2012). *The organization of higher education: Managing colleges for a new era.* Baltimore: Johns Hopkins University Press.

Bennis, W., Goleman, D., & O'Toole, J. 2008. *Transparency: How leaders create a culture of candor.* San Francisco, CA: Jossey-Bass.

Berger, J. B. (2001). Understanding the organizational nature of student persistence: Empirically-based recommendations for practice. *Journal of College Student Retention: Research, Theory & Practice, 3*(1), 3-21.

Bergquist, W. H., & Pawlak, K. (2008). *Engaging the six cultures of the academy: Revised and expanded edition of the four cultures of the academy.* San Francisco, CA: Jossey-Bass

Birnbaum, R. (1988). *How colleges work.* San Francisco, CA: Jossey-Bass

Bloom, J. L., Hutson, B. L., He, Y., & Konkle, E. (2013). Appreciative education. *New Directions for Student Services, 143,* 5–18.

Bolman, L. G., & Deal, T. E. (1991). *Reframing organizations* (Vol. 130). San Francisco, CA: Jossey-Bass.

Bolman, L. & Deal, T. (2008). *Reframing organizations: Artistry, choice, and leadership.* San Fransicso: Jossey-Bass.

Bolman, L. G., & Deal, T. E. (2013). *Reframing organizations: Artistry, choice, and leadership.* Hoboken, NJ: John Wiley & Sons.

Bolman, L., & Gallos, G. (2011). *Reframing academic leadership.* San Francisco, CA: Jossey-Bass.

Braskamp, L., Trautvetter, L. C., & Ward, K. (2008). Putting students first: Promoting lives of purpose and meaning. *About Campus, 13*(1), 26–32.

Buchanan, R. (1992). Wicked problems in design thinking. *Design Issues, 8*(2), 5–21.

Bui, H., & Baruch, Y. (2010). Creating learning organizations: A systems perspective. *The Learning Organization, 17*(3), 208–227.

Butler, J., & Gibson, D. (2013). Research universities in the framework of regional innovation ecosystem: The case of Austin, Texas. *Foresight-Russia, 7*(2), 42–57.

Cameron, K. S., Bright, D., & Caza, A. (2004). Exploring the relationships between organizational virtuousness and performance. *American Behavioral Scientist, 47,* 766–790.

Cameron, K., & Smart, S. (1998). Maintaining effectiveness amid downsizing and decline in institutions of higher education. *Research in Higher Education, 21,* 65–86.

Cameron, K., Dutton, J., & Quinn, R. E. (Eds.). (2003). *Positive organizational scholarship: Foundations of a new discipline*. San Francisco: Berrett-Koehler Publishers.

Cameron, K. S., & Quinn, R. E. (2011). *Diagnosing and changing organizational culture: Based on the competing values framework*. San Francisco: Jossey-Bass.

Christensen, C. M., & Eyring, H. J. (2011). *The innovative university: Changing the DNA of higher education from the inside out*. San Francisco: Jossey-Bass.

Cohen, M. D., March, J. G., & Olsen, J. P. (1972). A garbage can model of organizational choice. *Administrative Science Quarterly*, 1-25.

Colby, A., Ehrlich, T., Beaumont, E., & Stephens, J. (2003). *Educating citizens*. San Francisco: Josey-Bass.

Collins, J. C., & Hansen, M. T. (2011). Great by choice: Uncertainty. *Chaos, and Luck–Why some thrive despite them all*. New York: Harper Business.

Cooperrider, D. L., & Srivastva, S. (1987). Appreciative inquiry in organizational life. *Research in organizational change and development*, *1*(1), 129–169.

Cooperrider, D. L. (1997). Resources for getting appreciative inquiry started. *OD practitioner*, *28*(1), 28–33.

Cummings, T.G., & Worley, C.G. (2014). *Organization development and change*. Stamford: Cengage Learning.

Ely, D. P., & Atkinson, H. C. (1978). Creating the conditions for change. *Allerton Park Institute (22nd: 1976)*.

Fumasoli, T., & Stensaker, B. (2013). Organizational studies in higher education: A reflection on historical themes and prospective trends. *Higher Education Policy*, *26*(4), 479–496.

Gallup (2013, February 5). *America's call for higher education redesign: The 2012 Lumina Foundation study of the American public's opinion on higher education*. Washington, DC: Lumina Foundation. Retrieved from http://www.luminafoundation.org/publications/Americas_Call_for_Higher_Education_Redesign.pdf

Garrity, B. K. F., Garrison, M. J., & Fiedler, R. C. (2010). Access for whom, access to what? The role of the "disadvantaged student" market in the rise of for-profit higher education in the United States. *Journal for Critical Education Policy Studies*, *8*(1), 202–244.

Hamel, G. (2007). Management innovation: This can deliver top performance. *Leadership Excellence*, *24*(1), 5.

Hentschke, G. C., Lechuga, V. M., & Tierney, W. G. (2010). *For-profit colleges and universities: Their markets, regulation, performance, and place in higher education*. Herndon,: Stylus Publishing.

Kellogg Foundation, W. K. (2007). *The collective leadership framework: a workbook for cultivating and sustaining community change*. Battle Creek, MI: W. K. Kellogg Foundation.

Kezar, A. (2013). *How colleges change*. New York: Routledge.

Kezar, A., & Lester, J. (2011). *Enhancing campus capacity for leadership: An examination of grassroots leaders*. Stanford Press.

Kezar, A., & Lester, J. (2009). *Organizing for collaboration in higher education: A guide for campus leaders*. San Francisco: Jossey Bass Press.

Kezar, A. J. (2007). Tools for a time and place: Phased leadership strategies to institutionalize a diversity agenda. *The Review of Higher Education*, *30*(4), 413–439.

Kezar, A. J., & Eckel, P. D. (2002). The effect of institutional culture on change strategies in higher education: Universal principles or culturally responsive concepts? *The Journal of Higher Education, 73*(4), 435–460.

Khan, S. (2012). *The one world schoolhouse: Education reimagined.* Hachette Digital, Inc.

Kotter, J. (1998). Winning at change. *Leader to Leader, 10*, 27-33.

Kotter, J. P. (1996). *Leading change.* Boston, MA: Harvard Business Press.

Kuh, G. D., Kinzie, J., Schuh, J. H., & Whitt, E. J. (2005). *Assessing conditions to enhance educational effectiveness.* San Francisco: Jossey-Bass.

Lewin, K. (1947). Group decision and social change. *Readings in social psychology, 3*, 197–211.

Martinez, M. (2013). Perspectives on Innovation in Higher Education: A Framing Document for the Jandris Center for Innovative Higher Education.

Poister, T. H., & Streib, G. (1999). Performance measurement in municipal government: Assessing the state of the practice. *Public Administration Review*, 325–335.

Rawlings, H. (2012) 'Why research universities must change', *Inside Higher Ed.* Available online at: http://www.insidehighered.com/views/2012/03/30/essay-research-universities-must-pay- more-attention-student-learning.

Seligman, M. E., Ernst, R. M., Gillham, J., Reivich, K., & Linkins, M. (2009). Positive education: Positive psychology and classroom interventions. *Oxford review of education, 35*(3), 293–311.

Senge, P. M. (2006). *The fifth discipline: The art and practice of the learning organization.* Random House LLC.

Senge, P. (1999). It's the learning: The real lesson of the quality movement. *The Journal for Quality and Participation, 22*(6), 34.

Tucker, B. (2012). The flipped classroom. *Education Next, 12*(1), 82–83.

Ward, D. (2013). Sustaining strategic transitions in higher education. *EDUCAUSE review, 48*(4), 12–14, 16, 18, 20, 22.

Weerts, D. J., Rasmussen, C., & Singh, V. (2015). Using design thinking to drive collective impact in higher education. In J. E. Lane (Ed.), *Higher education reconsidered: Executing change to drive collective impact. SUNY Critical Issues Series, 3*, Albany, NY: State University System of New York (SUNY).

Wilson, R. (2010, February 7). For profit college change higher educations landscape. *The Chronicle of Higher Education.* Retrieved from http://chronicle.com/article/For-Profit-Colleges-Change/64012/#comments

Whitney, D. D., & Trosten-Bloom, A. (2010). *The power of appreciative inquiry: A practical guide to positive change (Revised, expanded).* Berrett-Koehler Publishers.

4 The Impact of Technology

Cause and Consequence

Ann Hill Duin, Bruce Maas, and Bradley Wheeler

The Duality of Technology

There is no mistaking that technology can assist in positioning public research universities for relevance and sustainability and students for success. We dare not ignore, however, the consequences of human action or inaction.

Consider Orlikowski's Structurational Model of Technology (shown in Figure 4.1) in terms of technology and the public research university where we have the following:

i human agents—technology designers, users, and decision-makers,
ii technology—material artifacts mediating task execution in the workplace; and
iii institutional properties of organizations, including organizational dimensions such as structural arrangements, business strategies, ideology, culture, control mechanisms, standard operations procedures,... competitive forces, vendor strategies,... state of knowledge about technology, and socio-economic conditions (p. 409).

According to Orlikowski (1992):

> Technology is physically constructed by actors working in a given social context, and technology is socially constructed by actors through the different meanings they attach to it and the various features they emphasize and use. However, it is also the case that once developed and deployed, technology tends to become reified and institutionalized, losing its connection with the human agents that constructed it or gave it meaning, and it appears to be part of the objective, structural properties of the organization.
>
> (p. 406)

DOI: 10.4324/9781315110523-5

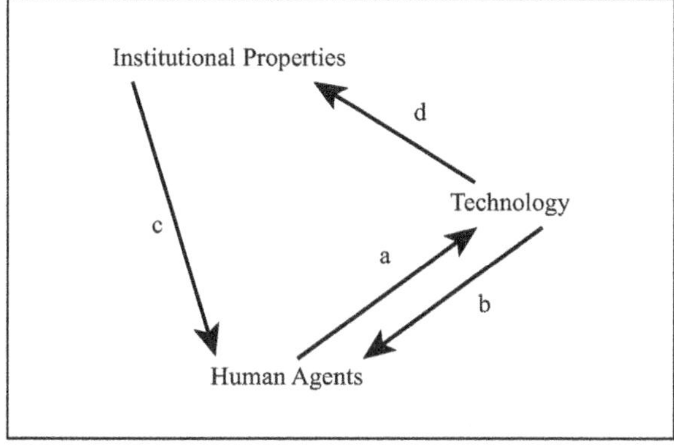

ARROW	TYPE OF INFLUENCE	NATURE OF INFLUENCE
a	Technology as a Product of Human Action	Technology is an outcome of such human action as design, development, appropriation, and modification
b	Technology as a Medium of Human Action	Technology facilitates and constrains human action through the provision of interpretive schemes, facilities, and norms
c	Institutional Conditions of Interaction with Technology	Institutional Properties influence humans in their interaction with technology, for example, intentions, professional norms, state of the art in materials and knowledge, design standards, and available resources (time, money, skills)
d	Institutional Consequences of Interaction with Technology	Interaction with technology influences the institutional properties of an organization, through reinforcing or transforming structures of signification, domination, and legitimation

Figure 4.1 Orlikowski's (1992) Structurational Model of Technology
Adapted from Orlikowski's (1992, p. 410) Structurational Model of Technology

Brad Wheeler, Vice President for Information Technology (IT) and Chief Information Officer (CIO) at Indiana University, summarizes Orlikowski's theory as follows:

> There is this notion that technology causes higher education to be different. A competing school says that organizations cause technology to be something other than what they intended it to be. In effect, technology is both cause and consequence of human action. We cause technology to be created, but once it exists, the consequences of it are based on our human behavior.

As an example, consider a university's need for a better student advising system and the technology we then design and deploy to meet this need. In the case of the University of Minnesota (UMN), our Academic Progress Audit System (APAS, 2017) is a technological artifact that lists student degree requirements, summarizes progress, and explains what a student needs to do to complete a declared degree program. As such, it facilitates and also constrains human action through its specific structure and service indicators. It reinforces and dominates the University's requirements for liberal education and writing intensive courses; students must use and update their APAS regularly to stay on track and ultimately, to graduate. In short, this system legitimizes their work.

Those who built the APAS system incorporated certain interpretive schemes, rules, and norms that define how the university operates; and as students, faculty, and staff use it for advising, it mediates this activity. Through its now many years of use, numerous institutional politics, properties and policies have been reinforced or transformed as a result. As Orlikowski emphasizes, "there are strong tendencies within institutionalized practices that constrain and facilitate certain developments and deployments with technology" (p. 423–424). In fact, anyone reading this chapter can point to examples of the technologies used daily for administrative and academic purposes. In each case, one can usually identify the need for the technology; how the technology facilitates and constrains activity in meeting that need; the institutional properties that influence one's interaction with the technology (intention, resources, and skills); and institutional and human consequences as a result of its use.

The point here, and the one used to frame this chapter, is that the impact of technology is a result of both cause and consequence of human action. The technologies we use and those we envision hold conditions and consequences; our design and use reinforce or transform "structures of signification, domination, and legitimation" (Orlikowski, p. 409). The ultimate tension and dilemma are this: A technology may be designed amid the best of intentions; it's consequences, however, are often startling.

So, what conditions loom largest at this point in time for public research universities? We next share the "Top 10 Issues" drawn from a yearly survey of membership in a national organization—EDUCAUSE—that includes over 1,800 colleges and universities and over 300 corporations. We then focus on those issues holding greatest importance to the co-authors of this chapter, issues that emerged as critical to consider and discuss as they represent the tensions and dilemmas facing public research universities.

The EDUCAUSE Top 10 IT Issues

EDUCAUSE is a nonprofit association comprising a community of IT leaders and professionals committed to advancing higher education. Every year since 2000, Educause has gathered issues from

TOP 10 IT ISSUES: 2000–2015

This graphic tracks the rankings of the top 10 IT issues since 2000. **Clicking or tapping a year** along the top will show the top 10 IT issues for that year. **Hovering over or tapping an issue** will highlight the trend in importance for that issue across years.

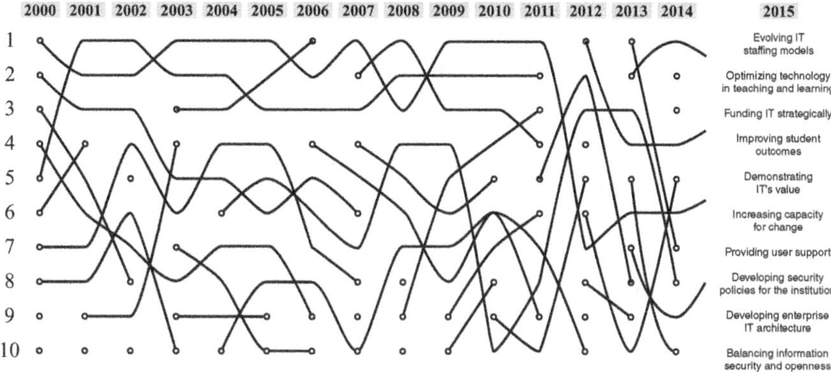

Figure 4.2 Top 10 IT Issues: 2000–2017 (from EDUCAUSE, 2017)
Adapted from Top 10 IT Issues: 2000–2017 (from EDUCAUSE, 2017)

a panel representative of its overall membership. The "Top 10 IT Issues" that are published and discussed broadly provide a glimpse of what the public research university needs to consider as we further incorporate technologies into our institutional fabric. An interactive graphic allows people to gain a sense of the change in technology issues across the last 17 years. Figure 4.2 provides a glimpse of the accelerated pace of change. Study the lines and note the increased pace of chaotic movement over the past 7 years.

Given the small print in this figure, we provide the 2017 Top 10 list here:

1. Information security
2. Student success and completion
3. Data-informed decision making
4. Strategic leadership
5. Sustainable funding
6. Data management and governance
7. Higher education affordability
8. Sustainable staffing
9. Next generation enterprise IT
10. Digital transformation of learning

Note the importance of "Data-informed decision making: Ensuring that business intelligence, reporting, and analytics are relevant, convenient, and used by administrators, faculty, and students" (EDUCAUSE, 2017). Because of technology, public research universities are now able to collect, store, and mine data business intelligence, descriptive and predictive analytics. This is changing the ways in which public research university leaders are making policy decisions.

According to Wheeler (2017), two forces are accelerating the demand for transforming and repurposing data for informed decision making: "Market forces are changing the economics of higher education as financing a college education becomes more of a private good…[and] the growing belief that computational analyses of big data from colleges and universities will yield formerly unknown insights regarding new efficiencies and effectiveness in the competitive market." Returning to the APAS advising system example, our institutions have an abundance of primary data from these many systems of record, yet, as Wheeler states, "few of us have made the substantial investments internally to repurpose our data for new insights". The future impact of technology depends on repurposing data—i.e., analytics—for new insight.

Analytics

> Analytics is one of the breakthroughs for us. We're moving from 'battleship' frameworks (registration systems) and shifting IT attention to the academic side. Cracking the code on the algorithms of the data/patterns. This is the 'game changer.' This is our decade of focusing on the data, but we don't know where our data is or how to mine it, study it, and make action plans accordingly. We are rushing into turning on all of this monitoring to help students, but are we crossing the line? Are we protecting privacy? Where is the line? We have to think clearly on these issues. We need to engage our students on these issues.
>
> (—Mark Askren, Vice Chancellor for Information Technology and CIO, University of Nebraska-Lincoln)

Maas and Gower (2017) define analytics as "the availability of data to make strategic, tactical, and operational decisions". For us, data is an immensely critical component for the public research university system (its people, processes, tools, and data). Our institutions must position themselves to secure value from data, i.e., the impact of technology depends on analytics. Institutions committed to remaining relevant are those that identify baselines and benchmarks, determine trend lines, and commit to pursuing a deep understanding of what matters and what makes a difference. Using data to drive decision-making behavior, these institutions identify patterns and take "actionable intelligence" to enhance student success and institutional achievement.

From interviews with 40 leading institutions that have developed analytics applications in support of student success, Norris and Bear (2013) emphasize that "Optimizing student success is the "killer app" for analytics in higher education. Intelligent investments in optimizing student success garner wide support and have a strong, justifiable return on investment (ROI). Moreover, improving performance, productivity, and institutional effectiveness are the new gold standards for institutional leadership. Enhanced analytics is critical to both optimizing student success and achieving institutional effectiveness" (p. 5).

In terms of consequence, look no further than Arizona State University (ASU) to see that the impact of technology depends on analytics. ASU has gone through a digital transformation to completely transform itself into what many consider to be "the model" for the next generation public research university. ASU started as a state teachers college, then its faculty developed PhD programs and started to conduct research. Michael Crow became ASU's 16th president in 2002, with the goal of transforming the institution into what he calls a "New American University—an institution combining the highest levels of academic excellence, inclusiveness to a broad demographic, and maximum societal impact" (Crow, 2012). Within 10 years, ASU had established over a dozen new transdisciplinary schools and large-scale research initiatives, nearly tripling its research expenditures. Amid an enrollment increase of 30% with minority enrollment increasing 52%, ASU also increased its graduation rate by 19.3%, and it is attracting some of the best faculty talent in the country and world.

President Crow attributes much of this success to the use of analytics. ASU is the model for using data to make decisions. Amid securing less funding from their state than most do, they have created a very large data analytics group (20+ individuals) along with investments in the infrastructure needed for this effort. They cut out inefficient and nonproductive expenditures, reinvesting in infrastructure to support the missions of teaching, research, and outreach. As a result, student success at ASU has been climbing steadily since making this major infrastructure (people, processes, tools, data) investment. Moreover, ASU is the "access campus" in the Arizona system; with digital infrastructure that can scale, it has lead to tremendous gains in student success.

Technology undergirds business intelligence, academic, and learning analytics. An Educause Center for Applied Research (ECAR) study by Goldstein and Katz (2005) emphasized that "a robust academic analytics environment is often associated with leaders who are committed to evidence-based decision making and to ensuring the existence of a well-trained cadre of analysts to work with information" (p. 7). Amid "(1) rising threats to revenue and downward pressure on costs; increased competition and increasing consumer power and choice; and (3) greater pressure on colleges and universities to demonstrate outcomes", public research institutions "with the best information and decision-making capacity can win" (p. 7).

In the years since this study, the expanding need for information and decision-making capacity has resulted in public research universities needing to adopt more sophisticated analytic technologies and techniques that analyze data and develop predictive models and assessment frameworks. Among these are the Predictive Analytics for Student Success (2017), Purdue's Course Signals (2017) project, and the Civitas Learning (2017) space. Analytics continues its advancement through the open learning analytics platform (Siemens et al., 2011), open standards through public and private partnerships, the IMS Global Learning Consortium (2017), and private funding support (Bill & Melinda Gates, 2017).

Despite evidence that analytics will pay significant dividends through increasing efficiency, effectiveness, and student success, far too many continue to see IT systems as being primarily about tools. As Maas and Gower state, institutions think they can "purchase a service from (name your company), and a campus will leapfrog years of data neglect. License tools from (name your company), and the college/university will instantly become a data-driven institution. Neither of these approaches will work unless significant additional investments are made. People, processes, tools, and data form the tetrahedron of a system and its value". People must possess up-to-date skills and have time for devoting attention to analytics; processes must be defined in consistent ways to ensure data quality; and data must be housed in ways that optimize it for analytics.

The cause and consequence of technology depends on how university leaders use analytics for data-based decision making. We urge readers, as Wheeler (2017) notes, to consider the problems or motivations driving current and future initiatives; e.g., whether your institution needs to

- rapidly remediate information reporting and dashboards to get everyone on a common basis of facts;
- accelerate student success goals in terms of graduation rates, retention, course sequencing, etc.;
- empower advisors and students with predictive information to support wise decisions in major and course selection;
- enable better financial decisions by deans and department chairs as they make choices in degrees to offer, frequency of courses, and teaching assignments; and
- benchmark an institution's performance on key performance indicator ratios for efficiency and effectiveness.

To assemble the analytics team, leaders should ask:

- How might my institution's Chief Business Officer (CBO) and CIO serve as foundational partners in this effort?

- How might CBOs and CIOs, along with Provosts, Deans, and faculty, get on the same page, throwing out "Magic" as a solution, and develop an architectural roadmap, complete with the need for process improvement and employee development needed to become a data-driven public research university? How might we get on the same page about the need for analytics infrastructure?

And among the many policy questions, leaders should ask:

- How might we clear policy hurdles such as archaic rules about course fees that prevent us from acquiring and charging back digital content to students at rates far below the cost of paper content?
- How might we address accessibility, so that all students have equal opportunity?

The future of the public research university depends on the courage, tenacity, and commitment to address these questions. And in doing so, we must also focus strongly on the potential consequences stemming from analytics. For example, Gerry McCartney, CIO at Purdue University, emphasizes that there is always a dark side: "We can railroad students with this data. We can segregate even more the able from the less able". In fact, numerous work discusses analytics and issues of privacy, security, and segregation (e.g., Pardo & Siemens, 2014; Tene & Polonetsky, 2013), providing codes of practice for learning analytics (Sclater, 2014) as well as matrices of strategies and choices for understanding ethical concerns in the design, application, and documentation of learning analytics are being developed. For example, in her dissertation research, Swenson (2015) deconstructed and surveyed the ethical concerns of learning analytics, finding that

> the inability of students to provide input into the learning analytics process was the concern most often revealed, followed by a lack of context for interpreting the data by both institutional users and students, and the potential inaccuracies in the predictive model caused by inaccurate or incomplete data. Secondary concerns included an undefined institutional responsibility to act on data, which could put the institution at risk for legal action, as well as the possibility for discrimination to occur during the learning analytics process. Concerns identified less frequently included the potential for students to become objectified (student viewed as data), the lack of an opt-out option for students, the potential for de-anonymizing the student as at-risk, and the failure to develop and communicate principles and policies college-wide. The final concerns identified included inadequate user training (for both students and institutional users), the potential for differential access, and a lack of a vision or mission statement, or code of ethics, created and communicated by the institution (iii).

Leaders of academic analytics initiatives such as Jones, Thomson, and Arnold (2014) emphasize that "technological progress and social enthusiasm for data analytics continues to outpace these concerns". In their focus on student data ownership, they contend that "Higher education must mind the gap: these problems are political, legal, and social land mines for institutions that continue to push forward without addressing them". Vince Kellen, CIO at the University of California, San Diego, agrees that "Data on learning has got to be free and open, not a black box. The student has to weigh in on its use. We must stress privacy and security. If we don't do that, the drawback is that our students and universities will walk away from the use of technology".

In short, as public research universities we most likely hold the greatest stockpile of student data; we also have the greatest stockpile of intellectual property. According to information from the massive database maintained by the Privacy Rights Clearinghouse (PRC, 2017) on data breaches, 19 educational institutions experienced data breaches in 2016, affecting 64,989 records. The PRC database includes information regarding the 5,400 data breaches made public since 2005. It should be of little surprise that the majority (63%) of these breaches are at doctoral institutions, even though doctoral institutions only represent 7% of all U.S. institutions. The recent breaches at Penn State and San Diego State came from governments (other countries) going after intellectual property. Kevin Morooney knows from experience as CIO at Penn State, sharing that "Right now they're WAY more sophisticated than we are".

Public research institutions——our research instrumentation, innovative online programs, exercise equipment, and even light bulbs with IP addresses—all have become vulnerabilities. Each digital artifact requires a lifecycle of maintenance and security applied to it. As we work to achieve "The Internet of Things", those who would do bad things now have an alarming capacity to go after anything: web cameras, exercise equipment, faculty and student data and discovery. According to Morooney:

> It's not that we should not take risk; rather, it's the need to understand all the risks that we're taking so that we can mitigate the risks, so that we can be more intentional about our risk profile. It's endeavoring to understand the risks and develop strategies to mitigate them.
>
> As we endeavor to connect everything, we develop enormous amounts of data of use to bad guys. As we instrument our campuses, and our people and their behaviors, are we having the right kinds of scholarly and operational conversations?

CIOs and IT leaders understand the significance of security, but this is not enough. We need every dean, every budget executive, every faculty member to have the insight that things are connected and enough understanding to be humbled by it. Too many administrative elements in our institutions continue to assume that they can function in a vacuum, and interconnectedness alludes most perspectives. Therefore, given the immense need to champion analytics coupled with the significance of security, as present and past CIOs, we issue a clarion call for intentional interdependence.

Intentional Interdependence

> Consider this: What if a very rich country bought all of higher education in the United States and said, "You run your academics any way you want, because your academic enterprise is unparalleled in the world. However, when it comes to back office stuff, that is ours".
>
> You see, anyone could take 25% out of the collective cost of higher education back office, but it would be because he or she had the authority to make the change.
>
> (– Brad Wheeler, Vice President for Information Technology and CIO, Indiana University)

Everything in the landscape of higher education at this juncture indicates that resources will continue to be constrained. Some public research universities are dealing with consistent and in many cases dramatic ongoing reductions in funding. Reducing the cost of what technology does is huge: it allows us to reduce the cost of both IT and other things. The need is to fund IT strategically through intentional interdependence as a means to increase the public research universities' capacity for ongoing and dramatic change. The promise comes in transformation: achieving a goal in a fundamentally different way.

For public research universities, a critical challenge is accessibility (cost). As Mark Askren shares,

> We have groupthink in higher education: States have decreased their contribution, so we have no alternative but to increase tuition. The bottom line is that we cannot continue this model. Is it worth it for kids to attend? Can technology make a difference? Are we automating existing processes and being more efficient? What can help us break the conundrum of public funding decline and increase in tuition? Technology is the one answer to become more effective and efficient at scale.

President Mitch Daniels (Purdue University, 2015) called on Congress "to join a growing movement to reform higher education, making it more accessible and accountable to students, parents and taxpayers". Strategic investments at Purdue are being made to "advance transformations that center around STEM leadership, world-changing research, transformative education, and affordability and accessibility". Amid this work, Gerry

McCartney shares that information technology has gone from "nice feature on the side" to "core of the business". Technology is central to all public research university strategic directions.

Critical to co-authors is the fact that public research universities for the most part continue to "go it alone", each working to solve problems independently rather than collaboratively. Askren (2013) emphasizes:

> The answer is clear. We have to collaborate. Substantially. And in ways that are far-reaching and very challenging. We have to change our core processes and our default approach, and we have to take some calculated risks. Our institutions, and perhaps our IT community, have largely resisted these changes to this point...
>
> We need to identify, and make, large-scale investments in strategic differentiators for our institutions. The core mission areas of learning, research, and community outreach are where the majority of our time and efforts should be focused. To do that, we need to drive the costs out of our core administrative commodity services, which is where the resources are. And we need to drive those costs out relentlessly.

Unfortunately, in an age when technology becomes more pervasive, public research universities often choose to disempower any individual in steering it collaboratively. In addition, executive leadership in public research institutions too often struggles under the assumption that technology or IT is what you do at Best Buy; the drawback is that executives and boards fail to understand the cause and consequence of the technology artifact. Technology is an artifact that causes things to happen, and at some point the tension will get deep enough to move beyond the double-speak of cost containment.

In his earlier article titled "Speeding Up on Curves", Wheeler (2014) stressed that

> In higher education, we are facing a series of unprecedented curves that our trustees, our senior academic leaders, our senior administrative leaders, and our deans have never seen before... Cost pressures and the increasing digitization of research and education are necessitating a greater shift from campus strategies of independence to dependence and interdependence...
>
> Who, then, are our higher education leaders who will dare to think differently? Who will foresee and shape the solutions for dependence and interdependence to address the challenges of our era rather than respond to these forces as they reshape us?
>
> (pp. 19–20)

As co-authors, we agree: The technological artifact is marching along, and the accelerating rate of the solutions space for any problem is staggeringly steep. The constant rate of acceleration is so great that the challenge comes in choosing which technology to pursue. It has accelerated to the point that making strategic technology decisions is an enormous challenge. As one co-author shared: "It's an arms race: the vendor community owns the solutions; we're in body bags".

A strategy of intentional interdependence is our best means for re-envisioning the future public research university. At some point the default strategy of independence by our public research universities must break. We must aggregate our resources and place control in the academy.

Unfortunately, for executive leadership in our public research universities, it's been much easier to just write the check. Case in point: $5B goes to Elsevier annually, and the main reason is because of the strategy of independence. The reward structures are just not there in the academy to do anything about this; companies like Oracle aggregate and take control. As stated in a news release at Indiana University in 2014:

> It [has become] increasingly clear that isolated, single campus-based approaches to deal with this path to scale would not favor institutions; rather, it would shift control and economic power to entities outside of academia that develop and own technologies and services at scale. These owners would be able to assert the terms for use of content and data on *their* platforms and would almost certainly add new costs to universities. In that shift of decision rights, long held faculty and student rights regarding control of intellectual property and privacy might no longer be decided in the Academy.

Fortunately, however, there's a critical mass of public research universities that have embarked on a digital ecosystem known as Unizin (http://unizin.org/). Unizin is about learning from the past (e.g., Elsevier cost) to create a true consortium that takes advantage of scale to create shared infrastructure to enable innovation. The Unizin site states:

> Higher education is facing a crisis of access, quality, and outcomes. Across the country, universities have invested in similar initiatives to reform their models of course design, delivery, measurement, and improvement. Unizin seeks to generate solutions that serve all consortium members… We want to support faculty and universities by ensuring that institutions and instructors have control of their own content, data, and communications…. Together, we can implement and start utilizing tools and services much faster than universities can on their own.
>
> (4.27.17, "Why Unizin?")

The Unizin vision is to provide key elements of the digital learning landscape that its public research universities can use to improve learning and advance all of higher education. Unizin is "the world's largest learning laboratory. Over half a million students are now part of it. With tagging at a fine level, you can really see what's going on" (Steve Fleagle). Unizin is an attempt to change the game, and it's already had impact. "Vendors are already acting differently with us because we're a part of Unizin. It's changing the academy around learning. We are creating the future digital learning ecosystem: we'll dictate the conditions, the terms, the integration. This will reduce switching costs (e.g., to other learning management systems) in the future. Moreover, we are in charge of our data" (Kevin Morooney).

According to John O'Brien, President and CEO of EDUCAUSE, collaborations like Unizin can be significant "game changers". In complex and emerging areas, public research universities have a strong track record of making investments at the front end, even at the "proof of concept" stage. With their collective breadth and depth, they can tackle analytics or exciting areas like the Internet of Things, where academic investments have not yet hit their stride. "I have no doubt", O'Brien adds, "that investments and explorations will likely begin with research universities leading the way–and in a way that benefits all sectors of higher education in the end".

Our public research universities can experiment and identify, given the scale, effective technological practices. Because of the research focus, our universities can generate findings and bring quantitative depth to this work. The impressive contribution is to bring empirical rigor to these conversations, to executive decisions, and to inter-institutional collaboration. The even greater consequence will come through collaboration.

What "structures of signification, domination, and legitimation" might we be able to reinforce or transform through intentional interdependence? In short, this consequential question demands attention: How is my public research university fostering intentional interdependence?

"Technology Is a Team Sport"

> The strength of higher education for a thousand years has been our innovation and independence to innovate. We now have challenges that come with digital advances. But the solution to these challenges doesn't have to mean all of us developing different infrastructure; let's innovate on advancing learning science together; let's respond more nimbly to the changing needs of our students, together; let's scale our infrastructure to hold costs down in a planned, designed way, together, so that we are not stifling faculty. Let's do so in a way that advances learning science and lifts the entire higher education boat. Together.
>
> (–Bruce Maas)

Technology spurs innovation and transformation in research, teaching/learning, and engagement/outreach. Our "next generation" environments, our very higher education ecosystems, are digital. Witness our active learning classrooms (Drake & Battaglia, 2014; International Forum on Active Learning Classrooms, 2017) and our flipped, hybrid, and online courses and curricula. There is no longer the need for "e" to be attached to our missions to somehow signal technology integration: all research, learning, and engagement includes "e". Technology makes "interoperability; personalization; analytics, advising, and learning assessment; collaboration; and accessibility and universal design" possible (Brown, Dehoney, & Millichap, 2015).

Based on a study of 17 large public research universities, Marcum, Mulhern, and Samayoa (2014) encountered a great deal of excitement about technology-enhanced work and some highly innovative practices, tempered by real limitations. They state that

> Administrators have pinned great hopes on technology as one solution to tightening budgets, recognizing that more work needs to be done to develop coherent, university-wide plans to leverage technology to 'bend the cost curve.' Faculty, meanwhile, endorse the idea of improving student learning, and many have developed sophisticated, technology-enhanced courses. At the same time, there is palpable trepidation….
>
> (p. 3)

Marcum et al. emphasize that "Universities should collaborate on the design and development of the infrastructure, and consider creating incentives for their faculty and units to facilitate cross-institutional collaboration" (p. 6). Wheeler (2017) reiterates this point, strongly encouraging institutions to look among their faculty and to draw on their expertise: "The underlying algorithms that power any predictive model for data enrichment are likely well understood within the academy…Many institutions, particularly research-intensive institutions, have within their ranks deep expertise in big data and modeling. Formally engaging the skills of faculty, post-docs, graduate students, and staff experts may be a very wise use of resources" (para. 49).

In 2012, the Research Universities Futures Consortium conducted a study on the current health and well-being of the American research university. Their first finding was that

> Scarcity of resources (relative to the demand for them) has engendered a hypercompetitive 'winner take all' environment and increased the difficulty of managing academic research activities. Growing regulatory requirements have increased the challenge. To enable impact-oriented research that addresses significant social

> challenges, universities and research sponsors must work together in providing flexible and adaptive strategies, tactics, and operational structures.
>
> (p. 11)

While scarcity of resources has no doubt engendered a hypercompetitive environment, and while universities and research sponsors must certainly work together, this study (sponsored by Elsevier) missed the mark. The future health and well-being of our public research institutions will come through collaboration and partnership, through intentional interdependence. As Burns, Crow, and Becker (2015) stress:

> Developing a successful model for collaborative innovation–for innovating together–is...the most sorely needed disruption in higher education. More than any particular technological development, improving the way that all technologies and innovations are shared and scaled throughout the sector has the potential to fundamentally change the way colleges and universities serve both students and society.
>
> (p. 12)

Both the cause and consequence of technology must come through collaboration. Intentional interdependence such as that evident in Unizin makes possible shared strategic investment for public research institutions to remain relevant amid the change underway across and the threats to higher education. Collaboration such as C-BEN (Competency-Based Education Network, 2017) addresses shared challenges in designing, developing, and scaling competency-based degree programs. Collaboration such as the University Innovation Alliance (UIA, 2017) focuses on making high-quality college degrees accessible to a diverse body of students. Indeed, the many issues and themes we could have also included—e.g., adaptive technology; accessibility standards; interoperability standards; content, authoring, and smart tools; all things mobile and BYOD; learning and research environment architectures—all must be addressed through collaboration and intentional interdependence.

Maas and Gower (2017) quote Keith McIntosh, vice president for information services and CIO at the University of Richmond when he states, "Technology is a team sport". The impact of technology depends on our "departure from the silo tendencies of many higher education institutions. We must move to a culture of data-informed decision making, and that can happen only with the effective use of data to provide actionable information...Partnerships ensure that we have a fighting chance, for the long haul, to find the sweet spot. Some level of investment is needed, and this does not happen by magic, nor does it happen on the cheap" (Maas & Gower, 2017).

To conclude, there is duality in technology, and to understand and envision its impact, one must identify both cause and consequence. According to Klara Jelinkova, current CIO at Rice University (and former IT leader in public research universities), there is also a duality of purpose that we have at the research university that private institutions do not necessarily have:

> Research universities must satisfy the public purpose while also being prestigious. This makes for great impact on the role of technology in a public research institution: Is there a way to be more inclusive at satisfying the public purpose while also moving the needle on the prestige side? This is where technology can help: it can lower the cost of education, the cost of educating the public and making research more available. This then allows for increased investment in its research capability.

Technology provides promise in advancing the public research university mission. Technology makes possible the promise of analytics as well as the security that is imperative for our public research mission to continue. As we near 2020, the promise or drawback will depend on how well our institutions position themselves to be intentionally interdependent. Once again: There is no mistake that technology can assist in positioning public research universities for relevance and sustainability and students for success. We dare not ignore, however, the consequences of human action or inaction.

Author note: With acknowledgement to these higher education leaders for their interviews and willingness to share their insight as part of this chapter:

- Mark Askren, Vice Chancellor for Information Technology and CIO, University of Nebraska-Lincoln
- Steve Fleagle, Associate Vice President and CIO, University of Iowa
- Klara Jelinkova, Vice President for Information Technology and CIO, Rice University
- Vince Kellen, Chief Information Officer, University of California, San Diego
- Gerry McCartney, Vice President for Information Technology and System CIO, Purdue University
- Kevin Marooney, Vice President for Trust and Identity, Internet2
- John O'Brien, President and CEO, EDUCAUSE

References

APAS (Academic Progress Audit System). (2017). Detail at https://onestop.umn.edu/academics/apas

Askren, M. (2013, October). Substantive collaboration: Are we ready to lead? *Educause Review*. http://www.educause.edu/ero/article/substantive-collaboration-are-we-ready-lead

Bill & Melinda Gates Foundation. (2017). Foundation invests in research and data systems to improve student achievement. http://www.gatesfoundation.org/Media-Center/Press-Releases/2009/01/Foundation-Invests-in-Research-and-Data-Systems-to-Improve-Student-Achievement

Brown, M., Dehoney, J., & Millichap, N. (2015). *The next generation digital learning environment: A report on research*. Educause Learning Initiative. http://www.educause.edu/library/resources/next-generation-digital-learning-environment-report-research

Burns, B., Crow, M. M., & Becker, M. P. (2015, March/April). Innovating together: Collaboration as a driving force to improve student success. *Educause Review*. http://www.educause.edu/ero/article/innovating-together-collaboration-driving-force-improve-student-success

Civitas learning space. (2017). https://www.civitaslearningspace.com/

Competency-based education network. (2017). A national consortium for designing, developing and scaling new models for student learning. http://www.cbenetwork.org/

Course signals. (2017). Purdue University. https://www.itap.purdue.edu/learning/tools/course-signals.html

Crow, M. M. (2012, July 18). "No more excuses": Michael M. Crow on analytics. EDUCAUSE Review. http://er.educause.edu/articles/2012/7/no-more-excuses-michael-m-crow-on-analytics

Drake, R., & Battaglia, D. (2014). Teaching and learning in active learning classrooms: Recommendations, research and resources. FaCIT Higher Impact Learning by Design. https://www.cmich.edu/colleges/cst/CEEIRSS/Documents/Teaching%20and%20Learning%20in%20Active%20Learning%20Classrooms%20-%20FaCIT%20CMU%20Research,%20Recommendations,%20and%20Resources.pdf

EDUCAUSE (2017). *Top 10 IT issues lists*. http://library.educause.edu/~/media/files/Library/2016/12/EDUCAUSE2017Top10ITIssuesAlmanacs.pdf

Goldstein, P. J., & Katz, R. N. (2005). Academic analytics: The uses of management information and technology in higher education. EDUCAUSE Center for Applied Research. https://net.educause.edu/ir/library/pdf/ers0508/rs/ers0508w.pdf

IMS global learning consortium. (2017). http://www.imsglobal.org/

International forum on active learning classrooms. (2017). https://cceevents.umn.edu/international-forum-on-active-learning-classrooms

Internet of things. (2017). In *Wikipedia*. https://en.wikipedia.org/wiki/Internet_of_things

Jones, K. M., Thomson, J., & Arnold, K. (2014). Questions of data ownership on campus. *EDUCAUSE Review*, August 25, 2015. http://er.educause.edu/articles/2014/8/questions-of-data-ownership-on-campus

Maas, B., & Gower, M. (2017, May/June). Why effective analytics requires partnerships. *EDUCAUSE Review 52(3)*.

Marcum, D., Mulhern, C., & Samayoa, C. (2014). *Technology-enhanced education at public flagship universities: Opportunities and challenges*. Ithaka S+R. http://sr.ithaka.org/sites/default/files/reports/SR_Technology_Enhanced_Education_Public_Flagship_Universities_121114_0.pdf

Norris, D., & Bear, L. L. (2013). *Building organizational capacity for analytics.* Educause. https://net.educause.edu/ir/library/pdf/PUB9012.pdf

Open learning analytics: An integrated & modularized platform. (2011). http://classroom-aid.com/wp-content/uploads/2014/04/OpenLearningAnalytics.pdf

Orlikowski, W. J. (1992). The duality of technology: Rethinking the concept of technology in organizations. *Organization Science, 3(3)*, 398–427. http://www.dourish.com/classes/readings/Orlikowski-DualityOfTechnology-OrgSci.pdf

Pardo, A., & Siemens, G. (2014). Ethical and privacy principles for learning analytics. *Brittish Journal of Educational Technology, 45(3)*, 438–450.

Predictive analytics for student success. (2017). http://www.parframework.org/

Privacy rights clearinghouse. (2017). *Data breaches.* https://www.privacyrights.org/data-breaches

Purdue University (2015). Purdue President Mitch Daniels calls on Congress to join higher education reformers http://www.purdue.edu/newsroom/releases/2015/Q1/purdue-president-mitch-daniels-calls-on-congress-to-join-higher-education-reformers.html

Sclater, N. (2014). *Code of practice for learning analytics: A literature review of the ethical and legal issues.* JISC. http://analytics.jiscinvolve.org/wp/category/code-of-practice/

Siemens, G., Gasevic, D., Haythornthwaite, C., Dawson, S, Shum, S.B., Ferguson, R., Duval, E., Verbert, K., & Baker, R.S.J. (2011). *Open learning Analytics: An integrated & modularized platform.* Society for Learning Analytics Research. https://solaresearch.org/wp-content/uploads/2011/12/OpenLearningAnalytics.pdf

Swenson, J. (2015). *Understanding ethical concerns in the design, application, and documentation of learning analytics in post-secondary education.* UMN: Dissertation.

Tene, O., & Polonetsky, J. (2013). Big data for all: Privacy and user control in the age of analytics. *Northwestern Journal of Technology and Intellectual Property, 11*(5), 239–273.

The Research Universities Futures Consortium (2012). *The current health and future well-being of the American research university.* http://www.researchuniversitiesfutures.org/RIM_Report_Research%20Future%27s%20Consortium%20.pdf

University innovation alliance. (2017). http://www.theuia.org/

Wheeler, B. (2014, January). Speeding up on curves. *Educause Review.* http://www.educause.edu/ero/article/speeding-curves

Wheeler, B. (2017, March). Who is doing our data laundry? *Educause Review.* http://er.educause.edu/articles/2017/3/who-is-doing-our-data-laundry

5 Public Research Universities as Engines for Economic Development and Innovation

Hiram E. Fitzgerald, Laurie A. Van Egeren, and Burton A. Bargerstock

Since the Morrill Act of 1862, public land-grant universities have reflected their states' priorities, exemplifying the statement, "Colleges are a mirror of the society they serve" (Quiggin, 2014). As states strive to compete in the 21st century global marketplace, their public research universities have accelerated changes in their educational programs, research and development objectives, and pursued global engagement in support of state economic, social, and global initiatives. States originally established public universities to meet local needs for an educated workforce and to increase agricultural production (Bonnen, 1998). However, global competitiveness forced state governments to shift from a relatively narrow focus to engaging outwardly in support of innovation and economic development. Local-to-global and global-to-local knowledge exchanges are critical for maintaining every state's ability to compete in world markets. Global competition requires a higher education infrastructure to advance state priorities and prepare students to participate in and lead global economies that directly benefit statewide workforce development.

In this chapter, we describe transformational changes in higher education that have stimulated research universities to integrate local and regional within-state collaborations with the worldwide competitiveness, connectivity, and innovation necessary to compete in the global economy. We illustrate how systems-focused approaches that link the four helixes of systems change (government, business, higher education, and civil society; Cooper, 2011; Etzkowitz, 2008) drive local innovation and sustainable change in support of global research and scholarly activities that enhance state economies, public health practices, K-12 education, business and economic development and the quality of urban and adult life. State-supported research universities expand competition for students beyond their state and national borders in order to enhance student language, cultural, and diversity skills, but also to expose them to international business practices, legal issues, socio-political infrastructures, and cutting-edge innovations in science, medicine, art, and culture. Higher

DOI: 10.4324/9781315110523-6

education today is preparing T-shaped graduates (Guest, 1991) who can compete for jobs in companies that are increasingly expanding their global reach. Faculty are engaged in trans-disciplinary, trans-university, and trans-national partnerships designed to produce mutually beneficial outcomes locally and globally. Higher education worldwide is relying on co-creative partnerships to merge local knowledge with university knowledge to tackle systemic problems that have local immediacy and global implications. The net result is that state public and land-grant research universities are increasingly aligned with state needs in the 21st century just as they were when they were integral to those needs in the 19th century.

Factors Binding Public and Land-Grant Research Universities to State Priorities

Contemporary emphasis on university–community partnerships and engagement scholarship (Fitzgerald & Simon, 2012; Fitzgerald et al., 2012; Fitzgerald, Allen, & Roberts, 2010; Van de Ven, 2007) can be traced to four-key developments that coalesced to shape a 50-year transformative change in higher education following the end of the Second World War: (1) the gradual integration of Triple Helix (university–industry–government) collaborations (Etzkowitz, 2008), primarily aimed at innovations in economic development; (2) the emergence of use-inspired basic research (Stokes, 1997) and more inclusive definitions of knowledge (Gibbons, Limonges et al., 1994); (3) the recognition that solutions to complex problems require the addition of civil society into the Triple Helix, creating a Quad Helix to stimulate regional community and economic development (Cooper, 2011); and (4) public criticism of higher education's mission drift (Boyer, 1990).

Triple Helix

First, the emergence of the university–industry–government Triple Helix (Etzkowitz, 2008) shifted federal funding away from state-defined priorities to those identified at the federal level. Direct investment into higher education as a major research and development arm of government linked faculty roles and responsibilities to federal priorities to build the nation's science and technology capacity and create a workforce focused on innovation and change (Dubb, 2007; Dzisah & Etzkowitz, 2012). The on-campus impact of the Triple Helix was multi-faceted. State responsiveness to federal funding priorities led to the creation of numerous centers and institutes that, while initially primarily independent from disciplinary departments, have in the past decades provided contexts for promotion of inter-disciplinary and trans-disciplinary research. Fueled by federal funding for workforce development in health, social, behavioral, and natural sciences as well as engineering and information technology, dramatic increases in graduate school enrollments occurred, further shifting research universities toward basic research (Dubb, 2007). Federal influence on higher education increased in proportion to its funding. Compliance monitoring expanded into every facet of university research including offices of grants and contracts administration, institutional review boards for the protection of human subjects and animal welfare, conflict of interest among researchers, responsible conduct of research, funding for student scholarships or loans, and all aspects of diversity and inclusiveness.

Use-Inspired Basic Research

Second, the establishment of the National Science Foundation in 1950 contributed to two funding strands, one of which focused on basic or disciplinary-focused research and the other on problem-focused or applied research, sometimes referred to as "use-inspired basic research" (Stokes, 1997). Use-inspired basic research is linked explicitly to Mode 2 knowledge production (Gibbons et al., 1994). Mode 2 knowledge refers to that which is cross-disciplinary, driven by application, methodologically diverse, societally accountable, and subject to broader quality control standards than provided by within-discipline metrics (Nowotny, Scott & Gibbons, 2001). Recognition that knowledge has multiple sources and is created as much outside the university as within required a new framework for conceptualizing the knowledge process (Hessels & van Lente, 2008; Sonka, Lines, Schroeder, & Hoofing, 2000). Sonka and colleagues adapted a decision-making process identified by Nonaka and Takeuchi (1995) which proposed that all individuals possess not only formal knowledge, which is systematic with definitions and theories (Explicit Knowledge), but also mental models of how the world works (Tacit Knowledge). These two forms of knowledge were proposed to be dynamically interconnected in a cycle of continual knowledge creation, application, and renewal.

Quad Helix

Third, the Triple Helix of university–industry–government was expanded into the Quad Helix (Cooper, 2011) with the inclusion of civil society: the common thread that binds university, government, and business through the intellectual capital it generates, the financial resources it invests into Triple Helix programs, and the quality of community that attracts the workforce needed to sustain community and economic development. The Quad Helix provides the framework for tackling complex or wicked problems through systems change. Systems thinking, innovation, change, and dynamic process are all concepts that are fueled by a philosophy of science that focuses on pragmatism, critical reflection, and non-linear systems dynamics (Fitzgerald & Zientek, 2015; McNall, Barnes-Najor, Brown, Doberneck, & Fitzgerald, 2015; Overton, 2015).

In the remainder of this chapter, we will illustrate how public/land-grant institutions in the 21st century have embraced the Quad Helix framework while continuing their historic alignment to societal needs framed within the context of state priorities, commitment to the co-creation of knowledge, and efforts to find solutions to complex societal problems, while also enhancing the quality of life for all. Although we will draw heavily from the programs and impacts of Michigan's public universities—with special attention to its research-intensive universities—we also include examples of public institutions in other states to convey the breadth of work across public universities in aligning their research, teaching, and service missions to state priorities in a world where global competitiveness is an everyday concern.

We have noted some of the historical events that fueled the emergence of tensions between state constituencies and the public universities they have created. Although tensions are ever-present, all public universities can point to successful initiatives that span local to global spheres across the domains of economic development (local businesses dependent on global supply chain effectiveness to get products to market), art and culture (museums and performing arts centers providing public access to local and global historical artifacts and performances), and overall well-being (research generated by a local pharmaceutical company or global health research that leads to elimination or prevention of disease).

Nevertheless, social critics attack the neoliberal economics of the Triple Helix triad of government, business, and education, its emphasis on unregulated marketplaces, disinvestment in social services, privatization of government-provided services, and devaluing community and public good while extolling the virtues of individualism (Fish, 2009; Lafer, 2017). During an interview conducted by Polychroniou (2013), Giroux argues that financial support for higher education drives many universities into partnerships with "vocational, military and economic considerations, while increasingly removing academic knowledge production from democratic values and projects." reminiscent of President Eisenhower's (1961) caution to the American public that, "In the councils of government, we must guard against the acquisitions of unwarranted influence, whether sought or unsought, by the military-industrial complex". Indeed, in this interview Giroux asserts that "Higher education may be one of the few public places left where knowledge, values, and learning offer a glimpse of the promise of education for nurturing public values, critical hope and a substantive democracy" (Polychroniou, 2013). Cooper's (2011) insertion of civil society into the Triple Helix adds a dimension to dampen the neoliberal view of higher education as career and job training, and preserve the values of liberal education that so positively contribute to innovation, creativity, and enhancement of the quality of life.

State Economic Impact of Michigan's Public Universities

The State of Michigan is a manufacturing state, and for the past 100 years or so, much of its manufacturing capacity has focused on automobiles. In part, the transition from local to global with respect to Michigan's economy can be linked to changes in the automotive industry. Historically, Michigan's automobile production was dramatically affected by two world wars. In each case the effect of war was to slow production and to convert factory production from automobiles to machines of war. Automobile production in 1941, as compared to 1942–1945, dropped from 3 million vehicles to 139,000, but during the 3 years of war, American manufacturing produced "297,000 aircraft, 193,000 artillery pieces, 86,000 tanks, and two million army trucks". (WETA & The American Lives II Film Project,2007, para. 2). A great deal of this production occurred at Ford, Chrysler, Hudson, and other auto plants in Detroit, including Willow Run, which itself employed 60,000 workers. Many of the components for these war machines required import of materials from other countries. For example, aluminum, a necessary metal for aircraft production, is extracted from bauxite, found almost exclusively outside of the United States. This catalyzed the expansion of global supply chains to import the quantities of aluminum for aircraft production.

When automobile production resumed after the war, supply chains for production and manufacturing continued to expand to provide materials for the reconstruction of Europe and Japan. Michigan's manufacturing capacity and its involvement in global reconstruction and automobile production gradually shifted from a heavy focus on within-state supply chains to those that today are interconnected to manufacturing plants throughout the world. For example, the Jeep Patriot is assembled in Illinois, but many of its critical parts are built in Mexico, Japan, and Germany. The Ford Mustang is assembled in Michigan, but its parts suppliers are in four other countries, and nearly half of the core parts of the Cadillac CTS are built in Canada and Mexico.

The point is that for 69 years following the end of the Second World War, the State of Michigan shifted from a local to a global economy, with expanded relationships with manufacturers located throughout the world. In order to support transitions in the state's economic base and increasing globalization, its public universities were required to make similar changes to align to the needs of a globally based economy. Instead of focusing on agricultural production and the development of engineers as required by the Morrill Act in 1862, public and public land-grant research universities broadened their academic and research portfolios to focus on programs aimed at building a work force prepared to be competitive in the global economic marketplace. To advance its competitive advantage in the global marketplace and provide jobs and economic opportunities for the people of Michigan, the state notes that, "Success is determined by the ability to attract and retain the best people and ideas. These 'knowledge workers' balance job opportunities with lifestyle, seeking more than just employment when deciding where to live. The concept of place making considers cultural and natural amenities, resources, and social and professional networks". (Michigan State Housing Development Authority, 2012; see Wyckoff, 2014).

For its public universities, this requires increased emphasis on teaching foreign languages; enhanced opportunities for students and faculty to experience other cultures through research, teaching, study abroad, and experiential learning; and increased attention to all aspects of diversity so that research universities mirror the diversification of the United States population as well as the diversity of world populations and cultures. Building the foundations for future intercultural commerce, nearly all public higher education institutions have aligned with their state's economic globalization efforts by increasing their enrollments of international students, both to encourage local talent development and to create opportunities for future collaborations with their international alumni who create and build successful businesses within their own countries and globally. On the other hand, critics of neoliberalism may argue that increasing international student enrollment reflects higher education's efforts to bolster the local parts of university-as-industry, thereby providing jobs and economic activity in the communities in which institutions are located.

Regardless of motive, United States public universities have been building global perspectives in support of state efforts to globalize their economies to produce local benefits. In order to find and develop new markets to grow the value of its $60 billion exports, Michigan established trade centers in Brazil, Canada, China, and Mexico. In concert, state public higher education has increased enrollments of students from these countries, provided more opportunities for study aboard, established or expanded partnerships with other universities, and broadened collaborations in research and creative programs. For example, Michigan State University has partnership agreements with 28 academic institutions in China and Hong Kong combined, which provide unique opportunities for student and faculty exchanges. As the second most diverse state in agricultural production, it should not be surprising that many of these university collaborations involve such topics as sustainable agriculture, agricultural production, and market expansions.

Economic Impact of Michigan's Public Universities

Michigan's current state-government dashboard includes eight priority domains for strategic development: Financial Health, Health and Wellness, Seniors, Energy and Environment, Public Safety, Talent Development, Infrastructure, and an omnibus category labeled MI

(Michigan) Performance (obesity, infant mortality, literacy, 4-year degree holders, and talent development/retention). Support for many of these priorities are reflected in the programs of its public universities. One approach has been the development of product centers. Such centers not only align with the State of Michigan's priorities but also with the business and economic growth agendas of groups like the Business Leaders for Michigan (2014). In many ways, product centers chase the cutting edge of innovation, collaboration, and community partnership development. For example, students and faculty at the Lake Superior State University Product Development Center have generated over 230 engineering projects for entrepreneurs and businesses in partnership with community businesses and economic development agencies in efforts to improve products or to take product development to scale and increase production capacity. Michigan Technological University has a highly diverse array of local and regional partnerships that have developed a series of integrated programs and services that support innovators and entrepreneurs to scale up their business reach and enhance economic impact. Product centers develop and bring to market consumer products and businesses in agriculture, natural resources, and sectors of the state's emergent bio-economies (Presidents Council State Universities of Michigan, 2014).

The State of Michigan identified advanced storage systems as a strategic growth cluster in order to generate an estimated 54,000 jobs. Wayne State University's partnerships with the Southeast Michigan Advanced Energy Storage Systems Initiative, the Michigan State Energy Sector Partnership, and the Michigan Academy for Green Mobility Alliance are responding to the needs of this rapidly emerging industry by strengthening communications with industry, workforce development agencies, and community college partners to define workforce requirements, developing technologically progressive curricula, and gathering and disseminating innovative educational materials to a broad network of national institutions. The University of Michigan-Flint's Innovation Center supports development of small business models and non-profit organizations that support regional and statewide growth. Through its Regional Economic Innovation program, Michigan State University's Center for Community and Economic Development collaborates with all Michigan colleges and universities, including community colleges, to develop local economic development initiatives through student-led, faculty-guided projects. The projects provide community and economic development professionals with access to technical assistance and data analysis that may not otherwise be available to them.

All of these examples provide students with opportunities to connect academic learning to real-world problems. At the same time, they increase the community and economic development skills of the graduates of

Michigan's universities and community colleges. Efforts such as these are linked to broader efforts to retain the talent, innovation, and workforce involvement of the graduates of Michigan's state supported higher education institutions, and each of these efforts strengthens Michigan's universities to successfully navigate the local to global nexus (Hudzik & Simon, 2012).

Michigan's public universities also contribute directly to Michigan's economy. For example, in 2012, Michigan's 15 public universities had an aggregate statewide economic impact of $24 billion, including nearly $10 billion in employee wages, $7 billion in non-wage expenditures, and $7 billion in student spending. The nearly 1.3 million alumni residing in Michigan generated $47 billion in salaries and wages (Horwitz & Superstine, 2013).

In 1998, Michigan was one of 45 states to share in a multi-billion-dollar settlement with the United States tobacco industry. The following year, Governor John Engler drew upon those resources to establish the Michigan Life Science Corridor, consisting of the state's three research universities (Michigan State University, University of Michigan, and Wayne State University), as well as the private Van Andel Institute in Grand Rapids. The purpose of the state's investment was to stimulate innovations in biotechnology research in the life sciences as a means to also create new industries and enhance economic growth. In 2002, Governor Jennifer Granholm added homeland security and alternative fuel research to the mission and simultaneously re-named the effort as the Michigan Technology Tri-Corridor. By 2006 yet another transformation occurred when the three research universities formed the University Research Corridor with three more generic goals (innovation, new business development, and new technologies) meant to make the Corridor more inclusive of disciplinary, cross-disciplinary, and cross-university initiatives (Sallee & Agemy, 2011).

The Corridor, thus transformed, became one of seven major tri-university research clusters in the United States. In 2011, the seven tri-university clusters in the United States received $115.5 billion to support research and development, the majority of which was directed to the life sciences (57%), engineering (15%), physical sciences (7%), environmental sciences (5%), and math/computer science (4%) 19 of the 21 institutions connected to the research clusters are public and/or public land-grant research universities (see Table 5.1). In 2015, the Corridor institutions enrolled 70 percent of all 4-year college students in Michigan (155,000), graduated 34,547 students, had an aggregate 1.2 million alumni, supported 66,134 employees, spent $2.15 billion on research, increased state tax revenue by $500 million, and had a $16.5 billion impact on the state's economy. Since 2002 they have fostered 210 start-up companies (Rosaen & Taylor, 2017; Superstine & Rosaen, 2014). What was originally initiated by state government has grown into a vibrant, self-sustaining, multi-university research incubator harnessing the intellectual capital of Michigan's public

Table 5.1 United States University Clusters Devoted to Stimulating Economic Development

Michigan	Michigan State University[d]	University of Michigan[c]	Wayne State University[c]
Northern California	University of California[c] San Francisco	University of California[d] Berkeley	Stanford University[e]
Southern California	University of California[c] Los Angeles	University of California[c] San Diego	University of Southern California[e]
Illinois	University of Chicago[e]	University of Illinois At Urbana-Champaign[d]	Northwestern University[e]
Massachusetts	Harvard University[e]	Massachusetts Institute of Technology[d]	Boston University[a,e]
North Carolina	Duke University[e]	University of North Carolina[c] Chapel Hill	North Carolina State University[dthat]
Pennsylvania	Pennsylvania State University[d] System	University of Pittsburgh[c]	Carnegie Mellon University[e]
Texas[b]	University of Texas[c]	Texas A & M University[d]	Rice University[e]

[a] In previous reports Tufts was included in the Massachusetts cluster. In 2014, the Anderson Group replaced Tufts with Boston University.

[b] University of Texas, Texas A & M, and Rice comprise an additional cluster added in 2014.

[c] Public University.

[d] Public Land Grant University.

[e] Private University.

research universities to foster discovery, economic development, and partnerships with business and industry throughout the state and beyond, in alignment with state priorities. Moreover, as we illustrate throughout this chapter, state and global priorities are deeply intertwined through international corporations, global supply chain transportation systems, and multi-lingual and multi-cultural employees, all of which are synergistically bound to state and public university priorities for economic and workforce development.

Economic Impact of Michigan's Public Land Grant University

Michigan State University alone reported a $5.1 billion impact, comparable to analyses published by other public universities around the United States (see Table 5.2). Although the number of employees, external grants

Table 5.2 Selected Sample of Public and Land Grant University Reports on Annual Economic Impact[a] (in billions of dollars), Number of Employees, and Full Time Students

			Employees		
University	*Individual*[b]	*System*[c]	*Individual*	*System*	*Students*
Georgia	2.16	14.10	22,196	139,263	309,469
Oregon State	1.93		15,000		24,393
Pennsylvania State	8.50			44,000	98,097
Minnesota	8.60		16,193		52,102
Michigan State	5.24		11,387		50,085
Colorado State	4.10		6,200		30,000
Wisconsin Madison	9.60		7,924		43,275
Arizona State	2.90		24,200		73,373
Maryland	3.40			23,508	37,272
North Dakota	1.30		3,502		15,143
Texas A&M	1.70				53,337

[a] Criteria determining economic impact varies from one institution to another. Wisconsin's impact includes its hospital/medical school. Arizona State's impact is based on its connection to the city of Phoenix only.

[b] Individual refers to single institution impacts.

[c] System refers to state university system impacts (2015 data).

and contracts received, and funds generated and spent collectively create estimates of economic impact, actual programmatic initiatives tell the on-the-ground story of how state universities align their student experiences and faculty research and development activities with state priorities more explicitly and illustrate the growing influences of Triple Helix (Etzkowitz, 2008) and Quad Helix (Cooper, 2011) approaches to university–community partnerships.

Creative Capital: Art, Culture, and Economic Development

Public universities also contribute to local economies and to public awareness of cultural diversity through support of folk, culture, natural history, science, and art museums, performing arts centers, public festivals, and community-based programs in music, dance, drama, and choir. Active children's programs in the arts provide opportunities for engagement with creative activities that often are missing or de-emphasized in public schools. Such programs enhance children's problem-solving and critical thinking skills, as well as stimulate neurobiological development that has spin-off effects on their mathematical and science skills and ultimately their potential for economic success.

Investigators at Michigan State University have attempted to discern whether engagement with the arts during childhood is predictive of innovation skills or future economic success. Their work suggests that there are strong relationships between childhood activities and post-graduate performance. LaMore et al. (2013) coined the term "creative capital" to capture the extent to which involvement with arts and crafts during childhood predicts such post-graduate outcomes as the creation of companies or obtaining patents for inventions. They found that college honors students who studied STEM disciplines were 3 to 8 times more likely than the general public to establish companies or obtain patents after graduation if they had been involved in creative activities during childhood (e.g., pottery, ceramics, photography, woodwork, electronics/computer programming for pleasure). Studies of individuals who have achieved recognition as Nobel Laureates or as members of prestigious national academies or honor societies indicate that they are 15 to 35 times more likely to have avocations involving the arts than are individuals who do not achieve such distinctions (Root-Bernstein & Root-Bernstein, 2004; Root-Bernstein et al., 2008). Investing in community music schools, children's choirs, and arts and crafts, and science festivals provide university faculty and students opportunities to engage directly with the publics they serve, and simultaneously contribute to the quality of place as an aspect of quality of life.

But creative capital that rests on home-spun talent suffers if not enriched by the creative capital that resides in locales broader than local community. If investment in the arts is to create dynamic and competitive creative capital, those who create performances, exhibits, and showings must experience art and culture beyond the borders of their local campus, state, or nation. Cultural exchanges provide reciprocal opportunities for residents to compete, innovate, and challenge local perspectives, beliefs, and values regarding the foundational meanings of culture and artistic expression. Tensions may arise regarding the selection of particular performers or performers from particular countries when members of the community do not value alternate belief systems or political entities. Such tensions may lead to deliberative dialogue about differences and values that can provide rich opportunities to deepen understanding of the meaning of civic responsibility in a democratic society, or a deeper understanding of how art and culture can often transcend other belief systems and illustrate a common humanity in expressive art. Thus, in creating a context for fostering the kinds of global cultural exchanges necessary to support vibrant local arts and culture, public universities are well-situated to convene dialogue, further understanding, enrich democratic citizenship, and expand markets for artistic performances and products.

Innovation and Entrepreneurial Development

Consistent with Michigan's priorities, many public universities have created innovation centers, often blended with university-created non-profit corporations focused on entrepreneurship and economic development. In contrast to the extensive number of centers and institutes located on campus and affiliated with specific colleges, universities also create non-profit corporations that are fully independent of the university, although closely aligned with its mission and anchored in community. To that end, all of the on-campus and community-anchored corporate entities are critical aspects of the institution's community engagement scholarship mission.

The examples of such activities at Michigan State University are illustrative of similar entities established by other public universities in their efforts to stimulate innovations in economic development and growth in their states. A defining feature of Michigan State University's (MSU) efforts is to create or co-create with community partners such as non-profit corporations that may initially be front-led by the university but located in communities with the goal of becoming fully self-sufficient.

Information Technology Empowerment Center (ITEC)

Information Technology Empowerment Center (ITEC) was developed through a university–community partnership, initiated by a resident of Lansing who convinced representatives of the core participating entities to invest in after-school educational programs designed to enhance creativity through exposure to computer games that require critical thinking and problem solving, and which, not so incidentally, are also fun. Faculty from engineering, education, psychology, and education, with support from MSU's office of University Outreach and Engagement, area information technology companies, Lansing Community College, and the Lansing School District collaborated to establish ITEC, a community-based non-profit corporation devoted to providing programs to stimulate problem-solving skills and creative thinking among middle-school age students involved in STEM-related course work. Over time, programs also targeted elementary-age students and math skills as well as adults seeking to develop or hone their skills with various computer software programs. Recent efforts have focused on helping girls (ages 9–13) to develop skills and interests in STEM for their personal and nascent professional development in response to the need for a more diverse and technologically skilled workforce for the broader Michigan economy.

Located in a community neighborhood center, ITEC has 18 training sites located throughout Greater Lansing, with partners such as the area public libraries, the Boys and Girls Club, YMCAs, Lansing Public Schools, and area churches. Children can work on computer program design at each of these locations, under the guidance of MSU graduate students in teacher education, computer science, and other campus departments and community members trained in the specific programs used in ITEC's educational programming. The success of the program is documented by improvements in children's skills as well as the investments in ITEC programs from various philanthropic funding agencies, informational technology companies, transportation companies, the City of Lansing, and area educational institutions.

Innovation Centers

One way for universities to promote the development of small businesses and support creative individuals to develop ideas into products that can compete in the marketplace is to provide opportunities for exposure to divergent views, experiences, and knowledge. Innovation centers provide the appropriate context for continual interaction and dialogue among individuals with varying levels of experience, diverse perspectives, and tolerance for risk who have a shared commitment to find new ways to compete in the New Economy and 21st Century Knowledge Economy.

For public universities to engage fully in New Economy and Knowledge Economy initiatives, they need to find answers to at least three questions. How do we: (1) effectively transfer university intellectual property to the marketplace?, (2) enable businesses to have access to university researchers?, and (3) encourage innovations that may lead to new intellectual property creation or new collaborations with businesses in the public sector?

The creation of the MSU Innovation Center provides one example of how public research-intensive universities attempt to address each of these questions. The MSU Innovation Center, located within the East Lansing Innovation Center, comprises three separate but closely interconnected organizations: Spartan Innovations, MSU Business Connect, and MSU Technologies. Spartan Innovations focuses on support for student, faculty, and community entrepreneurship and innovation development as well as commercialization support for businesses in the food, agricultural, and natural resource areas MSU Business Connect provides support for the development of research partnerships, economic development, and business support for university connections with established companies seeking to initiative new partnerships for economic development. MSU Technologies provides faculty and businesses with guidance on intellectual property rights and commercialization licensing of products produced through their partnerships. The collective focus of the Innovation Center is to support the development of new discoveries that can then be translated into new businesses and products, particularly within the domains of biotechnology, defense, energy, environment, informatics, and nanotechnology.

In order to bring new generations into the innovation center mix, MSU faculty created The Hatch, as a partnership with the MSU

Innovation Center, the city of East Lansing, and the Lansing Economic Area Partnerships (LEAP), an entity for which the university served as a co-founder with multiple government entities and businesses in Greater Lansing. The Hatch is part of the university's efforts to annually provide opportunities to cultivate a new cohort of innovative entrepreneurs. In addition to existing as an anchor serving institution promoting innovation and economic development through place-based organizations within communities, MSU also created new spaces to stimulate economic partnerships with university researchers.

Corporate Research Parks

Many universities have dedicated land to support development of corporate research parts primarily focused on the diverse areas of science and technology. The dramatic increase in such parks led to the creation of the Association of University Research Parks (AURP) in 2001 (Association of University Research Parks, 2014) Currently, 59 percent of AURP sustaining members are public universities, including Purdue, Wisconsin-Madison, Maryland, Montana State, Oklahoma, Virginia Tech, and the Research Foundation Triangle of North Carolina. There are more than 700 science and technology research parks worldwide that are already active or in various stages of construction and/or development. Research parks can facilitate development of new products (translating science into products through technology), facilitate scale-up for university inventions, serve as incubators for new small businesses development, or provide cutting-edge knowledge to enhance the quality of existing corporate products.

The mission of the MSU University Corporate Research Park is to mutually benefit the university and tenants through the advancement of research, technology, development of new knowledge, and commercialization of intellectual property. MSU Biotechnologies, a component of the MSU Foundation, is devoted to taking scientific findings and using technology to develop products of use to society, often through use-inspired basic research (Stokes, 1997). MSU Biotechnologies is a model for trans-disciplinary research with faculty from at least 13 disciplinary units working to create useful products from discoveries and partnering with organizations to facilitate creation of products of societal value, particularly within the State of Michigan and within the context of its global priorities.

Triple Helix and Quad Helix university–community partnerships, corporate parks, innovation centers, incubators, trans-disciplinary research activities, and projects such as the $700 million expansion of the Facility for Rare Isotope Beams (FRIB) challenge a number of Michigan State University's institutional policies and practices, many of which were established over a half century ago. Trans-disciplinary approaches to discovery scholarship may collide with structures such as disciplinary departments and functions such as evaluative criteria for faculty promotion and tenure. Combined with the democratization of knowledge through technology and increasingly open access to information, these approaches also cross traditional ways of educating students. In concert with changes throughout higher education, institutions like the University of Minnesota and Michigan State University are adopting the concept of the T-shaped professional (Alperovitz, 2011) to apply it to T-shaped faculty (trans-disciplinary scholars) and T-shaped students; that is, individuals who have both disciplinary depth in skills and knowledge, and the ability to work collaboratively and effectively across disciplines and systems. Tomorrow's talent must have the adaptive skills needed to work in teams, understand systems, negotiate boundaries across disciplines, and also to have deep knowledge within a discipline. Whereas economic development may be the driving force to create complex university–community partnerships, universities must devote the same level of innovation and boundary crossing needed to create learning environments and experiences that will assure that Triple and Quad Helix partnerships will be powered by a T-shaped workforce ready to meet the needs of their state's local and increasingly global economies.

After and End Thoughts

This chapter has shaped up to be a sweeping historical narrative of societal interconnection, institutional adaptation, and globalization. It also made us think about transformation and how it is not always easy to see up-close in real time. There have been large and small changes in the higher education environment—some succeeding, some not—but collectively producing altered contexts that shape assumptions and practices. All of this may be only vaguely perceptible at close range until someone makes sense of it in his or her own way and crafts that understanding into a story.

Our own story is multi-fold. It asserts that state-established public universities, particularly land-grant universities, accomplish specific goals within the context of state needs and priorities. Many years ago, needs focused on providing the public with access to higher education, particularly in domains that would accelerate food production, industrial capacity, and, somewhat less directly, quality of life. Architects assert that form follows function, and to some extent the metaphor applies to 21st century initiatives often broadly referred to as New Economy or Knowledge Economy. As federal and state governments and private businesses strive to be competitive in global marketplaces, they have increasingly invested in America's research universities to provide the research and development innovation necessary to generate the competitive edge and workforce needed to sustain success.

Drawing freely upon exemplars from Michigan's public universities, with special emphasis on its three research-intensive universities, we have focused on economic development to illustrate how higher education functions align with state strategic initiatives and priorities. We conclude, without apology and with some degree of assertiveness, that public research universities' alignment with state priorities is so strong, they not only have value as a public good locally and globally, but they reflect an extraordinary return on investment with respect to state financial support and university research output. We have provided an affirmation of Quiggin's (2014) assertion that universities mirror state needs and priorities. Moreover, through the generation of Triple Helix and Quad Helix partnerships, public research universities will continue to have significant impacts on state efforts to compete effectively in global economies. State global economies need state global universities!

What do the transformational changes in higher education and the increasing alignment of state and public university missions mean for the future? To answer this question, it is best to think of short- and long-term outcomes. In the short-term, tensions will likely continue between state legislative and public priorities that challenge the academic freedom and basic research traditions of higher education. The need for an educated workforce in highly specific domains will create continued tension between a "liberal arts" approach to education and an approach that focuses on generating a workforce with specific skills to meet the needs of business and industry, health care, and education. Resolution of such conflicting tensions may resolve in the short term as public higher education aligns more closely with state local–global needs. Nevertheless, the full impact of neoliberal economic policies and practices more than likely has yet to be realized.

In the long term, how can we predict systemic changes that may occur intentionally or unintentionally in public higher education? Who could have predicted the impact of the Morrill Act? Who could have predicted the impact of the creation of the National Science Foundation and shift of research priorities to federally focused needs? Who can predict how technology-driven access to knowledge will impact the public university of the future? What seems to be clear is that higher education needs to be intentionally part of the state and national conversation about public education of the future. What is easy to predict is that somehow, public higher education in 2050 will be different than it is today. The question is, how different and to whose benefit?

References

Alperovitz, G. (2011, June). The new-economy movement. *The Nation*. Retrieved from http://www.thenation.com/article/160949/new-economy-movement

Association of University Research Parks. (2014). AURP Sustaining Park Members. *Association of University Research Parks website*. Retrieved from http://www.aurp.net/sustaining-park-members

Bonnen, J. T. (1998). The land-grant idea and the evolving outreach university. In R. M. Lerner & L. A. K. Simon (Eds.), *University-community collaborations for the twenty-first century* (pp. 25–70). New York, NY: Garland.

Boyer, E.L. (1990). *Scholarship reconsidered: Priorities of the professoriate.* Lawrenceville: Princeton University Press.

Business Leaders of Michigan (2014). *Compete, invest, grow: Michigan turnaround plan.* www.businessleadersfor Michigan.com.

Cooper, D. (2011). *The university in development: Case studies of use-oriented research.* Cape Town, South Africa: Human Services Research Council.

Dubb, S. (2007). *Linking colleges to communities: Engaging the university for community development.* College Park, MD: The Democracy Collaborative at University of Maryland.

Dzisah, J., & Etzkowitz, H. (Eds.) (2012). *The age of knowledge: The dynamics of universities, knowledge and society.* Leiden, the Netherlands: Brill Academic Publishers.

Eisenhower, D. D. (1961, January 17). DDE's Papers as President, Speech Series. Box 38, Final TV1, NAID Number 594599.

Etzkowitz, H. (2008). *The triple helix: University-industry-government innovation in action.* New York, NY: Routledge.

Fish, S. (2009, March 8). Neoliberalism and higher education. The opinion page, *The New York Times.*

Fitzgerald, H. E., Bruns, K., Sonka, S. T., Furco, A., & Swanson, L. (2012). Centrality of engagement in higher education. *Journal of Higher Education Outreach and Engagement, 16*(*3*), 7–27.

Fitzgerald, H. E., & Simon, L. A. K. (2012). The world grant ideal and engagement scholarship. *Journal of Higher Education Outreach and Engagement, 16*(*3*), 33–55.

Fitzgerald, H. E., & Zeintek, R. (2015). Learning cities, systems change and community engagement scholarship. *New Directions for Adult and Continuing Education, 145*, 21–33.

Fitzgerald, H. E., Allen, A., & Roberts, P. (2010). Campus-community partnerships: Perspectives on engaged research. In H. E. Fitzgerald, C. Burack, & S. Siefer (Eds.), *Handbook on engaged scholarship: Contemporary landscapes, future directions. Community-campus partnerships* (Vol. 2, pp. 5–28). East Lansing, MI: Michigan State University Press.

Gibbons, M., Limoges, C., Nowotny, H., Schwortzman, S., Scott, P., & Trow, M. (1994). *The new production of knowledge: The dynamics of science and research in contemporary societies.* San Francisco, CA: Sage.

Guest, D. (1991, September). The hunt is on for the Renaissance Man of computing. *The Independent.*

Hessels, L. K., & van Lente, H. (2008). Re-thinking new knowledge production: A literature review and a research agenda. *Science Direct: Research Policy, 37*, 740–760.

Horwitz, J. & Superstine, S. (2013). *The economic footprint of Michigan's fifteen public universities. Presidents Council State University of Michigan.* East Lansing: Anderson Economic Group.

Hudzik, J., & Simon, L. A. K. (2012). From a land-grant to a world-grant ideal: Extending public higher education core values to a global frame. In D. M. Fogel, & E. Madson-Huddle (Eds.), *Precipice or crossroads? Where America's great public universities stand and where they are going midway through their second century.* Albany: NR: University of New York.

Lafer, G. (2017, May 5). The corporate assault on higher education. *The Chronicle Review*, B8–B10.

LaMore, R., Root-Bernstein, R., Root-Bernstin, M., Schweitzer, J. H., Lawton, J. L., Roraback, A. P. … Fernandez, L. (2013). Arts and crafts: Critical to economic innovation. *Economic Development Quarterly, 27*, 221–229.

McNall, M. A., Barnes-Najor, J. V., Brown, R. E., Doberneck, D., & Fitzgerald, H. E. (2015). Systemic engagement: Universities as partners in systemic approaches to community change. *Journal of Higher Education Outreach and Engagement, 19*, 1–25.

Michigan State Housing Development Authority. (2012). *MI Place website.* Retrieved from http://www.miplace.org

Nonaka, I., & Takeuchi, H. (1995). *The knowledge creating company.* New York: Oxford University Press.

Nowotny, H., Scott, P., & Gibbons, M. (2001). *Rethinking science: Knowledge and the public in an age of uncertainty.* Cambridge: Polity.

Overton, W. F. (2015). Processes, relations, and relational-developmental-systems. In W. F. Overton, P. C. M. Molenaar, & R. M. Lerner (Eds.), *Handbook of child psychology and developmental science: Theory and method* (pp. 9–62). John Wiley & Sons, Inc.. https://doi.org/10.1002/9781118963418.childpsy102

Polychroniou, C. J. (2013, March 30). Neoliberalism and the politics of higher education: An interview with Henry A. Giroux. C. J.Polychroniou (/author/itemlist/user/45668), Truthout (http://truth-out.org)\Interview

Presidents Council State Universities of Michigan. (2014). Community-University partnerships invested in Michigan's future. *Presidents Council State Universities of Michigan website.* Retrieved from http://pcsum.org/MichigansFuture

Quiggin, J. (2014). Campus reflections. *The Chronicle Review.*

Root-Bernstein, R. S., & Root-Bernstein, M. (2004). Artistic scientists and scientific artists: The link between polymathy and creativity. In R. Sternberg, E. Grigorenko, & J. Singer (Eds.), *Creativity: From potential to realization* (pp. 127–152). Washington, DC: American Psychological Association.

Root-Bernstein, R. S., Allan, L., Beach, L., Bhadula, R., Fast, J., Hosey, C., & Weinlander, U. (2008). Arts foster success: Comparison of nobel prize winners, royal society, national academy, and sigman xi members. *Journal of the Psychology of Science Technology, 1*(2), 51–63.

Rosaen, A. L., & Taylor, T. (2017). *Empowering Michigan: Tenth annual economic impact report of Michigan's university research corridor.* East Lansing, MI: Anderson Economic Group, LLC. Retrieved from http://www.andersoneconomicgroup.com/Portals/0/upload/URC_Econ%20Impact_1-24-2017.pdf

Sallee, C. M., & Agemy, E. (2011). *The university research corridor's support for information and communication technology in Michigan.* East Lansing, MI: Anderson Economic Group, Inc. (www.AndersonEconomicGroup.com).

Sonka, S. T., Lins, D. A., Schroeder, R. C., & Hofing, S. L. (2000). Production agriculture as a knowledge creating system. *International Food and Agribusiness Management Review, 2*(2), 165–178.

Stokes, D. E. (1997). *Pasteur's quadrant: Basic science and technological innovation.* Washington, DC: The Bookings Institution.

Superstine, S. L., & Rosaen, A. L. (2014). *Empowering Michigan: Seventh annual economic impact report of Michigan's university research corridor.* East Lansing, MI: Anderson Economic Group, Inc. Retrieved from http://www.andersoneconomicgroup.com/Portals/0/upload/URC_EconImpact_2013_Jan%207%20for%20website.pdf

Van de Ven, A. H. (2007). *Engaged scholarship: A guide for organizational social research*. Oxford, UK: Oxford University Press.

WETA, & The American Lives II Film Project (2007). *War production*. Retrieved from http://www.pbs.org/thewar/at_home_war_production.htm

Wyckoff, M. A. (2014). Definition of place making: Four different types. *Planning and Zoning News*, *32*, 10–13.

6 The Iron Triangle Revisited

Re-Envisioning Public Research University Financing

David J. Weerts and Nichole Sorenson

Research universities are important cultural institutions that develop local, national, and global economies and act as centers for social commentary and critique. Because of their global significance, research universities are considered "among the central institutions of 21st-century knowledge economies" (Altbach & Salmi, 2011, p. 3). Yet, the anxiety about the future of public funding for research universities in the U.S. is palpable. A mix of cultural, economic, political, and demographic changes has led to a contentious higher education policy environment with no end in sight.

This chapter explores the tensions and dilemmas related to financing public research universities in the U.S. and possibilities for re-envisioning the financing these institutions in the future. We begin our chapter by describing the complex changes that have shifted the higher education financing landscape significantly in the past three decades. We then discuss how public research university leaders have responded to these shifts in the realm of governance reform proposals and revenue growth strategies. The strengths and limitations of these strategies are discussed. We conclude this chapter by imagining ways in which a re-envisioned public research university might alleviate current tensions and promote a productive way forward.

Public Research Universities in a Shifting Financial Landscape

The landscape of financing American higher education continues to shift in complex and unpredictable ways. Mountains of commentaries, reports, and scholarly articles paint a gloomy picture about the future of funding public higher education. Most prominent in this discussion is evidence about the relative decline in state support for public colleges and universities. While state spending on higher education increased in absolute terms by $10.5 billion from 1990 to 2010, it has not kept up with escalating costs of services and a growing population of students entering the system. The amount states spent on higher education per full time equivalent student

DOI: 10.4324/9781315110523-7

enrollment declined by 26.1 percent between 1990 and 2010 (Quinterno, 2012). Experts in the field of higher education finance conclude that the current model of funding higher education at the state level is unsustainable due to unresolved structural deficits, growing Medicare costs, and financial pressures on families for goods and services that exceed their income growth (Finney, 2014).

A confluence of cultural, social, economic, demographic, and political shifts that have contributed to the relative decline in levels of public support for higher education since the mid-20th century. Between the end of World War II and the 1960s, access to higher education was expanded significantly and the nation invested heavily in educational infrastructure (Cohen & Kisker, 2010; Jencks & Reisman, 1968). However, this "golden age" came to an end in the 1970s as fallout from campus riots coincided with soaring inflation, high unemployment, oil crises, wage and price controls, and corporate downsizing (Freeman & Holloman, 1975; Lazerson, 1997). Out of this cultural, political, and economic disruption emerged a new conservatism in the 1980s which promoted an alternative vision of higher education primarily focused on preparing students for jobs. Consequently, higher education soon became widely viewed as a private good rather than a public good (Berrett, 2015; St. John & Parsons, 2004). With this shift, the burden of financing higher education shifted drastically to students and parents, especially at leading public research universities (see Mitchell, 2015).

By the late 20th century, a perfect storm was brewing that began to sour public confidence in higher education. As institutions were getting more expensive for students and families, public research universities were especially seen as bloated, elite, out of touch, and not organized to meet the needs of a changing society (Kellogg Commission on the Future of State and Land-Grant Universities, 1999; St. John & Parsons, 2004; Thelin, 2004). In general, the country was beginning to lose patience with many large American institutions of all types. Discontent with public research universities mirrored growing public skepticism of public schools, unions, churches, medical, and legal professions (Heclo, 2008). In addition, the country grew increasingly politically polarized (Abramowitz, 2013; Jacobson, 2010), and in some cases, higher education became wedge issue accentuating these divisions (Cramer, 2016).

Adding to this contentious political environment, national demographic shifts almost ensure that public funding for higher education will face additional hurdles in the future. Research shows that state funding for higher education is especially strained in states with large populations of older Americans since demands for health care and other services among this group crowd out education funding (McLendon, Hearn, & Mokher, 2009; Rizzo, 2006; Stinson, 2012). One can predict that the growing population of older Americans will have a significant negative impact on funding higher education in the future.

Public research universities are uniquely situated within these funding shifts as compared to other sectors of public higher education. A 20-year longitudinal study of state support for higher education found that state appropriations for public research universities have been the least stable over the past two decades as compared to regional and 2-year colleges. In interpreting their findings, authors suggested that legislators may view public research institutions as more expensive, less accessible, and better able to generate their own money through gifts and grants. Especially in tough economic times, public research universities may be viewed as most independent in weathering financial storms and have the ability to tap into other sources of revenue (Weerts & Ronca, 2012).

Overall, a range of forces have been a game changer in financing public research universities over the past four decades. The relationship between higher education leaders, public officials, and the general public is increasingly contentious and reflects broader cultural and political divisiveness in the nation. The legacy of these shifts is a growing anti-tax sentiment and heightened attention to accountability, productivity, and cost controls (Bruininks, Keeney & Thorp, 2010; Immerwahr, Johnson, Ott, & Rochkind, 2010).

Key Tensions and Dilemmas: Revisiting the Iron Triangle

Several tensions are deeply felt in debates about financing public higher education, especially in the public research university context. The concept of the "iron triangle" is particularly illustrative in animating the core tensions and dilemmas related to financing public research universities. Scholars associated with the National Center for Public Policy in Higher Education invoked the iron triangle metaphor to discuss the zero-sum approach to the pursuit of higher education quality, access, and affordability. The key dilemma of the iron triangle is that the pursuit of one of these three goals often comes at the expense of the other (see Immerwahr, Johnson, & Gasbarra, 2008). These tensions are illuminated in the following paragraphs.

Above all, differing views of quality constitutes a core tension within the iron triangle. On one hand, the public and policymakers are more likely to view classroom teaching and educating state resident students as key measures of quality. On the other hand, public research universities may view research outcomes—such as grants acquisition, patents and licensing—as the most salient metrics of quality. Total research expenditures are an important measure of prestige among research universities (Smith, 2013).

Uneven expectations or views about quality often put institutions and policymakers in tension with one another. Faculty rewards systems at public research universities may prioritize research over teaching in tenure and promotion since such institutions are comprised of cosmopolitan faculty hired for their national and international reputations (Birnbaum, 1988). These pursuits are often met with criticisms of faculty teaching loads; since research university faculty members are given release time to pursue scholarship. For example, Missouri legislators questioned why a third of the faculty at the University of Missouri were granted waivers from their teaching requirements. Missouri legislators sought to align faculty productivity—defined as teaching loads—to institutional requests for state appropriations (Keller, 2015).

Traditional conceptions of quality also pose difficult questions about access. Public research universities become more prestigious as they become more selective and enroll better prepared students. Winston (1999) explains that "…the quality of education any student gets from college depends in good measure on the quality of that student's peers" (p. 17). From this vantage point, institutions that limit their access to the most academically prepared student may be viewed as those that promote high quality. As such, students from underrepresented backgrounds may be further underrepresented as selectivity increases (Bergquist, 1995). Furthermore, strategies to increase access such as tuition discounting for target student populations may increase access and affordability for targeted populations, but often at the expense of higher tuition to full-paying students. This strategy puts access and affordability at odds with one another.

In an effort to diversify the student body and increase tuition revenue, many public flagship universities are recruiting and enrolling international students who pay a higher tuition rate than in-state resident students (Redden, 2017). Similarly, universities recruit out-of-state students who pay higher tuition than their own state residents. For example, the University of Alabama altered their out-of-state recruiting and merit aid program to vastly increase their enrollment of out-of-state students. This strategy has helped the institution weather significant state budget cuts (Burd, 2015). However, aggressively recruiting out-of-state students is often criticized by state policymakers as limiting access to the state's public flagship universities among resident students (Read, 2012). Increasing student selectivity fuels debate about public research universities as a public good (widespread consumption) versus a private good (limited consumption).

Finally, questions about quality and access are directly are in tension with those focused on affordability. Building world class research universities requires significant resources, and institutional leaders seek these resources from multiple sources (Altbach & Salmi, 2011). A self-perpetuating loop exists between quality and resource acquisition which, in part, explains the escalating costs of college. Howard Bowen's classic "revenue theory of costs" suggests that colleges and universities raise all the money they can, and spend all the money they make in pursuit of prestige (Bowen, 1980). As research institutions become more prestigious and viewed as high quality, they are likely to be more competitive for resources through gifts, grants or the tuition of students who are willing to pay more for a prestigious degree. These shifts can be seen in the growth of tuition at public flagship universities across the U.S. between 1995 and 2015, in-state tuition and fees at public national universities ranked in *U.S. News and World Report* grew by an astounding 296 percent (Mitchell, 2015).

A Culture of Blame-Shifting

As these iron triangle tensions are left unresolved, a culture of blame-shifting has gripped the nation. On the institutional side, research university leaders often blame short-sighted legislators for breaking the social contract in supporting their institutions. President emeritus Mark Yudof articulated this perspective in the early days of the 21st century:

> "More than a century ago, state governments and public research universities developed an extraordinary compact. In return for financial support from taxpayers, universities agreed to keep tuition low and provide access for students from a broad range of economic backgrounds, train graduate and professional students, promote arts and culture, help solve problems in the community, and perform groundbreaking research. Yet over the past 25 years, that agreement has withered, leaving public research institutions in a purgatory of insufficient resources and declining competitiveness".
>
> (Yudof, 2002, p. 2)

Yudof articulates a common view among research university presidents, which is that the public has not lived up to their part of the bargain, and that states have left their research institutions to fund for themselves financially. One colorful quip often used by leaders of research university campuses is that "We used to be state-supported, then we became state-assisted, and now we are state-located" (Breneman, 2002 p. B7).

Meanwhile, public officials offer an opposing narrative, suggesting that public universities have not earned their support, and have neglected their duty to provide accessible, affordable, high quality education that benefits society. Legislators especially point out the sub-par graduation rates at many public universities, suggesting that these institutions have not served students well in ensuring their success (Kelderman, 2012; Walters, 2012). In addition, presidents face scrutiny about institutional investment in amenities while simultaneously denouncing state budget cuts. For example, Louisiana State University (LSU) went forward with building an $85 million state-of-the-art "lazy river" recreation area while at the same time drafting an academic bankruptcy plan in response to state budget cuts (Shaheed, 2015). While LSU leaders explained that the project is completely financed by student fees, the project fuels skepticism among the public and legislative leadership about the use of scarce resources. Projects like the LSU lazy river are a part of an "arms race" of facilities, amenities, and services to attract students raise the profile of the institution (Newlon, 2014). To maintain competitiveness with other institutions, LSU and other public research universities are in a difficult position where they seek to satisfy consumer demand in ways that ultimately increase the cost of attendance. Tensions such as these are playing out in the media and public forums across the county.

Leadership Responses and Strategies

Multiple strategies are being pursued simultaneously to manage these tensions within the iron triangle. At the policy level, leaders of public research universities are working with state policymakers in designing new governing structures that promote the financial health of their institutions and hold them accountable for various outcomes. For example, Virginia passed the Restructured Higher Education Financial and Administrative Operations Act in 2005 which gave a select group of public research universities more autonomy over their operations in exchange for agreeing to meet specific performance goals (Couturier, 2006). Similarly, higher education institutions in Oregon have sought more freedom from state oversight and flexibility in decision making. In 2011, the legislature altered the governance structure, allowing the three largest institutions to be independent public organizations (Graves, 2011). Across the country, many leaders of public research universities are seeking greater freedom from their states, especially in cases where the institution receives only 10 percent of their budget from state appropriations (Stripling, 2011).

Yet, these governance reforms have been met with mixed reviews. In Oregon, critics argue that the reforms will result in less accountability for these institutions. Conversely, supporters tout the increased efficiencies that will result from being more flexible and responsive (Kelderman, 2013). Proposals pushing these governance reforms are often politically contentious. In documenting these reforms, an unflattering headline appeared in a *Chronicle of Higher Education* article which read, "Flagships just want to be alone". The article brought to light the tensions that many public research university leaders face in managing their institution's financial future (Stripling, 2011).

At the campus level, entrepreneurial campus leaders are experimenting with several strategies to maintain quality, keep college affordable, and ensure access. For example, leaders are increasingly pursuing open textbook platforms that are free to students. Many institutions now encourage faculty to contribute to open textbooks and to select resources that are available at no cost to students (American Council on Education, 2015). Another innovation aimed to promote access and affordability is Massive

Open Online Courses (MOOCs) and the more recently developed MOOC-based master's degrees. MOOCs are free to participants, with student opting to pay a learning assessment exam fee to receive a certificate recognizing their mastery of the content. Some public research institutions such as Georgia Tech have started offering entire MOOC-based master's degrees where the exam fees for the program are considerably less than the cost of the corresponding traditional on-campus master's degree (Straumsheim, 2016; Straumsheim, 2017). The University of Illinois at Urbana-Champaign is partnering with Coursera to offer a number of MOOC-based masters degrees that cost less than their traditional masters degrees (Young, 2015). For students that can afford the fees without student aid (MOOCs course are currently ineligible for federal aid), this new model may be increasing access to a degree. This is particularly relevant for students who are working full-time, have families, or engaged in other commitments that limit their ability to participate in the traditional on-campus programs.

One particularly headline grabbing move to increase access and generate revenue is seen in Purdue University's recent acquisition of Kaplan University. Purdue opted to buy the existing online institution after an analysis on starting their own online college showed that it would be cost-prohibitive. For Purdue administrators, buying Kaplan is viewed as an opportunity to reach a different student population than their traditional on-campus programs and create new revenue stream. This decision however, has been challenged by Purdue's faculty senate as many Purdue faculty worry about whether the move will diminish the reputation of the institution (Blumenstyk, 2017). The situation unfolding at Purdue University is another example of addressing the tensions within the iron triangle. The institution's pursuit of revenue and broadening access is perceived as being in conflict with its traditional view of quality. Only time will tell whether Purdue's approach can be reconciled within these ongoing tensions.

Another popular approach to generating revenues in a time of declining public resources is to invest heavily in offices of technology transfer. Since the passage of the Bayh–Dole Act of 1980, many public research universities have invested heavily in these offices as a means of generating significant income from patents and other licensing arrangements. While some institutions have found success with technology transfer divisions, studies find that the majority of institutions lose money on these ventures. Only well financed institutions with a history of robust technology transfer activity are most likely to succeed (Powers, 2006).

In some cases, enterprising public research university leaders have executed aggressive institution-building strategies which have inadvertently harmed the institution and its students. For example, University of Massachusetts–Boston invested heavily in new programs to raise the profile of the institution from a regional research university/commuter school to a top-tier research university. Campus leaders predicted that these investments would yield a $2.3 million surplus. Instead, it resulted in a budget gap of approximately $30 million. The result has been cancelled courses, hiring freezes, and layoffs of instructional staff (Krantz, 2017). The UMass–Boston case reveals that investment in innovations can be risky as a strategy to secure long-term financial grounding.

Finally, public research universities are doubling down on tried and true efforts to bolster revenue through fundraising and large-scale capital campaigns. In 2015, giving to higher education hit a historic high of $40.3 billion (Council for Aid to Education, 2016). Fundraising campaigns among public research universities are increasingly aggressive and on par with the top private universities. For example, the University of Washington (UW) recently announced a historic $5 billon campaign. UW communications staff made the case for its ambitious campaign by explaining the shifting financial landscape that makes philanthropy necessary to sustaining a world-class university:

> "A generation ago, major fundraising campaigns for public universities were rare. This began to change as state support began to erode and tuition was relied upon more to support basic functions of universities. As public universities' quest for excellence intensified, philanthropic support began to take on a more prominent role in university funding. It is these dollars that often spell the difference between being a very good institution and being an exceptional one".
>
> (Balta, 2016)

The messaging for the UW campaign brings to light the significant shift in financing public research in recent decades. The narrative explicates how relative declines in state support combined with an intensified push for "excellence" necessitates robust private support. Overall, aggressive fundraising campaigns, the pursuit of new business models, online course offerings, and technology transfer will continue as primary strategies to position public research universities for success in the future.

Resource Dependence and Shifting Institutional Identities

In pursuing this array of revenue generating strategies, leaders of public research universities perform a high wire act in retaining their identities as state institutions. Many state flagship institutions were founded as land-grant universities that were created to expand educational opportunity for the working class and give them access to affordable postsecondary training. Yet, as the preceding paragraphs illustrate, such institutions have become more selective and revenue-focused, prompting critique about the sector as increasingly elitist, privatized, and profit-serving (Martin, 2005).

Institutions that are striving to join the ranks of world-class research universities may do so at the expense of harming their relationship with their regions and communities. As previously discussed, unrealized gains in revenue at UMass- Boston has led to layoffs and course cancellations. Equally troubling, however, is its damaged relationship with the city which historically viewed the institution as providing a key niche in Boston's robust higher education ecosystem. *Boston Globe* reporter Laura Krantz declared, "It is a body blow to the mission and image of a university that plays a critical role in a city known as a higher-education capital, offering undergraduate and graduate school opportunity to students with high aims but limited means" (Krantz, 2017).

Telling the story of institutional ambitions in a way that ties together state and global contexts is one interpretative strategy used by leaders to build local and international support for their campus. For example, in the case of the UW's $5 billion drive, the campaign theme reads, "Be Boundless—For Washington, For the World" (Balta, 2016). The campaign theme can be interpreted as supporting both institutional and state interests in a way that has global impact. The campaign positions UW for securing private support for bold initiatives that are simultaneously local, national, and international in scope.

In sum, pressures associated with resource dependency have shaped institutional identity in multiple ways over the past four decades. State and research university leaders have responded in multiple ways through reforms in governance, policy, and escalation of campus-level entrepreneurial activity. While some small gains have been made that makes the college experience more affordable (e.g., open textbooks) and maintains quality and access (MOOCs, fundraising campaigns, etc.), there are also unintended effects related to the character of the institutions themselves and changing historic relationships with their regions. Ultimately, the cumulative impact of these disconnected strategies inadequately addresses the broader iron triangle dilemma. To get at these root issues, we suggest that the public research university must be re-imagined in a way that re-establishes its role in society as one of worthy of public trust and support. It is from this basis that financing might be re-envisioned for the future.

Re-Envisioning Public Research University Financing

What would a re-envisioned university look like that addressed the financial tensions and dilemmas within the iron triangle? We conclude that "more of the same" (e.g., large-scale fundraising, board restructuring, pursuing nominal cost efficiencies) will not result in a re-envisioned public research university. Past studies show that public research universities that have pursued these technical or structural strategies continue to clash with residents who view them as being disconnected from state needs and concerns (see Cramer, 2016). In this context, public support for higher education continues to dwindle and the cycle of blame shifting continues.

A challenge for many campus leaders to move beyond viewing the financing dilemma as a public relations problem but rather a large cultural or systemic problem. A common exhortation among campus leaders is, "Legislators just don't understand the impact we make on this state and region. We need to do a better job of getting our message out. If we only told our story better, we could get more support from the legislature" (Weerts, 2011, p. 1). However, such a stance further fuels a view of research universities as arrogant and out-of-touch with the public. For example, the University of Wisconsin–Madison is well known for its historic commitment to the state through the Wisconsin Idea—a Progressive Era concept which knitted the state and institution together in a way that contributed to economic prosperity and self-governance (Drury, 2011). However, the Wisconsin Idea has fallen on hard times. In a scathing critique, *Isthmus* writer Dave Blaska declared, "…the narrative behind the Wisconsin Idea, is that the 'experts' on Bascom Hill would instruct their lessers, especially legislators popularly elected by the rabble, to scrape the manure off their boots before they enter the State Capitol" (Blaska, 2010).

This view of Wisconsin's state flagship university as elitist is not unique to Wisconsin, but representative of public views of state flagship universities nationally. Ironically, the early foundations of the Wisconsin Idea emphasized egalitarian, theologically anchored values toward building a good society (Hoeveler, 1997). Wisconsin Idea historian Gwen Drury explains that the Wisconsin Idea was never a mission, but a *vision* jointly shared by the state and university. "The vision—of using knowledge and education to create a balance that would keep our citizens at the heart of their own governance and of their own economy—was like nothing that had been seen before" (Drury, 2010, p. 4).

Creating Virtuous Research Universities: Re-Establishing Public Confidence and Support

The lessons of the Wisconsin Idea—its early conceptions and later negative perceptions—are instructive to re-envisioning public research university financing in the future. We believe that the central task is for public research leaders to prioritize relational restoration with state leaders in ways that promotes generative conversations about how their institutions will serve the future needs of the nation and states. It is from this position that financing the public research university might be re-envisioned. Toward this end, the task at hand is developing institutional cultures that foster public trust and position research universities as entities worthy of public investment.

The emerging field of positive organizational scholarship provides perspectives on how institutions might be re-envisioned in this way. Management professor Kim Cameron and his colleagues at the University of Michigan coined the term "organizational virtuousness", exploring the attributes of organizational cultures that pursue higher order objectives and focus on human impact and social betterment. Virtuous organizations perform at high standards and engender loyalty and trust among organizational actors. They go beyond asking, "Are we achieving our goals, creating value, and performing successfully?" Rather, they inquire, "Is there profound purpose in our objectives? Are we pursing the highest human potential?" (Cameron, 2003). In pursuing these questions, the virtues of charity and humility can form the basis for an intellectual community that is committed to truth seeking and the common good (Ebels-Duggan, 2016).

We suggest that the re-envisioned public research universities would model such virtues in ways that promote listening, responsiveness, and transparency with the public. We offer one example of how these values might be expressed in the realm of public policy. In 1999, the North Dakota Higher Education Roundtable was launched to engage stakeholders in a discussion about the needs of North Dakota. Sixty-one representatives from higher education, state government, business, and industry convened to create a vision for higher education in the state and mechanisms to achieve that vision. In response to the Roundtable goals, the University of North Dakota—the state's leading public research university—required all departments to submit annual reports illustrating how they were fulfilling Roundtable cornerstones. During its time of operation, the Roundtable brought many positive changes to the North Dakota State University System including an enhanced public perception of the value of the higher education system, revision of old policies to promote institutional effectiveness, and new policies that promote campus entrepreneurship and innovation (Lane, 2008).

The Roundtable was successful due to a significant effort made to define the compact or the nature of the relationship between higher education, state government, and business and industry. A key strategy was that the cross-sector relationships were carefully nurtured by Roundtable leaders, and the needs of North Dakota—as opposed to the ambitions of the universities—were salient driver of the agenda. Other key ingredients leading to successful outcomes include strong leadership, effective use of data, private sector engagement, diverse membership on the Roundtable, a focus on planning, and clear responsibilities (Lane, 2008).

The North Dakota Higher Education Roundtable provides an example of how public research universities might revision the relationship with their regions and the broader public. It created a new venue for which key relationships could be developed and nurtured in relationship to common interests. It is in this context that a common vision was developed, and policies were created that brought collective benefits to the state, institutions, and business and industry. David Longanecker, past president of the Western Interstate Commission for Higher Education declared that the Roundtable raised public confidence in higher education in the state, "....the Roundtable's work helped changed the climate toward higher education in North Dakota from skepticism and occasional hostility to greater trust and collaboration. North Dakota's efforts in this respect have provided an example for other states to emulate..." (Longanecker, 2008, p. iii)

Evidence suggests that public research universities that are responsive, active listeners, frame and execute their work around broader public priorities are attractive entities for public and private investment (see Langseth & McVeety, 2007; Strickland, 2007; Weerts, 2014). For example, one study of state appropriations for public research universities found that institutions that received higher than predicted levels of state support over two decades leveraged public engagement as a strategy to increase state funding for their institutions. These innovative campus leaders situated their institutions within the larger social and economic priorities of the region as a means to sustain ongoing political and financial support (Weerts, 2014). Being fully engaged and attuned to public needs has also shown to positively impact philanthropy in higher education. Institutions that align campus fundraising campaigns with key public priorities have been successful in expanding their donor base (Langseth & McVeety, 2007).

Virtuous institutions that promote and value listening, responsiveness, and transparency are poised to pose larger questions such as, "What are the most pressing needs, challenges, and opportunities facing our state and region? What is the unique role of the state's public research universities in addressing these challenges and opportunities?" From these larger questions could flow more specific questions about funding: "What level of financial support is needed to achieve these goals? What are the sources from which this investment should be secured?" Institutional leaders that pose such questions may unearth creative strategies to leverage financial partnerships for mutual interests. For example, university advancement leaders and those in the non-profit sector might create synergistic campaigns resulting in broader public impact. Major donors are attracted to opportunities that maximize the impact of their giving, and thus, collaboration across sectors may yield stronger outcomes for all parties.

Finally, institutions operating from a place of organizational virtue would be more attuned to concerns about cost containment and stewardship of public resources. In an effort to promote a culture of financial stewardship, leaders could develop strategies for rewarding cost containment such as recognizing members of the community that have been innovative in creating efficient, cost-effective operations and services. In the same vein, institutions must be willing to invest in developing new prototypes that may lead to breakthroughs in breaking the iron triangle. As discussed in detail in chapter two in this book, design thinking methodologies have been proven useful in reducing costs and improving services in a variety of sectors. Institutional leaders that prioritize and create a culture of cost containment demonstrate that they understand and care public concerns and are responsive to them. In sum, re-envisioning public research university financing requires fostering other-centered behaviors that build public confidence and trust.

Conclusion: Courageous Choices Ahead

In this chapter, we have revisited the iron triangle metaphor and the ways in which the goals of quality, access, and affordability are constantly in competition. To date, state and institutional leaders have engaged in multiple strategies to address the seemingly unsolvable dilemmas within the triangle. At the state level, new governance structures that introduce institutional freedoms alongside performance measures offer mixed results. At the institutional level, the creation of new business models, expansion of technology transfer, and aggressive fundraising campaigns remain the salient strategies to expand sources of revenue. While some of these tactics may result in nominal gains, it will not result in a re-envisioned university that breaks the iron triangle. Rather, we suggest that leaders of public research universities must do culture changing work that promotes organizational virtue, and in so doing, reaffirm their unique place in society. In doing so, institutions can make gains in challenging the current "deficit versus abundance" mindset which prohibits leaders from thinking creatively about higher education financing.

In making these recommendations, we are not naive to the political and market realities that make such counter cultural efforts extremely difficult. The forces pushing against a re-envisioned research university in this manner are sure to be met with opposition. For example, the leadership of one private research university, Syracuse University, re-envisioned itself as an anchor intuition focused on building up the social and economic fabric of the region. However, such efforts became associated with Syracuse's slide in national rankings and dropping out of the prestigious Association of American Universities (Wilson, 2011). No doubt the Syracuse experience gives pause to leaders of public research universities who may seek to reinvigorate commitments to their regions.

Recognizing these realities, we are not suggesting that public research universities abandon their international ambitions and adopt a more localized view of themselves. Instead, we posit that institutional leaders would more intentionally leverage their international relationships to bring direct benefits to their local regions. For example, as state businesses and industries seek to expand their work into international markets, research universities can play a critical role in helping their regions become attractive centers in a global economy. Public research universities that operate from a position of generosity would broker opportunities to connect faculty and staff with local partners toward these efforts.

We also acknowledge that shifts like the ones are proposing are difficult to sustain over long periods of time. This is evident in the historical ups and downs of the Wisconsin Idea and example of the North Dakota Higher Education Roundtable. Lane's (2008) case study posed questions about whether the initiative could be sustained far into the future. The author shared insights about managing turnover of participants and communicating the public value of the initiative. In making this case, Lane (2008) emphasized that the success of the work should not be measured in the number of "products" (e.g., reports) created by the Roundtable. Instead, success relates to its ability to create a guiding force—a public agenda—to guide decision making as opposed to a "sum of competing interests" (p. 9). Yet, sustaining these initiatives remains difficult, and a central challenge is to incorporate sustainability into the charter of the relationship (Lane, 2008).

Creativity and compromise are necessary to rethink current funding models and must become valued in higher education and across sectors. There are many challenges in financing initiatives that require a long-term, collaborative change process. In their analysis of collective impact ventures, Kania and Kramer (2011) suggest that funders need to have patience, and invest in the capacity of the collaborative to flourish and result in change. They state, "Until funders are willing to embrace this new approach and invest sufficient resources in the necessary facilitation, coordination, and measurement that enable organizations to work in concert, the requisite infrastructure will not evolve" (p. 41). While our chapter does not call for a complete overhaul of the current funding model for higher education, we are suggesting a new spirit of collaboration that is necessary to facilitate common commitments. Resource providers—including state governments—must be willing to embrace new approaches to funding research universities that show promise for bringing about innovation and change. Virtuous universities could model and nurture this collaboration.

Higher education policy expert, Aims McGuinness (2011) has lamented that "there is 'no one at home' when it comes to the responsibility to articulate and defend basic public purposes [of higher education]" (p. 164). Who will take the helm of leading this effort for the good of the nation? We echo the call of public research university executives who declare that university leaders must take the lead in deepening the societal commitments of their institutions if they expect them to be well financed, vibrant entities in the future (Crow, 2010; Duderstadt, 2000; Zimpher, 2006). Put simply, leaders must engage in the hard and courageous work of developing virtuous organizations that renew a spirit of collaboration and goodwill in meeting key societal challenges. Indeed, it may be the greatest challenge and opportunity facing higher education leaders moving into the mid-21st century.

References

Abramowitz, A. I. (2013). *The polarized public? Why American government is so dysfunctional*. New York: Pearson.

Altbach, P. G., & Salmi, J. (Eds.). (2011). *The road to academic excellence: The making of world class research universities*. Washington, DC: World Bank.

American Council on Education. (2015, April). *Open textbooks: The current state of play*. Washington, DC Retrieved from: http://www.acenet.edu/news-room/Documents/Quick-Hits-Open-Textbooks.pdf

Balta, V. (2016, October 21). University of Washington launches historic $5 billion philanthropic campaign. *UW today*, University of Washington. Retrieved from: http://www.washington.edu/news/2016/10/21/university-of-washington-launches-historic-5-billion-philanthropic-campaign/

Bergquist, W. H. (1995). Quality through access, access with quality. The new imperative for higher education. *The jossey-bass higher and adult education series*. San Francisco, CA: Jossey-Bass.

Berrett, D. (2015, January 26). The day the purpose of college changed. *Chronicle of Higher Education*, Retrieved from: http://www.chronicle.com/article/The-Day-the-Purpose-of-College/151359/

Birnbaum, R. (1988). *How colleges work: The cybernetics of academic organization and leadership*. San Francisco: Jossey Bass.

Blaska, D. (2010, November 22). Blaska's Blog is 'stupid' for voting for Scott Walker and Ron Johnson. *Isthmus The Daily Page*. Retrieved from http://www.thedailypage.com/daily/article.php?article=31347

Blumenstyk, G. (2017, May 4). Purdue's faculty senate seeks to rescind Kaplan deal. *The Chronicle of Higher Education*. Retrieved from http://www.chronicle.com/blogs/ticker/purdues-faculty-senate-seeks-to-rescind-kaplan-deal/118201

Bowen, H. R. (1980). *The costs of higher education*. San Francisco: Jossey-Bass.

Breneman, D. W. (2002, June 14). For colleges, this is not just another recession. *Chronicle of Higher Education, 48*(40), B7. Retrieved from http://chronicle.com.ezp3.lib.umn.edu/article/For-Colleges-This-Is-Not-Just/27351/

Bruininks, R. H., Keeney, B., & Thorp, J. (2010). Transforming America's universities to compete in the "new normal." *Innovative Higher Education, 35*(2), 113–125.

Burd, S. (2015). *The out-of-state student arms race: How public universities use merit aid to recruit nonresident students*. Washington, DC: New America Foundation. Retrieved from https://static.newamerica.org/attachments/3120-out-of-state-student-arms-race/OutOfStateArmsRace-Final.b93c2211cdfb4c3da169d-668fbb67cc1.pdf

Cameron, K. (2003). Organizational virtuousness and performance. In K. Cameron, J. Dutton, & R. Quinn (Eds.), *Positive organizational scholarship: Foundations of a new discipline*. San Francisco: Berrett-Koehler Publishers.

Cohen, A. M., & Kisker, C. B. (2010). *The shaping of American higher education: Emergence and growth of the contemporary system* (2nd ed.). San Francisco, CA: Jossey-Bass.

Council on Aid to Education (2016, January 27). *Colleges and universities raise record $40.30 billion in 2015*. Press release: Author.

Couturier, L. K. (2006). *Checks and balances at work: The restructuring of Virginia's public higher education system (national center report #06-3)*. San Jose, CA: National Center for Public Policy and Higher Education.

Cramer, K. (2016). *The politics of resentment: Rural consciousness in Wisconsin and the rise of scott walker*. Chicago: University of Chicago Press.

Crow, M. (2010, November 14). *Future of public research universities*. Dallas, TX: Plenary session, annual meeting of the Association of Public and Land-Grant Universities [APLU].

Drury, G. (2011). *The Wisconsin idea: The vision that made Wisconsin famous*. Madison, WI: University of Wisconsin Community Partnerships and Outreach Staff Network. Retrieved from http://www.ls.wisc.edu/documents/wi-idea-history-intro-summary-essay.pdf

Duderstadt, J. J. (2000). *A university for the 21st century*. Ann Arbor, MI: University of Michigan Press.

Ebels-Duggan, K. (2016). Autonomy as intellectual virtue. In H. Brighouse, & M. McPherson (Eds.), *The aims of higher education: Problems of morality and justice* (pp. 74–90). Chicago: University of Chicago Press.

Finney, J. (2014). Why the finance model for higher education is broken and must be fixed. *Wharton Issue Brief. University of Pennsylvania. 2*(6). Retrieved from: https://publicpolicy.wharton.upenn.edu/live/files/145-a

Freeman, R. B., & Holloman, J. H. (1975). The declining value of college going. *Change*, 24–31.

Graves, B. (2011, June 27). Legislature gives Oregon University System freedom from agency status. *The Oregonian*. Retrieved from http://www.oregonlive.com/education/index.ssf/2011/06/oregon_university_system_wins.html

Heclo, H. (2008). *On thinking institutionally*. Boulder, CO: Paradigm publishers.

Hoeveler, J. D. Jr. (1997). The university and the social gospel: Intellectual origins of the "Wisconsin idea. In L. F. Goodchild, & H. S. Wechsler (Eds.), *The history of higher education* (2nd eds.). ASHE reader series). Old Tappen, NJ: Pearson.

Immerwarhr, J., Johnson, J., & Gasbarra, P. (2008). *The iron triangle: College presidents talk about costs, access, and quality (national center report # 08-2)*. San Jose, CA: National Center for Public Policy and Higher Education. Retrieved from http://www.highereducation.org/reports/iron_triangle/IronTriangle.pdf

Immerwahr, J., Johnson, J., Ott, A., & Rochkind, J. (2010). *Public agenda, squeeze play 2010: Continued public anxiety on costs, harsher judgments on how colleges are run*. National Center for Public Policy and Higher Education and Public Agenda. Retrieved from http://www.publicagenda.org/files/SqueezePlay2010report.pdf

Jacobson, G. (2010). *A divider not a uniter: George W. Bush And the American people*. New York: Longman.

Jencks, C., & Riesman, D. (1968). *The academic revolution*. Chicago: University of Chicago Press.

Kania, J., & Kramer, M. (2011). Collective impact. *Stanford Social Innovation Review, 1*(9), 36–41.

Kelderman, E. (2013, April 29). Oregon considers recasting governance of higher education. *Chronicle of Higher Education*. Retrieved from http://chronicle.com/article/Oregon-Considers-Big-Changes/138867/

Kelderman, E. (2012, January 22). States push even further to cut spending on colleges. *Chronicle of Higher Education*. Retrieved from http://chronicle.com/article/States-Push-Even-Further-to/130416/

Keller, R. (2015, November 29). Legislative questions about faculty teaching loads add to University of Missouri woes. *Columbia Daily Tribune.* Retrieved from http://www.columbiatribune.com/005504f7-1ce0-516a-bd94-9e75ae94d5cb.html

Kellogg Commission on the Future of State and Land-Grant Universities. (1999). *Returning to our roots: The engaged institution.* Washington, DC: Association of Public and Land-Grant Universities. Retrieved from http://www.aplu.org/library/returning-to-our-roots-the-engaged-institution/file

Krantz, L. (2017, March 18). Growth spree has the UMass Boston campus in a bind. *Boston Globe.* Retrieved from: https://www.bostonglobe.com/metro/2017/03/18/growth-spree-has-umass-boston-bind/VWvSjoFBbdMiIYCN362qfJ/story.html

Lane, J. E. (2008). *Sustaining a public agenda for higher education: A case study of the North dakota higher education roundtable.* Boulder, CO: Western Interstate Commission for Higher Education. Retrieved from http://www.wiche.edu/info/publications/ND_Roundtable.pdf

Langseth, M. N., & McVeety, C. S. (2007). Engagement as a core university leadership position and advancement strategy: Perspectives from an engaged institution. *International Journal of Educational Advancement, 7*(2), 117–130.

Lazerson, M. (1997). *Discontent in the field of dreams: American Higher education, 1945-1990. (publication number NCPI-3-01).* Stanford University: National Center for Postsecondary Improvement.

Longanecker, D. A. (2008). Foreword. In J. Lane, *Sustaining a public agenda for higher education: A case study of the North Dakota higher education roundtable (p. iii).* Boulder, CO: Western Interstate Commission for Higher Education. Retrieved from http://www.wiche.edu/info/publications/ND_Roundtable.pdf

Martin, M. (2005, February 25). A drift toward elitism by the "people's universities." *Chronicle of Higher Education, 51*(25), B26. Retrieved from http://chronicle.com/article/A-Drift-Toward-Elitism-by-the/15465/

McGuinness, A. C. Jr. (2011). The states and higher education. In P. G. Altbach, P. J. Gumport, & R. O. Berdahl (Eds.), *American Higher education in the 21st century: Social political and economic challenges* (3rd ed., pp. 139–167). Baltimore, MD: Johns Hopkins University Press.

McLendon, M. K., Hearn, J. C., & Mokher, C. G. (2009). Partisans, professionals, and power: The role of political factors in state higher education funding. *The Journal of Higher Education, 80*(6), 686–713.

Mitchell, T. (2015). *Chart: See 20 years of tuition growth at national universities.* US News and World Report. Retrieved from: http://www.usnews.com/education/best-colleges/paying-for-college/articles/2015/07/29/chart-see-20-years-of-tuition-growth-at-national-universities

Newlon, C. (2014, July 31). The college amenities arms race. *Forbes.* Retrieved from: https://www.forbes.com/sites/caranewlon/2014/07/31/the-college-amenities-arms-race/#1a55219d4883

Powers, J. B. (2006). Between lab bench and marketplace: The pitfalls of technology transfer. *Chronicle of Higher Education, 55*(5), B18.

Quinterno, J. (2012). *The great cost shift: How higher education cuts undermine the future middle class.* New York, NY: Demos.

Read, B. (2012, May 25). Proposal would require U. of California to cap out-of-state enrollments. *The Chronicle of Higher Education.* Retrieved from http://www.chronicle.com/blogs/ticker/bill-would-require-u-of-california-to-cap-out-of-state-enrollments/43588

Redden, E. (2017, May 26). Perceptions of pathway programs. *Inside Higher Ed.* Retrieved from https://www.insidehighered.com/news/2017/05/26/report-looks-perceptions-third-party-pathway-programs-international-students

Rizzo, M. J. (2006). State preferences for higher education spending: A panel data analysis, 1977-2001. In R. G. Ehrenberg (Ed.), *What's happening to public higher education?* (pp. 3–36). Westport, CT: Praeger.

Shaheed, A. (May 17, 2015). LSU's $85M 'lazy river' leisure project rolls on, despite school's budget woes. *Fox News*, Retrieved from: http://www.foxnews.com/us/2015/05/17/lsu-85m-lazy-river-leisure-project-rolls-on-despite-school-budget-woes.html

Smith, J. (2013, March 4). The world's most reputable universities. *Forbes.* Retrieved from https://www.forbes.com/sites/jacquelynsmith/2013/03/04/the-worlds-most-reputable-universities-2/#7465cddb66b7

St. John, E. P., & Parsons, M. D. (2004). *Public funding of higher education: Changing contexts and new rationales.* Baltimore, MD: The John Hopkins University Press.

Stinson, T. (2012, October 4). *The economic future of public research universities: Why don't citizens and public officials see a research university as worthy of state investment?* Panelist, University of Minnesota Faculty Senate Centennial Convocation, University of Minnesota-Twin Cities.

Straumsheim, C. (2016, September 20). MicroMasters on a global scale. *Inside Higher Ed.* Retrieved from https://www.insidehighered.com/news/2016/09/20/mooc-based-masters-degree-initiative-expands-globally

Straumsheim, C. (2017, January 12). Georgia Tech's Model Expands. *Inside Higher Ed.* Retrieved from https://www.insidehighered.com/news/2017/01/12/georgia-tech-launches-second-low-cost-online-masters-degree-program

Strickland, S. (2007). Partners in writing and rewriting history: Philanthropy and higher education. *International Journal of Educational Advancement, 7*(2), 104–116.

Stripling, J. (2011, March 13). Flagships just want to be alone. *Chronicle of Higher Education.* Retrieved from http://chronicle.com/article/Flagships-Just-Want-to-Be/126696/

Thelin, J. R. (2004). *A history of American higher education.* Baltimore, MD: Johns Hopkins University Press.

Walters, G. (2012). It's not so easy: The completion agenda and the states. *Liberal Education, 98*(1), 34–39.

Weerts, D. J. (2011). *"If only we told our story better…": Re-envisioning state-university relations through the lens of public engagement. (WISCAPE viewpoints).* Madison, WI: University of Wisconsin–Madison, Wisconsin Center for the Advancement of Postsecondary Education (WISCAPE).

Weerts, D. J., & Ronca, J. M. (2012). Understanding differences in state support for higher education across states, sectors, and institutions: A longitudinal study. *Journal of Higher Education, 83*(2), 155–185.

Weerts, D. J. (2014). State funding and the engaged university: Understanding community engagement and state appropriations for higher education. *Review of Higher Education, 38*(1), 133–169.

Wilson, R. (2011, October 2). Syracuse's slide. *Chronicle of Higher Education.* Retrieved from: http://www.chronicle.com/article/Syracuses-Slide/129238

Winston, G. C. (1999). Subsidies, hierarchy, and peers: The awkward economics of higher education. *Journal of Economic Perspectives, 13*(1), 13–36.

Young, J. R. (2015, May 4). U. of Illinois to offer a lower-cost M.B.A., thanks to MOOCs. *Chronicle of Higher Education.* Retrieved from http://www.chronicle.com/article/U-of-Illinois-to-Offer-a/229921

Yudof, M. G. (2002, January 11). Is the public research university dead? *Chronicle of Higher Education.* Retrieved from http://chronicle.com/article/Is-the-Public-Research/14345/

Zimpher, N. L. (2006). Institutionalizing engagement: What can presidents do? In S. L. Percy, L. Zimpher, & M. J. Brukardt (Eds.), *Creating a new kind of university: Institutionalizing community-university engagement* (pp. 223–241). Bolton, MA: Anker Publishing Company.

7 Knowledge Without Boundaries Revisited Beyond the Walls of Academia

The Role of Engagement

Mary L. Walshok, Lorilee R. Sandmann, and John Saltmarsh

Knowledge Without Boundaries

The publication of *Knowledge Without Boundaries: What America's Research Universities Can Do for the Economy, the Workplace, and the Community* by Mary Walshok in 1995 coincided with a surge in interest among public research universities in their "public-serving role." The book asserted that research universities were increasingly becoming anchor institutions in communities across the United States because of the ever-increasing value of knowledge to the economy and the seismic implications of globalization. The book's premise was that knowledge "originates from myriad sources" and can be effectively organized and disseminated through the university (p. 24). In this role, universities have an obligation to find ways to generate knowledge differently, in collaboration with nonacademics, and to make their resources accessible to the growing publics who need knowledge, yet to do so without compromising their autonomy in the discovery and development of knowledge. Walshok wrote *Knowledge Without Boundaries* to point out that America's continued economic and social well-being was increasingly dependent on the new knowledge being generated and organized by the nation's research universities, but also by others outside the academy. Today, 20 years later, this is a commonly accepted fact: that solving seemingly intractable and complex social problems—"wicked problems"—requires bringing together academic knowledge and community knowledge.

We want to be clear about how we are using the term community engagement or the shortened version "engagement" in this chapter. When *Knowledge Without Boundaries* was published in 1995, the term "engagement" was not commonly used in describing the university's interaction with communities. Co-curricular connections were framed as "community service." In discussing curricular connections, "service-learning" was prominent. Campuses with outreach missions used the language

DOI: 10.4324/9781315110523-8

of "public service," and their faculty often had a public service role. In the area of research, the dominant framing was that of "application," the knowledge generated within the university being applied externally. All of these framings were university-centric and implied a one-way transaction of service, knowledge, and expertise in the academy being provided to external audiences. The language used in *Knowledge Without Boundaries* is that of "exchange," "interactions," "networking," and "mutual understanding, cooperation and collaboration" (pp. 260–261). The terminology speaks to Walshok's assertion that "knowledge comes from many places" and that "a flexible view of knowledge and the recognition of multiple sources of expertise as needing to be factored into any institutional initiative is central" (p. 261). This is what we mean when we use the term "engagement" in this chapter. It refers to relationships between those in the university and those outside the university that are grounded in the qualities of reciprocity, mutual respect, shared authority, and co-creation of goals and outcomes. Such relationships are by their very nature transdisciplinary (knowledge transcending the disciplines and the university) and asset-based (valid and legitimate knowledge exists outside the university). Also, from this definition of engagement, consistent with Boyer (1996) and Boyer's (1990) scholarship of engagement, the organizational logic that follows is that universities will need to change their policies, practices, structures, and culture in order to enact engagement and support scholars involved in engaged knowledge generation.

Engagement in this framing is not the same thing as "outreach," which has a long history in higher education, particularly in the public land grant universities even as they became heavily research focused. In the post-war period, research universities were fundamentally shaped by cold war science and the infusion of federal funding that fueled the military, industrial, and university complex. Their research was shaped by Vannevar Bush's *Science, the Endless Frontier* (1945), which framed an epistemological and methodological case for "basic scientific research" (p. 6) which, secondarily, could lead to "application of existing scientific knowledge to practical problems" (p. 6). Applied research involved university research and knowledge flowing from the university outward to the society (Stokes, 1997). The outreach function of research universities mirrored the framing of application, that the knowledge and resources of the academy would be shared with the public for its betterment. It involved the reaching out, in a one-way fashion, from the university to society.

The kind of knowledge generation that Walshok (1995) describes in *Knowledge Without Boundaries*, research guided by "mutual understanding, cooperation, and collaboration" (pp. 260–261) with knowledge experts outside the university, points to a new approach to community outreach and re-positioning of the university: from being the sole place where knowledge is generated, organized, and disseminated, to becoming a central place where knowledge is organized and disseminated. However, this method of generating new knowledge for public problem-solving occurs only through authentic engagement.

Collaborative research signals an opportunity for counterbalancing traditional academic knowledge generation (pure, disciplinary, homogeneous, expert-led, supply-driven, hierarchical, peer-reviewed, and almost exclusively university-based) with engaged knowledge generation (applied, problem-centered, transdisciplinary, heterogeneous, hybrid, demand-driven, entrepreneurial, network-embedded, etc.; Gibbons et al., 1994). Collaborative knowledge generation legitimizes knowledge that emerges from experience, what Donald Schön (1995) called practice knowledge, or actionable knowledge: "The epistemology appropriate to [engaged scholarship] must make room for the practitioner's reflection in and on action. It must account for and legitimize not only the use of knowledge produced in the academy, but the practitioner's generation of actionable knowledge" (p. 26). Legitimate knowledge, writes Walshok (1995), "is something more than highly intellectualized, analytical, and symbolic material. It includes working knowledge, a component of experience, of hands-on practice knowledge" (p. 14). This reconceptualization is also central to collaboration and reciprocity. It is associated with campus-community "partnerships that possess integrity and that emphasize participatory, collaborative, and democratic processes" (Bringle, Hatcher, & Clayton, 2006, p. 258). Collaboration reinforces—and instills—"the norms of democratic culture…determined by the values of inclusiveness, participation, task sharing, lay participation, reciprocity in public problem solving, and an equality of respect for the knowledge and experience that everyone contributes to education and community building" (Saltmarsh, Hartley, & Clayton, 2009, p. 6).

Knowledge Without Boundaries also provided examples of the ways universities could build meaningful linkages with multiple constituencies in a manner that embraced their curriculum and their scholarly work. To that end, the book was organized around ideas and programs that addressed three critical dimensions of social life: (1) economic activity, (2) human development, and (3) civic capacity, the ability of citizens to be informed and engaged in the major social, cultural, and economic trends shaping their personal and community lives.

Now that more than 20 years have passed, what kind of progress has been made? On the economic development front, universities have engaged as never before in research partnerships, technology transfer, and technology commercialization initiatives that have produced significant returns for local communities and the nation as a whole. However, much remains to be done in terms of the lifelong education needs of citizens whose work lives are affected daily by continuous and sometimes radical changes.

As important as economic development and talent development are, the third dimension, knowledge relevant to the civic sphere, is where we would argue that we continue to fall short of our responsibility to the sponsoring society in which we operate. If anything, over the past 20 years, knowledge within the academy has become even more specialized and fragmented. The social scientists of the 1940s, 1950s, and 1960s, for example, engaged in community-anchored research that focused on many of the issues affecting society and its challenges: race relations, union/management issues, marriage and the family, and challenges faced by inner-city children. Paradoxically, as society's problems have become more complex, the social sciences and humanities have become more remote: deeply anchored in historicism and identity politics on the one hand or abstract statistical/analytical forecasting models on the other. The consequence is a decreasing ability among typical humanists and social scientists to engage in meaningful dialogue with urban planners, mayors, and school district superintendents, much less the general public. Society struggles to understand how migration and immigration, increasing forms of inequality, access to health care, and constantly changing employment imperatives shape regional futures. The majority of academics are oriented toward peer communities of discourse and focused on research questions and scholarly pursuits that enhance academic disciplines rather than civic capacity. As Boyer wrote in 1996, the public perception is that higher education is "part of the problem rather than the solution" as "the overall work of the academy does not seem particularly relevant to the nation's most pressing civic, social, economic, and moral problems" (p. 14). The contentious civil discourse and policy debates over the last decade, culminating in the 2016 U.S. Presidential election, suggest there may be some truth in Boyer's observation.

The importance of university leaders' revisiting these three issues—economic activity, human development, and civic capacity—cannot be overstated. Universities to a large extent have gotten comfortable with the idea that they are "serving" the larger society because of the increased role they now play in economic development and in curricular service-learning. However, the data are compellingly clear that the tremendous innovations and breakthroughs that have been created through much of the research and development at universities have disproportionally benefited certain groups in society (Reich & Kornbluth, 2013). This is manifest in the growing income gap between those who create and manage the technologies and industries that are based on advances in research and development and those whose jobs are disappearing because of the efficiencies and productivity gains the new technologies have introduced into all forms of production and service, whether in the automobile industry, small appliance manufacturing, or accounting and financial services. The effects of globalization have also powerfully impacted these spheres, creating a globally competitive landscape for industries and workers. Citizens in local communities across the country are struggling to find a path toward sustained prosperity and community well-being under radically changed conditions of production and the exponential growth in global markets.

Universities continue to have an important engagement mission that goes beyond educating undergraduates and graduate students and contributing to research that creates new businesses and industries. They need to make active lifelong learning resources available to a wider audience than the affluent professionals and large corporations that can pay high fees for executive Master of Business Administration (MBA) programs and industrial affiliate programs. They need to be participants in the civic life of their communities, not just through prestige events that appeal to elites, but through a variety of forms of engagement that touch the lives of the increasingly diverse populations they serve.

Current Unbalanced Approach

The unbalanced approach to engagement characterizing so many public research universities is in no small part attributable to the challenges in securing resources to support specific kinds of research and education activities. Industry-focused programs such as research partnerships, technology commercialization, and executive MBAs are typically funded by for-profit organizations, many of which have been the direct beneficiaries of the economy's recent growth in innovation clusters such as software, pharmaceuticals, medical devices, and Information Technology. In other words, these spaces offer a ready customer for what the university has to offer. However, universities need to think not simply in terms of customers, but also in terms of constituencies. A variety of constituencies remain underserved, either because they lack the personal resources to take advantage of the knowledge that research universities offer or because they are involved in organizations such as small businesses, not-for-profit institutions, museums, and symphony orchestras that lack the same level of discretionary funds for philanthropic purposes or personal development.

Theoretically, these developments are clear examples of higher education's response to neoliberal pressure. Broadly defined, neoliberalism, as political and economic practices, emphasizes free markets, free trade, and movement away from the public good toward an emphasis on private benefits, individual interests and responsibility, competition, and efficiency (Harvey, 2005; Newfield, 2008). Slaughter and Rhoades (2004) suggest that due to various political, economic, and social policies relating to neoliberalism, higher education is shifting from a Public Good Regime, characterized by "communalism, universality, the free flow of knowledge, and organized skepticism" (p. 28) to an Academic Capitalism Knowledge Regime that commodifies knowledge and aligns more closely with the market. Practically, three trends over the last 20 years have exacerbated and further exemplify this movement.

First is the decreased support for public research universities across the country, as discussed in other chapters, which has yielded an increased emphasis on privatization. Widespread public perceptions of higher education as a private benefit instead of a public good along with rising costs and diminishing support from the state have led to funding shortfalls that call for innovative approaches to revenue generation. Given the resultant increasing privatization and monetization of many public university activities, it is not surprising that the paying "customer" ends up trumping constituencies that lack resources. Recruitment of international students has grown significantly among public research universities, in large part because these students will pay premium tuition fees that represent a significant new source of income to campuses. Similarly, the professional school, high-fee executive education programs targeted toward major industries and employers represent a significant flow of new capital into research universities. For many campuses, the growth of online learning represents not only pedagogical innovations and efficiencies, but also new renewable income streams. Finally, the increased staffing of technology transfer offices and technology commercialization initiatives is in no small part motivated by the expectations of patent and licensing royalties, return on investments in product development, and the spinning-out of profitable companies. The extraordinary growth in fund-raising functions across all public universities represents a critical expansion of the emphasis on private donors.

The good news at one level is that these efforts have in fact produced significant returns to America's research universities, and many of these institutions have not only closed the gap, but exceeded their expectations in private fund-raising revenues, from high-tuition programs and expansion of corporate support. The bad news is that this exceedingly market-driven approach means the primary investors in the university's new initiatives typically represent corporate interests and/or donors who have been the beneficiaries of the wealth created by the innovation economy. This is not to cast aspersions on their generosity or the university's success. Nonetheless, these donors have contributed disproportionately to science, technology, medicine, and business activities that tend to reinforce their economic and corporate interests. Because they cannot offer the same potential for direct economic returns, many community-anchored programs, arts and humanities initiatives, and public policy and social science research initiatives do not attract the same financial benefits, and their base of funding as a percentage of the university's total budget is diminishing while they are encouraged to develop revenue generating or fee-based partnerships (Brown, Otto, & Ouart, 2006).

The second factor is that this shift in how universities are financed and what the private sector is willing to finance has increased demands on faculty time. After faculty have enjoyed multiple decades of increasing time for research and scholarship, the last decade has seen them asked to take on more instructional or advisement load and to be more productive in achieving high levels of scholarship and research (Colbeck, 2002; Fairweather, 2002). As a consequence, public-serving activities that may be perceived as contributing little directly to the financial well-being of a department or the professional evaluation of an academic get short shrift. Furthermore, faculty experience increased pressures to be entrepreneurial and raise money to fund their faculty line, base activities, and support. Even the most liberal, social-minded faculty find it hard to respond to the multiple demands they face in today's public university.

A third factor that has shaped this skewed idea of public engagement and service in the modern research university is the relative lack of infrastructure that can support programs that are not "customer-oriented"; that is, non-fee-based programs. Anecdotally, it appears public research universities have significantly expanded their international outreach, their executive education programs, their advertising budgets, and the size of their development offices, but they have made relatively less investment in community engagement activities (Demb & Wade, 2012). As a result, the kind of translational, management, and delivery systems that are required to serve lifelong learners and specific publics, much less the general public, are still primarily within specialized units such as Co-operative Extension, continuing education, offices of community engagement, and the like. Even when community engagement can be framed as a scholarly act, both faculty and administrators hesitate to invest resources or effort in this arena because it offers less apparent immediate financial return. Faculty increasingly support the growth of a "customer service" infrastructure, because they see it as providing the resources needed for their traditional work. Community engagement and outreach present a challenge because they are not typically interpreted as a core part of the faculty mission, nor do they produce revenues that support that core mission. Only by devoting increased levels of resources to various forms of support can university leadership bring about a renewed institution able to meet the lifelong learning needs of workers and citizens in their region and contribute in a meaningful way to civic life. These activities can be partially monetized, that is, in the arts, humanities and social sciences, but probably not to the extent possible for programs such as engineering or management that have garnered significant levels of investment over the last 20 years (Massey, 1996; Newfield, 2010; Slaughter & Leslie, 1997; Slaughter & Rhoades, 2004).

Re-Envisioning the Public Research University

In order for research universities to achieve the multiple forms of engagement that a democratic, competitive economy requires, university leadership needs to think deeply about the challenges related to how their structure, governance, constituents, leadership and workforce, curricula and its delivery, and overall culture either facilitate or inhibit new forms of engagement. As an economy, we are transitioning from reliance on goods to reliance on knowledge. As a country, we have begun to recognize that the prevailing economy, especially manufacturing, involves very different technologies and forms of organization from vertically integrated Fortune 500 companies or modes of manufacturing that became standard during the industrial age. Industry is moving from assembly line technologies and models of organization to networked suppliers and developers of components. Although digital technologies have made for dramatic changes in curriculum development, program delivery, and assessment, as more fully examined in other chapters, public research universities continue to struggle to be leaders of the needed change.

Given this context for today's public research universities and drawing on the original *Knowledge Without Boundaries'* key contributions in rethinking where knowledge exists and generating new knowledge through networked collaboration, as well as envisioning the kinds of organizational structures that are needed in the modern research university to support new ways of generating knowledge, the rest of this chapter addresses the current challenges public research universities must confront in order to be civically engaged with their local, national, and global communities. Specifically, building on some of the issues described in the previous chapters, we address the needed re-envisioning about (1) what networked knowledge generation means for teaching and learning and for rethinking who are the learners, (2) the finances of community engagement, and (3) changing not only structures, but the academic culture and its knowledge workforce at the core of a research university.

Content and Constituencies—the Learners

American research universities have been slow to recognize the extent to which their engagement with students must be lifelong. We are very good at organizing 4-to-6-year undergraduate living and learning experiences as well as coherent and focused professional school and Ph.D. programs, preferably for young adults with high potential. At most of America's large research universities, all other categories of students tend to be either marginalized or treated as "cash cows" for university revenue. The latter approach is most clearly manifest in the exorbitant fees business schools charge for their executive MBA programs. For decades, lifelong learning has tended to occur in departments or schools that are themselves marginalized because of the largely practice-focused curriculum they offer. Further, the professionals and practitioners who teach many of their courses typically are not embraced by the academic departments and full-time faculty as part of the "real university." The "real university" in current and future contexts will have very different characteristics.

a Universities will engage potential stakeholders in identifying what skills and knowledge are needed and where employment opportunities are. This engagement with the larger society will not crowd out the core commitment to building a strong liberal arts foundation into the undergraduate experience or providing the skills and knowledge important to civic participation and quality of life. In a knowledge economy, these foundations are essential. What is missing, however, are experiences that show students how to put their general knowledge to work in professional and organizational settings.

b Professionals and practice-anchored instructors will be incorporated at higher rates and in more meaningful ways into the learning experiences of undergraduates and graduate students. They will be an integral part of the learning and credentialing experience as opposed to the occasional guest lecturer in a course taught by a faculty member with minimal knowledge of the economic and social forces affecting the lives of students outside the university setting.

c Project-based learning and meaningful internships will become an integral part of every undergraduate degree and postgraduate certificate. Engineers need to have experience with machines, tools, and engineering problems; sociology students need to have experience doing demographic research, interviewing citizens, and profiling communities; music, art, and theater students need to have opportunities to engage in performance, and perhaps also to learn about production and management issues in the arts.

d Universities will have many more approaches to documenting competency, certifying mastery, and credentialing experience. Co-curricular activities, internships, and project-oriented learning will be properly documented and transcripted. Certificates in specialized areas such as science communications or museum management can be awarded simultaneously with a solid liberal arts degree in theater or biology.

Finance and Organization

a Collaborative approaches to curriculum development will of necessity require new kinds of public–private partnerships for financing and validating programs. Curriculum committees in the future will include practitioners, and the financing of innovative programs that build competencies in students will increasingly include corporate underwriting and support.

b Scholarships and stipends for a much wider array of students will be available. The student in a certificate program will be eligible for financial support, particularly if he or she is bridging into a company, an economic sector, or a career that offers public benefits, such as teaching or urban planning. Currently, most financial support is focused on the young and full-time student. Moving forward will involve broadening such support across a wider variety of fields as well as throughout a student's lifespan.

c On-the-job training and credit for workplace projects will increasingly be financed and underwritten by worksites as a way to offset the costs of delivering new forms of education in order to complement the core academic knowledge and skills being imparted by full-time faculty.

d Online learning will be ubiquitous and will be used in occasional, hybrid, and exclusive forms based on the appropriateness of the skills and knowledge being delivered. The ability to validate the gains from online learning will be embedded in new assessment tools as well as student transcripts.

e New communities of learning will be built across research university campuses. The promise of this approach is reflected in the Osher Lifelong Learning programs that have proliferated across the United States to support serious "learning in retirement." Parallel learning communities could be built around communities of practice, enabling medical doctors in specific fields, or museum directors and curators, to form learning collaboratives through which courses, lectures, and new forms of certification are delivered simultaneously with the development of a robust community of practice at the regional level. In arenas such as health and medicine, urban planning, K-12 pipelines in STEM, retooling a technical workforce, research universities have much to offer.

Academic Culture and Faculty Rewards

Across higher education, the reconsideration of epistemology that comes from forms of knowledge that are relational, contextual, participatory, and localized is emerging alongside traditional academic epistemologies, revealing the significance of broadening ways of knowing so as to challenge the academy to create organizational cultures and institutional structures that will support them and the underlying epistemology of engagement. This epistemological shift points to the need for changes in academic culture and in the reward policies that function as perhaps the most tangible artifact of academic culture. This is particularly true for public research universities because of a dedicated mission to generate knowledge with public good purpose.

An increasing number of campuses are working to build systems of incentives and supports for faculty who undertake community-engaged scholarship. Recognizing that the policies and cultures that shape faculty behavior for career advancement have not kept pace with changes in knowledge production and dissemination, many campuses are at some stage in the process of reconsidering and revising their reward structures to provide recognition for new forms of scholarship, including community-engaged, digital, and interdisciplinary scholarship. Such revisions are necessary to validate faculty work that, although inadequately rewarded, is already occurring. Findings from 2013 to 2014 national Faculty Survey (based on responses from 16,112 full-time undergraduate teaching faculty at 269 four-year colleges and universities) from Higher Education Research Institute at the University of California–Los Angeles demonstrate the scale of community-engaged scholarship now taking place. Among faculty respondents to the survey, 48.8% reported that they have "collaborated with the local community in research/teaching" during the past 2 years (Eagan et al., 2014, p. 26). As Tierney and Perkins (2015) observe,

> the professional reward structure needs to shift. Institutions need a diversity of routes to academic excellence and some of them will pertain to being involved outside the ivory tower.... Academic work needs to have an impact in order to provide society's return on investment.... For that to happen, the reward structure and those practices that socialize faculty need to shift in a way that supports engagement rather than disdains it.
>
> (p. 186)

Community-engaged research brings with it explicit cultural norms that are counter to the dominant norms of academic culture:

- Participatory epistemology: the co-creation of knowledge that shifts the position of students from knowledge consumers to knowledge producers and shifts community groups from being subjects or spectators of the research process to collaborators in knowledge generation and problem solving (Rendon, 2009).
- Collaborative research: recognizing an ecosystem of knowledge and acknowledging that the new generation of knowledge requires bringing together academic knowledge with community-based knowledge, eliminating a hierarchy of knowledge and a one-way flow of knowledge (Gibbons et al., 1994; Lynton, 1994).
- Scholarly artifacts as publications: expanding the understanding and valuing of scholarly products beyond publication in highly specialized disciplinary journals (Ellison & Eatman, 2008).
- Nonacademic knowledge experts (peers): along with a valuing of the knowledge and experience that both academics and nonacademics bring to the processes of education and knowledge production comes the reframing of who is a peer in the peer review process and the recognition that in certain circumstances the expert will be a noncredentialed, nonacademic collaborator.
- Transdisciplinarity: recognizing that interdisciplinary inquiry remains bounded by academic disciplines and that transdisciplinarity is fundamentally different in that it combines multiple disciplines within the university with knowledge that exists and is generated outside the university (Tress, Tress, & Fry, 2006).
- Impact: broader impact is conceived as "the advancement of scientific knowledge and activities that contribute to achievement of societally relevant outcomes" (National Science Foundation,

2014, p. 11) and is shaped by examining the nature of the system within which knowledge is transformed into public policy or social action and how scholars engage others to transform research into actionable and useful knowledge.
- Reconfigured tenure clock: the acknowledgement that contextual, relational, collaborative knowledge generation through participatory research methodologies requires a different time frame for results.

This attention to a different set of cultural norms, and concurrently a different set of criteria, brings faculty rewards to the center of changes in academic culture. As the 2013 white paper *Academic Review and Engagement at Tulane University* states, "given the centrality of engagement to Tulane's mission and to the ongoing strategic planning process, we cannot continue to sustain a culture of academic review that is silent on engagement" (p. 3).

Evidence of the importance of change in faculty rewards is reflected in the 2015 documentation framework for the Carnegie Foundation's Elective Community Engagement Classification. Whereas in earlier cycles of the classification, questions on faculty rewards were "optional" and then "supplemental," starting in 2010 they were part of the core questions on institutional culture and commitment. The Carnegie framework focuses on "institutional level policies for promotion (and tenure at tenure-granting campuses) that specifically reward faculty scholarly work that uses community-engaged approaches and methods"; whether "community engagement [is] rewarded as one form of scholarship"; and whether "there [are] college/school and/or department level policies for promotion (and tenure at tenure-granting campuses) that specifically reward faculty scholarly work that uses community-engaged approaches and methods" (pp. 9–10). Of the total of 361 campuses that have the Carnegie Community Engagement Classification in 2015, 85 (or just less than 24%) are public universities that have the Carnegie Basic Classification of either RU/H (research university—high research activity) or RU/VH (research university—very high research activity).

As part of a strategic planning process, the University of North Carolina at Chapel Hill (UNC-CH) —a RU/VH campus—in 2009 formed a Task Force on Future Promotion and Tenure Policies and Practices. The task force recommended that emerging forms of scholarship be considered in tenure and promotion processes. Specifically,

1 Faculty engagement with the public outside the traditional scholarly community should be valued and evaluated during the tenure and promotion process. Faculty "engagement" refers to scholarly, creative or pedagogical activities for the public good, directed toward persons and groups outside UNC-CH.

2 New forms of scholarly work and communication made possible primarily by digital technology should be included in evaluations of scholarship.
3 Work across disciplinary lines should be supported. Expectations of all involved parties should be articulated at the outset, and referred to as tenure and promotion decisions are made. (p. 2)

In its *Academic Plan 2011* UNC-CH set forth the strategic priority of building engaged scholarship into the core culture of the campus. The plan states that:

> because the tenure and promotion policies and criteria for most units on campus do not recognize engaged scholarship, the University should adopt the recommendations of the May 2009 University-wide Task Force on Future Promotion and Tenure Policies and Practices, which call for the inclusion of engaged scholarship and activities in departmental tenure and promotion policies and criteria. Following these recommendations, each academic unit should review and revise its tenure and promotion criteria to include engaged scholarship and activities appropriate for their discipline.

At the University of Minnesota—a RU/VH campus, with a revision in 2007 of its promotion and tenure guidelines, included language in policy documents establishing tenure criteria for research and teaching that states "public engagement…should be applied when applicable" (University on Minnesota, Faculty Tenure. Section 7.11). Following the revision, each department has been charged with developing specific language of how it will interpret and apply "public engagement." A similar process has unfolded at the University of North Carolina at Greensboro (UNCG)—a RU/H campus. In 2011 the university revised its "University-wide Guidelines for Promotion and Tenure" to specifically include language and criteria for "community engaged teaching," "community engaged research," and "community engaged service" (University-Wide Evaluation Guidelines For Promotions And Tenure The University Of North Carolina At Greensboro). As was the case with the university of Minnesota, at UNCG, departments have been charged with translating the university wide guidelines to the department level.

These are just a few examples of the ways campuses are responding to the need to have rewards in place that recognize, legitimate, and honor the work of faculty who are collaborating with the community in their research. Reward policies that create incentives for faculty to perform transdisciplinary, collaborative, public problem-solving research have to provide legitimacy for publications and scholarly artifacts other than academically peer-reviewed articles in journals with high impact factors. Such policies will need to support recognition of the knowledge expertise of those outside the academy as peers in peer review. They will need to include recognition and reward for research that takes longer due to the relational and collaborative basis of knowledge generation. Only a change in cultural norms, including the norms related to education of the knowledge workforce, can make this possible.

The Engaged Knowledge Workforce

Re-envisioning the public research university means re-envisioning both its academic knowledge workers and its preparation of such workers of tomorrow. This re-envisioning is actually well under way and vividly evident in the radical shift in the demographics, values, and roles of the academic workforce (Trower, 2010). The ranks of baby boom generation faculty are shrinking, and smaller numbers of millennial generation faculty are taking their place. Because millennials bring with them a greater interest in work–life balance, a more intense emphasis on the relevance of their work, and a higher level of social networking savvy than previous generations, some aspects of transformation are inherent in the academic workforce itself. Furthermore, many early career faculty have come through K-16 programs that have embraced community-based learning and inquiry and have expectations to continue such engaged pedagogies and research approaches as academics.

The starkly apparent changes in the number and type of faculty positions also form an important aspect of this transformation. As the number of full-time tenured professorships declines, the number of part-time and nontenure-track faculty appointments is increasing (Schuster & Finkelstein, 2006). The "proliferation of part-time faculty members" is demonstrated by the 376 percent increase in part-time faculty members from 1969 to 2001, as well as the majority of full-time faculty hires since 1993 having been for off-track positions (Schuster & Finkelstein, 2006, p. 40). This trend has continued in contingent faculty hires, and continues to gain momentum (Hearn, Milan, & Lacy, 2012). While this fundamental shift may be less pronounced in public research universities as compared to other institutional types, they turn to nontenure track faculty and graduate assistants for coverage of instructional activities so faculty can focus on research, publication and educating graduate students (Kezar & Maxey, 2012).

Relevant to the "engaged" academic workforce, growth has also occurred in the roles and identities of professionals operating in what Whitchurch (2013) calls the *third space.* Her research in institutions of higher education in Australia, the United Kingdom, and the United States found those in this third space to be the "insider and outsider voices" (p. 21). These professionals view themselves as managers and leaders operating in areas formerly described as "fringe specialisms." However, their command of "in-between spaces" (p. 21) has led to utilization of their talents in a spectrum of identities that provide specialist contributions on topics ranging from governance, intellectual property, and commercialization to just-in-time academic support and donor or partner relationship management. Third space professionals work not only between professional and academic types of activities but also "between functions and project, between internal constituencies, and between institutions and their external partners" (p. 138). These individuals serve important roles, whether acting as internal cultural integrators and boundary spanners to ensure positive student experiences and outcomes or as external cultural integrators and boundary spanners to facilitate the local, regional, and global research and engagement partnerships described above. The professionals in these roles are characterized by their affinity for change, talent for innovation, collaborative skills, and client-centered or partnership-centered approaches to the provision of value within and across the boundaries of organizations.

A re-envisioned public research university needs to attract, retain, manage, and motivate this new cadre of knowledge workers. Doing so will require more supportive organizational cultures, academic leadership, and institutional structures. The following descriptions reflect representative developments for institutions supporting the engagement that is concomitant with the needed re-envisioning of higher education.

a There will be a reaffirmation of the importance of integrating more engaged practice-oriented activities and expertise into the life of departments on every university campus. This will occur as academia comes to encompass a wider circle of instructors, academic professional, and faculty, not as second-rate citizens, but as carriers of information, knowledge, and insights that are viewed as essential to students and potentially even to the research and scholarly enterprise by engaging increasing numbers of professors of practice. The presence of clinical faculty in medicine and the growing number of practice-oriented faculty in schools of engineering presage what many would argue needs to occur throughout the social sciences and the humanities as well.
b Helping the faculty connect, not just to real-world problems but to real-world expertise and leadership, will be a core value on campus. High-level officials from chancellors to deans will project a sense of responsibility for supporting the faculty not only in their independent, scholarly, and research activities but in forums, programs, and activities that allow them to connect with "real world" expertise and leadership on a regular basis.
c As a result, research universities will support and where necessary expand offices, programs, and divisions that represent intermediaries and enabling mechanisms in this process of growing a truly transdisciplinary and collaborative academic institution. Many if not most campuses have some kind of infrastructure for interacting with the

community. The key question is not one of whether to have such an office, but how the work of the office is oriented, and whether it is designed to facilitate reciprocity, mutual respect, shared authority, and co-creation of goals and outcomes. For extension schools, community development offices, economic development offices, and related programs, isolation from the central conversations of the campus will be a thing of the past. The chancellor and provosts will no longer separate their academic deans from deans who are involved in putatively more "practical matters," because those "practical matters" involving the education needs of K-12 systems, adult learners, and lifelong learners will be part of the university's core commitments alongside undergraduate and graduate education.

d Furthermore, academic leaders and managers will become more adept at working with mixed teams that include knowledge experts from outside the university. This will be especially important when expertise may reside in those in third space boundary-spanning roles or when the teams have no formal status.

e Finally, professional and career development and support will be provided to the professionals who move in and out of an institution's third space, or even higher education, as they often do. They will be able to receive this support at different stages in their careers and in different locales.

In addition to institutional re-positioning for the academic workforce, public research universities will have an opportunity to take the lead in building a new cadre of engaged professionals, whether faculty or knowledge workers in other positions, within both the university and the community. This implies a number of necessary developments for advancing education, training, and research to support such professionals.

a Graduate programs will abandon the academic and nonacademic preparation binary, expanding their curricula to groom doctoral students not only for increasingly elusive faculty roles but for a multiplicity of professional roles with a more diversified skill set. The Pew Charitable Trusts are showing leadership with their Re-envision the Ph.D. Project, which supports an extensive repository of best practices in doctoral education, having catalogued approximately 350 strategies for change employed at nearly 100 institutions of higher education (Nyquist, n.d., 2002). These innovative strategies are intended to better prepare doctoral students for the responsibilities and trajectories of nonfaculty careers. Likewise, the Carnegie Project on the Education Doctorate is a consortium of 80 institutions involved in redesign and critical evaluation of the professional doctorate in education. The project seeks to improve that degree's relevance for "school practitioners, clinic faculty, academic leaders and professional staff for schools, colleges, and learning organizations that support them" (CPED, 2014, Mission section, para 1).

b Engagement will be embedded in graduate education to attract students who are eager to connect their studies to societal needs, to develop knowledge, skills, and values of an engaged scholar, and to "grow as professionals who find satisfaction in integrating different kinds of faculty work" (O'Meara, 2008, p. 40). In "Graduate Education and Community Engagement," O'Meara outlines the critical experiences needed in four phases of graduate education to insert community engagement into the socialization and preparation of future faculty. One such approach is currently offered by Michigan State University (MSU). Modeled after teaching certification offered by many graduate schools, MSU's Graduate Certification in Community Engagement is designed to help graduate students and professionals "develop systemic, thoughtful, and scholarly approaches to their community engaged work" (Matthews, Karls, Doberneck, & Springer, 2015, p. 168). Completing the certification involves showing mastery of core engagement competencies, finishing a 60-hour mentored community engagement experience, and writing a portfolio. This builds on MSU's broad local and global engagement agenda described in Chapter 5.

c Higher education doctoral programs will teach a continuum of scholarship. Beyond the typical qualitative and quantitative methods courses, programs will be required to include a community-based participatory research course and feature community-engaged scholarship, action research, translational research, and other forms of what Gibbons et al. (1994) called Mode 2 knowledge generation, as described earlier. By becoming facile with more engaged methods of scholarship, future knowledge workers will experience the connection between research and addressing the problems of the larger society while also broadening their own knowledge through interactions with leaders in business, government, health, education, nonprofit, and other sectors.

d The changing identities and roles of current and future knowledge workers in a reimagined public research university is an area ripe for further research. One thread of needed research will focus on those taking up these roles. What is their optimal education and continuing education, particularly the training needed to manage the dual domains they span, whether cross-discipline, cross-project, or cross-organization? What expectations and accountability measures are appropriate for such professionals, who typically answer to multiple stakeholders? How do individuals and institutions navigate the paradox of the third space as an environ for experimentation and creativity producing new forms of activities and relationships, and also

> a milieu of risk, uncertainty, and disconnection? Should such faculty roles be to some extent "hybrids," additive to other faculty functions, or should the activities of designated knowledge workers release faculty to focus on mainstream teaching and research? If, as Whitchurch (2013) suggests, relationships rather than structure are the way of engaged knowledge work, what are the implications for investment in network and relationship development? What does that look like? Who champions, leads, and supports such efforts?

Only by bridging the divide between the value of thinking and the value of doing, which exists in many academic departments, will it be possible to integrate practitioners and professionals from the larger society into the development and delivery of campus programs, whether curricular or co-curricular. The only way to transform an undergraduate and graduate institution into the central, lifelong learning resource of a community is to include the voices of people who represent and serve this wider constituency. Achieving this transformation will require a cultural shift, one that will lead academia to recognize the intellectual as well as the political and social value of that inclusion. This re-envisioned culture will honor the distinctive skills and competencies that allow people and offices to serve as effective interlocutors, intermediaries, and bridgers between the world of the academy and the world of the sponsoring community. In *Scholarship Reconsidered*, Boyer (1990) discussed the importance of the scholarship of integration, which requires "making connections across disciplines, placing specialties in larger context, illuminating data in a revealing way" (p. 18), and it has become clear that critical connections between institutions of higher education and their communities, facilitated both by internal and external boundary spanners and by working in a transdisciplinary, adaptive manner, are essential to addressing society's difficult problems (Ramaley, 2014).

Knowledge Without Boundaries Revisited

In the 20 years since *Knowledge Without Boundaries* was published, the core issues addressed in this book vis-à-vis the role of the public research university have moved center stage. When it was published, the book appealed primarily to practitioners of adult and continuing education, including leaders of large extension schools or professional studies programs, but we believe that its value was and continues to be much broader. Its value relates in powerful ways to the challenges the contemporary American university is facing today.

The modern American university must find new models of curriculum development, introduce new organizational and financing mechanisms, and embrace new forms of talent in order to thrive in what is an increasingly difficult environment in the face of global trends and the diminishing significance of the American economy in the global marketplace. Given the decrease in public funding, the rush to monetize services through such sources as tuition increases, high-fee-paying international students, and aggressive technology transfer and commercialization offices will not produce the results that are needed. These new fiscal imperatives have brought about increased demands on faculty members' time that inhibit their ability to engage in public service. The absence of a supportive engagement infrastructure makes it difficult for universities to engage new forms of knowledge and new stakeholders, much less deliver knowledge in new ways to broader constituencies. Unquestionably a new model is required.

We contend that integral to this new model will be a networked approach to developing bodies of knowledge and curriculum that honors the input of the users of knowledge as well as the producers of knowledge. The model will support broader forms of documentation of skills, competencies, and knowledge gains. In addition, the delivery of learning will be more hybrid in terms of content that is accessible online and will reflect a stronger focus on project-based learning that occurs in groups with significant leadership and direction from expert faculty. In order to create an environment that supports this kind of dynamic development and dissemination of knowledge, we must revisit the organization and financing of our public research universities. This chapter has described a variety of practices that could engage new kinds of investment in the teaching and learning process as well as accreditation opportunities for on-the-job training and participation in communities of practice.

However, the critical factor in our judgment to making all of this happen is a fundamental shift in faculty culture. For centuries universities have been seen as the source of knowledge for all of society. However, contemporary conditions clearly suggest that knowledge resides in multiple places and that universities must be the "hub" rather than the exclusive source of knowledge. As a hub, the university generates important academic, analytical, and scholarly knowledge, but it also has to harvest practice-based knowledge and tap into a much more diverse array of experts in order to deliver the sorts of knowledge required in a global economy. To do this requires not only traditional tenured faculty and a system of rewards and incentives focused on their lives, but the integration of a new cadre of knowledge workers into all the activities of the university, including the delivery of knowledge directly to students at the undergraduate, graduate, and lifelong professional development stages. Without this kind of re-imagination, America's public research universities will fall short in serving the needs of a democratic society.

References

Academic Plan 2011. (2011). Chapel Hill, NC: University of North Carolina–Chapel Hill. Retrieved from http://academicplan.unc.edu/

Boyer, E. L. (1990). *Scholarship reconsidered: Priorities of the professoriate*. Princeton, NJ: Carnegie Foundation for the Advancement of Teaching.

Boyer, E. L. (1996). The scholarship of engagement. *Journal of Public Service and Outreach*, *1*(1), 11–20.

Bringle, R. G., Hatcher, J. A., & Clayton, P. H. (2006). The scholarship of civic engagement: Defining, documenting, and evaluating faculty work. *To Improve the Academy*, *25*, 257–279.

Brown, P. W., Otto, D. M., & Ouart, M. D. (2006). A new funding model for extension. *Journal of Public Service Outreach and Engagement*, *11*(2), 101–116.

Bush, V. (1945). *Science, the endless frontier*. Washington, DC: U.S. Government Printing Office.

Carnegie Foundation (2015). *The Carnegie Foundation for the Advancement of Teaching elective community engagement classification, first-time classification documentation framework*. Retrieved from http://nerche.org/images/stories/projects/Carnegie/2015/2015_first-time_framework.pdf

Carnegie Project on the Education Doctorate. (2014). About CPED. Retrieved from http://cpedinitiative.org/about

Colbeck, C. L. (2002). State policies to improve undergraduate teaching: Administrator and faculty responses. *The Journal of Higher Education*, *73*(1), 3–25.

Demb, A., & Wade, A. (2012). Reality check: Faculty involvement in outreach and engagement. *The Journal of Higher Education*, *83*(3), 337–366.

Eagan, M. K., Stolzenberg, E. B., Berdan Lozano, J., Aragon, M. C., Suchard, M. R., & Hurtado, S. (2014). *Undergraduate teaching faculty: The 2013–2014 HERI faculty survey*. Los Angeles, CA: Higher Education Research Institute, UCLA.

Ellison, J., & Eatman, T. K. (2008). *Scholarship in public: Knowledge creation and tenure policy in the engaged university*. Syracuse, NY: Imagining America.

Fairweather, J. S. (2002). The mythologies of faculty productivity: Implications for institutional policy and decision making. *The Journal of Higher Education*, *73*(1), 26–48.

Gibbons, M., Limoges, C., Nowotny, H., Schwartzman, S., Scott, P., & Trow, M. (1994). *The new production of knowledge: The dynamics of science and research in contemporary societies*. London, UK: Sage.

Harvey, D. (2005). *A brief history of neoliberalism*. New York: Oxford University Press.

Hearn, J. C., Milan, M. C., & Lacy, T. A. (2012). The contingency movement: A longitudinal analysis of changing employment patterns in U.S. higher education. TIAA-CREF Institute Research Dialogue, (105). Retrieved from https://www.tiaa-cref.org/public/pdf/institute/research/dialogue/105a.pdf

Kezar, A., & Maxey, D. (2012). *The changing faculty and student success: National trends for faculty composition over time*. Los Angeles: The Pullias Center for Higher Education. Retrieved from http://www.uscrossier.org/pullias/wp-content/uploads/2012/05/Delphi-NTTF_National-Trends-for-Faculty-Composition_WebPDF.pdf

Lynton, E. A. (1994). Knowledge and scholarship. *Metropolitan Universities: An International Forum*, *5*(1), 9–17.

Massey, W. F. (Ed.) (1996). *Resource allocation in higher education*. Ann Arbor, MI: The University of Michigan Press.

Matthews, P., Karls, A., Doberneck, D., & Springer, N. (2015). Portfolio and certification programs in community engagement as professional development for graduate students: Lessons learned from two land-grant universities. *Journal of Higher Education Outreach and Engagement, 19*(1), 157–184. Retrieved from http://openjournals.libs.uga.edu/index.php/jheoe/article/view/1396/845

National Science Foundation. (2014). STEM + Computing Partnerships program solicitation (NSF 15-537). Retrieved from National Science Foundation website: http://www.nsf.gov/pubs/2015/nsf15537/nsf15537.htm

Newfield, C. (2008). *Unmaking the public universities: The forty-year assault on the middle class*. Cambridge, MA: Harvard University Press.

Newfield, C. (2010). The end of the American funding model: What comes next? *American Literature, 82*(3), 611–635.

Nyquist, J. D. (n.d.). Promising practices. Retrieved from http://depts.washington.edu/envision/practices/index.html

Nyquist, J. D. (2002). The Ph.D.: A tapestry of change for the 21st century. *Change: The Magazine of Higher Learning, 34*(6), 12–20.

O'Meara, K. A. (2008). Graduate education and community engagement. In C. L. Colbeck, K. A. O'Meara, & A. E. Austin (Eds.), *Educating integrated professionals: Theory and practice on preparation for the professoriate* (New Directions for Teaching and Learning, No. 113, pp. 27–42). Wiley Online Library. doi:10.1002/tl.306

Ramaley, J. (2014). The changing role of higher education: Learning to deal with wicked problems. *Journal of Higher Education Outreach and Engagement, 18*(3), 7–22. Retrieved from http://openjournals.libs.uga.edu/index.php/jheoe/article/view/1286/783

Reich, R., & Kornbluth, J. (Director). (2013). *Inequality for all*. USA: 72 Productions.

Rendon, L. I. (2009). *Sentipensante (thinking/feeling) pedagogy: Educating for wholeness, social justice, and liberation*. Sterling, VA: Stylus Publishing.

Saltmarsh, J., Hartley, M., & Clayton, P. H. (2009). *Democratic engagement white paper*. Boston, MA: New England Resource Center for Higher Education.

Schön, D. (1995). The new scholarship requires a new epistemology. *Change, 27*(6), 26–35.

Schuster, J. H., & Finkelstein, M. J. (2006). *The American faculty: The restructuring of academic work and careers*. Baltimore, MD: The Johns Hopkins University Press.

Slaughter, S., & Leslie, L. L. (1997). *Academic capitalism: Politics, policies, and the entrepreneurial university*. Baltimore, MD: The Johns Hopkins University Press.

Slaughter, S., & Rhoades, G. (2004). *Academic capitalism and the new economy: Markets, state, and higher education*. Baltimore, MD: The Johns Hopkins University Press.

Stokes, D. E. (1997). *Pasteur's quadrant: Basic science and technological innovation*. Washington, D.C: Brookings Institution Press.

Task Force on Future Promotion and Tenure Policies and Practices. (2009). *Report of the UNC* Task Force on Future Promotion and Tenure Policies and Practices (Final report 5-8-09). Retrieved from http://provost.unc.edu/files/2012/10/Taskforce-on-Future-Promotion-and-Tenure-Policies-and-Practices-FINAL-REPORT-5-8-09.pdf

Tierney, W. G., & Perkins, J. F. (2015). Beyond the ivory tower: Academic work in the 21st century. In G. G. Shaker (Ed.), *Faculty work and the public good: Philanthropy, engagement and academic professionalism* (pp. 185–198). New York, NY: Teachers College Press.

Tress, B., Tress, G., & Fry, G. (2006). Defining concepts and the process of knowledge production in integrative research. In B. Tress, G. Tress, G. Fry, & P. Odam (Eds.), *From landscape research to landscape planning* (pp. 13–26). Dordrecht, The Netherlands: Springer.

Trower, C. A. (2010). A new generation of faculty: Similar core values in a different world. *AAC&U Peer Review, 12*(3). Retrieved from http://www.aacu.org/publications-research/periodicals/new-generation-faculty-similar-core-values-different-world

University on Minnesota, Faculty Tenure. Section 7.11. http://regents.umn.edu/sites/regents.umn.edu/files/policies/FacultyTenure1_0.pdf

University-wide evaluation guidelines for promotions and tenure the University of North Carolina at Greensboro. http://provost.uncg.edu/documents/personnel/evaluationPT.pdf

Walshok, M. (1995). *Knowledge without boundaries: What America's research universities can do for the economy, the workplace, and the community*. San Francisco, CA: Jossey-Bass.

Whitchurch, C. (2013). *Reconstructing identities in higher education: The rise of third space professionals (research into higher education, society for research into higher education)*. London, UK: Routledge.

8 Interdisciplinarity and the American Public Research University

Karri Holley and Karen Brown

From the establishment of the Morrill Acts of 1862 and 1890, to serving as a platform for post-World War II era scientific advancement, and now cultivating innovative start-up and not-for-profit organizations, public research universities reflect the changing cultural, economic, and political norms of society (National Science Board, 2012). As underscored by contemporary debates regarding the balance between the public good and the private benefits of higher education, the public research university fulfills several key social functions: ensuring access for all students, training professionals in multiple fields of study, and offering bodies of knowledge relevant to a dynamic and healthy society (McPherson, Gobstein, & Shulenberger, 2010). These functions have long been carried out through disciplinary traditions of the university. The dynamic growth of knowledge over the past century brought concurrent growth in the complex organization of higher education and the academic catalogue that forms the core of the public research university. These public institutions produce 62 percent of the nation's academic research, graduate 70 percent of professionals in such fields as teaching and engineering, and educate 85 percent of the American undergraduate students (National Research Council, 2012, p. 57).

The work of the public research university extends beyond such tangibles as the conferral of degrees, the number of graduates, or publications by the faculty. For such institutions with land grant status, the Smith-Lever Act of 1914 formalized cooperative extension programs, delivering knowledge about home economics, agriculture, and public health into hundreds of communities (Rogers, 1988). This focus on high-priority needs of community stakeholders directly shapes the institutional public mission (Rhoten & Calhoun, 2011). In addition, federal investment through Research and Development Centers (often identified as national laboratories) as well as university affiliated Research Centers demonstrate the university–government partnership in producing knowledge relevant to persistent and multifaceted problems (Galison, 1992). Research universities increasingly prioritize an international focus as part of their mission, seeking to globalize the curriculum, connect students with global

DOI: 10.4324/9781315110523-9

knowledge networks, and fulfill their role as "a key international link for science, scholarship, culture, and ideas" (Altbach, 2008, p. 13). The dual emphases on addressing public policy challenges and extending the reach of engagement to a global sphere helped spur the growth of new strategies such as interdisciplinary education and research initiatives as integral institutional components.

As the American public research university sets its course for the remainder of the century, knowledge production as a public good serves a crucial function (National Science Board, 2012). Whether universities effectively carry out this function depends upon institutional academic structures. In this chapter, we examine the growth of interdisciplinary academic structures and their prospective role in the public research university. While certain fields of study have a substantial history of interdisciplinary inquiry (e.g., public policy and feminist/women's studies), universities typically carry out teaching and research functions within academic disciplinary structures. Disciplines provide a context for the development of specialized academic communities and the production of particular forms of knowledge that correspond to disciplinary paradigms. However, instead of providing a home for faculty and students to engage in this type of work, the disciplines are more and more perceived as structural, cognitive, and cultural barriers to knowledge production (Holley, 2009).

Given the origins of academic work and organizational form in the disciplines, and the pressing demands of a changing social and economic environment, how might interdisciplinary endeavors be conceptualized for the public research university of the future? In considering this question, we explore the rise of interdisciplinarity and transdisciplinarity and how these approaches shape (and are shaped by) public research universities. We first outline the historical foundations of disciplinarity, noting how different university functions are conceptualized through disciplinary and interdisciplinary lenses, and the external environment influencing university knowledge production practices. We then focus on those skills and activities that cut across disciplinary boundaries and respond to the new environment, such as critical thinking and global problem-solving. We conclude with examples of how institutions can best facilitate such interdisciplinary behavior and consider how interdisciplinarity might shape the future research university.

Academic Disciplines as Building Blocks of the Public University

The academic disciplines have served and continue to serve as the primary structure of knowledge production and educational processes of higher education. For centuries, they have structured institutional academic practices in significant ways. They remain the central organizing feature of higher education today. Consider, as one example, the traditional arrangement of the physical campus, which is compartmentalized by disciplinary areas of study. Blocks of space are devoted to the sciences, engineering, the humanities, agricultural studies, and so on. Students engage with the institution through these distinct spaces and are socialized to the norms of disciplinary behavior by their work with faculty and peers (Harris & Holley, 2008). An institution's academic catalogue illustrates the segmented nature of the curriculum, demonstrating the specialized bodies of knowledge relevant to individual fields of study. Perhaps one of the strongest visual indicators of the disciplinary foundation of higher education is the commencement ceremony. Faculty and student regalia, academic banners, and conferral of degrees present evidence that a single institution is comprised of many different disciplinary groups. This disciplinary structure takes on added significance in the contemporary economic context.[1] Public research universities increasingly prioritize unit-level revenue generation (e.g., by departments and colleges) in an environment of more scarce public resources and more competitive internal economies of universities. University revenue generation and distribution, as well as faculty hiring, promotion and tenure decisions, often follow *and* strengthen disciplinary distinctions. Leaders of academic units face an incentive structure that frequently discourages collaboration across institutional boundaries.

The organization of the university by these distinct bodies of knowledge continues to offer numerous advantages for student learning and scholarly engagement. This organization enables institutions to offer a well-defined course of study, allowing students to chart their course from the start of studies to graduation. Scholars find intimate communities with like-minded peers, which can foster in-depth study of intricate disciplinary subject matter. This knowledge is woven into the curriculum and imparted to students and the larger community. Revenue is generated by, and frequently allocated to, units based on their enrollment as well as their role within the institution. These multiple key functions allow the inherently complex (and frequently volatile) organization of higher education to function. Beyond the limitations imposed by revenue distribution, disciplinary cultures also facilitate varied perspectives on the role, work, and culture of higher education. In reflecting on the university and knowledge, Clark (1983) summarized, "Psychologists may see it as a place where people undergo personality development; sociologists as a central institution for status attainment or denial; political scientists as the locus for political recruitment; economists as a developer of human capital" (p. 12).

In addition, traditional disciplines have played key roles in knowledge development. Distinctions between basic and applied knowledge, as one example, took hold in the early 20th century, fueled by the work of the Social Science Research Council and other private foundations as well as the influential *Science: The Endless Frontier*, penned by Vannevar Bush (1945). These efforts solidified the value of all disciplines, including those focused on application or issues of practice. As part of the disciplines, the notion of peer review evolved, defining, and validating the role of a specialist community (typically disciplinary in character) in documenting knowledge. Disciplinary communities fostered the development of paradigms and other guiding theoretical orientations that focused the work of community members; these frameworks also gave a sense of order to sprawling bodies of knowledge, rendering them comprehensible for faculty and students in terms of the curriculum and research endeavors.

The Case for Interdisciplinarity: The Limits of Disciplinary Knowledge

Despite the important role of academic disciplines in building American higher education, critics highlight their inherent tensions and limitations. Some scholars assert that disciplinary structures assume knowledge gains occur in a linear, straightforward direction, not allowing for the messy and frequently unpredictable nature of knowledge production (Stehr & Weingart, 2000). Others suggest that those same boundaries that give the disciplines meaning also exclude new ideas, collaborations, and conversations among scholars from related fields of study (Palmer, 2001). Still others have noted that the disciplinary foundation does not reflect the dynamic and ever-changing nature of knowledge, instead privileging areas that may no longer be relevant to society (Parker, Samantrai, & Romero, 2010).

Two particular examples illustrate motivations for interdisciplinary scholarship. First, the critique of existing disciplinary structures and the kinds of questions facilitated by them provides the basis for teaching and research without an obvious disciplinary foundation, an approach that has been labeled as "conceptual interdisciplinarity" (Lattuca, 2001, p. 83). Such critique, and the related emphasis on posing novel questions outside of existing disciplines, has led to the development of new fields of study not rooted in disciplinary knowledge creation. Examples of this type of interdisciplinary field of inquiry include feminist, ethnic, and cultural studies. In some cases, these emerging fields have resulted in university academic structures paralleling discipline-based departments and producing their own bodies of work united by shared paradigms.

A second motivating factor in the growth of interdisciplinary scholarship relates directly to the globalized context of higher education and of the policy world. So-called "wicked" global challenges with multiple and interconnected dimensions provide a compelling illustration of the limits of disciplinary knowledge in addressing the public good. What Barnett (2000) terms "supercomplexity" requires universities to offer new frameworks for understanding the world and acting in a critical, reflective, and purposive manner. Social and policy issues often demand multiple perspectives (and the integration of these perspectives) to identify solutions. In addition to their value in generating nuanced perspectives on pressing policy challenges, interdisciplinary approaches provide additional institutional and social benefits. Interdisciplinary education and research programs typically connect closely to social identities and social movements, particularly in the social sciences and humanities. As argued by Brint, Bicakci, Proctor and Murphy (2009), interdisciplinary programs can offer a niche space for scholars focused on social identity and promoting social change. This capacity can help universities respond to an increasingly diverse student population.

Arguments Against Interdisciplinarity

Interdisciplinary work can come at some cost to the individual faculty, the academic institution, and the process of knowledge production. For example, critics of burgeoning interdisciplinary initiatives point to tensions between disciplinary and interdisciplinarity knowledge (e.g., Graff, 2017). One concern relates to using, or "importing," concepts and theories from one field to another where they might not possess the same explanatory power. As a context-specific element, and one responsive to such issues as power, knowledge is transformed when lifted from one context to another. This transformation could have negative consequences (Kellert, 2009). A second tension concerns what critics see as inflated claims for the power of interdisciplinary research. In this view, interdisciplinarity in itself does not necessarily produce innovation. Interdisciplinarity instead relies upon the foundation of academic disciplines for theories and methods. A balance of resources between interdisciplinary and disciplinary efforts is necessary for future knowledge efforts. This balance can be upset by issues such as faculty hiring or resource allocation. How should institutions choose to allocate finite (and increasingly scare) resources in a way that promotes a balanced enterprise? Ultimately, proponents of the continued centrality of traditional disciplines fear that interdisciplinary initiatives will siphon away resources that could be used to enhance the strength and reputation of discipline-based departments and research. Neglecting disciplinary areas in favor of interdisciplinary efforts risks a discrepancy in such essential activities as undergraduate education, graduate education, faculty hiring and research, and outreach efforts (Jacobs, 2014).

Fostering Interdisciplinarity Through University Structures and Practices

The value of the disciplines, it seems, must be balanced with an understanding of their inherent limitations. As an institutional type, the public research university is particularly vulnerable to these limitations. Consider its mission: ensuring student access, educating students in multiple fields of study, and producing knowledge of benefit to a range of institutional stakeholders. Surely individual academic disciplines have the capacity to respond to these different aspects of the institutional mission. Indeed, for over a century, they have done just that.

But when faced with the intricate and daunting challenges of contemporary society, we must consider whether the potential of the disciplines might be enhanced by fostering engagement across boundaries and integrating knowledge from multiple fields of study. Many such efforts appear in a historical review of American higher education. The emergence of department-less institutions such as Evergreen State College and Hampshire College in the 1960s and 1970s provide one example, as do the more recent efforts by such universities as Duke, Minnesota, Southern California, Stanford, Washington, and Wisconsin to integrate interdisciplinary behavior as part of the organizational culture (Klein, 2010). Even transdisciplinary approaches have long held a role in higher education. Transdisciplinarity, defined as "the engagement of different academic disciplines and practitioners in solving real-world problems" (Holley, 2009, p. 22), fosters conversations among academicians, other experts, and community members. This emphasis on real world problem-solving has the potential to privilege interdisciplinary solutions.

These efforts reveal common trends toward facilitating interdisciplinary work. Promotion of interdisciplinarity initiatives by organizations central to the U.S. public research context (such as the National Academy of Sciences' 2004 report and Association of American Universities' 2005 report) demonstrate the importance of these trends. Interdisciplinary programs typically occupy institutional spaces between or across formal academic departments. These programs, such as cluster colleges, learning centers, and research institutes, bring scholars out of their disciplinary communities for sustained interdisciplinary conversations. Cluster colleges, derived from the learning models of Oxford and Cambridge, integrate students and faculty into living and learning communities. These communities can even extend beyond institutional boundaries, as evidenced by the consortium of five undergraduate and two graduate colleges that form The Claremont Colleges in California. A more recent effort has been seen with cluster hires, or the strategic efforts of an institution to bring in groups of faculty with complementary expertise, often targeted toward an interdisciplinary area. Beyond cluster hires, institutions have also developed research clusters, which include multiple faculty, departments, universities, and often for-profit corporations as a way to engage in knowledge production. "Cluster models leverage local and regional strengths and resources to benefit the university and surrounding community," concluded Birx, Anderson-Fletcher, and Whitney (2013, p. 13). A common characteristic across these various initiatives is the importance of organizational flexibility and innovation, the recognition of key external and community stakeholders, and the willingness for personnel to participate in activities beyond disciplinary or departmental boundaries. Institutions seek to incentivize participation in a variety of ways including faculty grants for interdisciplinary and collaborative research, interdisciplinary institutes offering residencies and research infrastructure to scholars, and interdisciplinary graduate fellowship programs. In addition, the growing number of interdisciplinary fields of study and departments provides institutional spaces for dialogue and education around questions that might not be central in discipline-based units. Sustaining and supporting intellectual engagement across disciplinary boundaries whether through institutional spaces, support or incentives is critical to address what Myra Strober (2011, p. 153) describes as the "tough work" of interdisciplinary dialogue and to foster productive conversations.

Interdisciplinary Knowledge Production: Dilemmas of Integration

The challenge of defining interdisciplinarity frequently relates to the extent of integration required between the multiple disciplines. While such integration is crucial to producing interdisciplinary outcomes, oft-cited definitions of the term focus on both the process and the end result. Effective interdisciplinarity, then, might suggest not only that relevant knowledge from multiple disciplines can be identified, but also that such knowledge can be applied in a way that furthers shared understanding. Mansilla and Duraisingh (2007) define interdisciplinary understanding as

> the capacity to integrate knowledge and modes of thinking in two or more disciplines or established areas of expertise to produce a cognitive advancement—such as explaining a phenomenon, solving a problem, or creating a product—in ways that would have been impossible or unlikely through single disciplinary means.
>
> (p. 219)

However, it can also be argued that some interdisciplinary work results not from combining knowledge from multiple existing disciplines or operating at the intersection of disciplines, but from the recognition of questions to be posed that are not comfortably at home in any existing discipline. In such cases, interdisciplinary dialogue and research promote rethinking of worldviews and paradigms for knowledge production. Post-structural perspectives offer an example of such an approach, offering a new lens on long standing social, political and economic challenges.

Public universities operating in resource-constrained environments face the dilemma of needing to support scholarship in traditional academic disciplines while also fostering innovative, interdisciplinary knowledge production. While fields of inquiry not closely linked to disciplines have grown in number and importance, we must recognize the power of disciplinary knowledge cultivated through the interaction of expert communities. Rather than dismissing the academic disciplines as cultural barriers or out-dated organizational forms, some approaches to interdisciplinarity seek to utilize disciplinary strengths to achieve cognitive advancements. In this sense, interdisciplinarity offers a means for the modern public research university to extend its impact and further its mission. The ways in which these efforts should be institutionalized depends on the individual campus culture and the motivating research or pedagogical problem. One example can be seen through undergraduate interdisciplinary studies programs, which have existed for decades in American higher education (Klein, 2010). At one institution, such programs might be part of the College of Arts and Sciences, while at another institution, they are free-standing or autonomous units. The individual nature of the programs and the institutional capacity to support them remain significant influential variables.

Advantages of Interdisciplinary Education

Although the assessment of interdisciplinary outcomes is still a young field, ample evidence suggests the positive influence of interdisciplinarity on students, faculty, and the institution. For students, enhanced critical thinking skills are typically associated with interdisciplinary engagement (Vess, 2001) as well as the ability to engage in meta-cognitive reflection (Haynes & Leonard, 2010). These gains can in part be attributed to the complexity required from the integration of multiple disciplines. While knowledge from the disciplines might overlap, they may also be contradicting, requiring students to grapple with ambiguity and uncertainty. This ambiguity prompts students to engage in intellectual risk-taking in ways that might not be possible in a strictly disciplinary environment. Students "must move beyond the view of disciplines as fixed bodies of information and understand the constructed and dynamic nature of knowledge production" (Mansilla, Duraisingh, Wolfe, & Haynes, 2009, p. 338). Other common components of interdisciplinary programs include inquiry-based learning and reflective assignments. These forms of learning encourage students to be active contributors to the interdisciplinary enterprise (Haynes & Leonard, 2010) and to think in ways that transcend a particular disciplinary framework. In this view, the messy process of knowledge production escapes strict categories.

For faculty and graduate students, the opportunity to participate in interdisciplinary partnerships can potentially enrich and strengthen a scholarly career. Recognizing that scholars build networks of peers through their disciplinary communities, institutions offer avenues toward innovative and cross-disciplinary scholarship by providing an interdisciplinary platform. Knowledge is produced through the interaction of people, ideas, and objects. The support of interdisciplinary graduate training initiatives, from individual centers or programs focused on content areas to federally funded projects such as the National Science Foundation's Research

Traineeship Program (NRT), influences a future generation of academics who will possess the skills and motivations to facilitate interdisciplinary scholarship. Investments in the interdisciplinary development of doctoral students hold immense promise for the growth of interdisciplinary initiatives into the next century. While complicated by a troubled academic job market and a changing notion of the professoriate, socializing scholars to interdisciplinary work early in their career builds the foundation so crucial to cross-disciplinary knowledge. For doctoral students, and those faculty who work with them, the experience gained by working with interdisciplinary research or participating in an interdisciplinary curriculum shapes future institutional behavior (Holley, 2009). Doctoral students can take their experiences working on an interdisciplinary project to their new institution as part of their faculty role. They might also potentially create an environment for their future students conducive to interdisciplinary scholarship. Institutional investment in doctoral students and future faculty can have long-ranging positive influences on the undergraduate student experience, the research enterprise, and academic culture.

The institutional structures that house interdisciplinary communities and promote interdisciplinary scholarship and teaching provide the physical, social, and intellectual space to continue boundary-crossing work. Jasanoff (2004) concluded, "[Knowledge] is embedded in social practice, identities, and norms… in short, in all the building blocks of what we term social" (p. 3). Cognitive advancements are possible when these building blocks are used in new and innovative ways (or, in the case of conceptual interdisciplinarity, where new blocks are created). Public research universities, and the faculty within them, hold a historical obligation to produce knowledge of value and relevance. By facilitating interdisciplinary opportunities, knowledge moves beyond disciplinary boundaries to address complex, contemporary problems.

Interdisciplinarity and the Future Public Research University

We conclude this chapter with reflections on steps that could be taken by public research universities to support, institutionalize, and further notions of interdisciplinarity. Given their intellectual, social, and cultural histories, these institutions are uniquely poised to assume a leadership role in advancing interdisciplinarity within American higher education. The past decade has evidenced strides in cultivating interdisciplinary work by this institutional type, as noted by Sa (2008) and Holley (2009). "Most leading universities boast commitments to fostering interdisciplinary activity on their campuses, while some universities aspire to differentiate themselves as propitious places for interdisciplinarity," concluded Sa (p. 538). These efforts have been bolstered by federal funding, political support, and a social interest in the kinds of issues conducive to interdisciplinary analyses. If analyzed by such measures as new degree programs, institutional planning, or new research structures, then we have seen a substantial level of investment in interdisciplinarity by public research universities in recent years. But the incorporation of interdisciplinarity into an institution's mission, culture, and structure defies easy solutions. Public research universities are positioned to set the standard for high quality and publicly valued interdisciplinary scholarship and teaching. We offer two specific areas for progress.

Internationalization as a Companion to Interdisciplinarity

Public research institutions respond to changing social demands through innovative programs—often interdisciplinary in nature and increasingly global in focus. Internationalization initiatives commonly cross disciplinary and institutional boundaries and involve faculty, students, and other institutional stakeholders in conversations about pressing global problems. Kofi Annan, the former Secretary General of the United Nations, described these global demands as "problems without passports" that could only be solved by "blueprints without borders" (1998). The global concerns are ripe for the types of advantages drawn from interdisciplinary engagement. Consider the issue of climate change, the consequences of which impact communities across the globe. The University of Wisconsin in Madison recently launched a competition for interdisciplinary teams drawn from faculty and others within the community to design practical, high-impact solutions for climate change that can be adopted on a large scale. Noting that challenges such as climate change "demand innovation, usually crossing disciplinary boundaries," the project administrators added, "Great solutions can come from unexpected partnerships" (Sakai, 2014).

Public research universities face tension in defining the balance between obligations to their local community and commitment to advances on a global scale. Rather than viewing such a balance as an either/or option, these institutions are well-served to consider a synergistic approach to internationalization. Economic and technological advances have made globalization a reality for many communities, ensuring that physical distances are no longer always obstacles to learning as well as bringing both negative and positive effects of global connections. Students benefit from an institutional commitment to internationalization, when they learn to think of themselves as citizens of the world and understand the myriad connections among local and global. Institutions can also find a revitalization of purpose as well as an expansion of research opportunities. Ultimately, for the local community, internationalization commits local and regional resources to a global conversation (NASULGC, 2004). In this way, universities can adopt strategies that understand internationalization and interdisciplinarity as linked and interconnected goals.

Funding Dilemmas and Solutions

Like numerous other segments of higher education, public research universities have been increasingly troubled by changing state funding patterns and expectations. Observers have noted a sustained change to the nature of higher education as a public good, as opposed to a private benefit. Put simply, states are contributing less to public higher education, leaving students and their families to contribute more. If institutions are unable to raise tuition rates, making cuts in spending is one option, which potentially reduces the quality and depth of academic programs. Public institutions are asked to do more with less. For public research universities comprising the heart of the research and development effort, these cuts have serious implications for knowledge production, innovation, and dissemination. Beyond reductions in public funding for universities, the contemporary post-industrial economic context has driven an increased focus by universities on the promotion of entrepreneurial and applied approaches to research and formation of linkages between academic institutions and markets (Slaughter & Rhodes, 2010). Understanding this increasingly constrained economic landscape is critical, as scholars and policymaker alike call for a re-evaluation of how universities produce a public good (Kezar, Chambers, & Burkhardt, 2005).

Borrowing from organizational theory, times of crisis lend themselves well to new ways of behavior. For public research institutions, one option to support research and development functions in an era of reduced state funding is through privatization. Privatization requires public institutions to look toward private sources of funding to fuel operations, such as for-profit industry and other market-based resources. Concern has been raised about the potential of such behavior to damage the quality, focus, and autonomy of academic research (Altbach, 2008). This concern is important to acknowledge, as the innovations made possible through university research have in part depended on the autonomy of the institutions and scholars. Public universities can develop future funding strategies that seek to leverage private support for interdisciplinary initiatives. For instance, multiple stakeholders (including public, private, and nongovernmental organizations) could support research and education related to complex social and environmental challenges including water resources, human rights, and global food security. For a growing number of public institutions, initiatives of this kind define "grand challenges" that draw together resources from multiple source and scholars from multiple fields of study. The University of Minnesota, Washington State University, Indiana University, and Texas A&M University are among the public research universities framing their work in a set of grand challenges. At Texas A&M University, research foci include issues related to energy, the environment, economic development, and democracy. One result of these efforts is a selective undergraduate program designed to graduate future leaders in these areas. Another result is a competitive internal grant program to promote collaborative and transformative research. Similarly, a grand challenges research program at the University of Minnesota seeks to support interdisciplinary approaches to complex, global problems such as clean water, food security, and building equitable communities through grants to interdisciplinary faculty groups.

Cultures and Practices of Interdisciplinarity

How might public research universities create an environment that fosters the success of the kind of interdisciplinary education and research initiatives described in this chapter? Beyond the issues of internationalization and funding discussed in this section, universities can look ahead to adopt policies and practices more friendly to interdisciplinary knowledge production. Faculty incentive and reward structures (promotion and tenure, awards, intramural research funding, merit pay increases) must reflect an institutional priority for interdisciplinarity. In short, universities must find ways to recognize and reward work across disciplinary boundaries in both research and curriculum development. In addition, universities can create physical and administrative structures that cross and link disciplinary fields. Such spaces—in the form of interdisciplinary centers and institutes, interdisciplinary research grant programs, professional development (e.g., teaching workshops, research proposal development guidance) as well as financial (e.g., interdisciplinary research grants or curriculum development grants) support for the development of interdisciplinary research and teaching teams—will help to create future public research universities that not only accept but value interdisciplinary scholarship.

Conclusion

This chapter built upon the history of interdisciplinarity as an institutional component of the American public research university to construct an argument for its relevance to the pressing contemporary challenges of internationalization and privatization. Traditional academic disciplines continue to play a key part in knowledge production, student engagement, and connections with broader communities. However, interdisciplinarity offers a particular set of advantages in addressing complex problems, producing innovative approaches and perspectives, and developing new knowledge at the intersection of and by integrating disciplinary fields. Public research universities will advance their mission by identifying and supporting institutionally defined strategies to support and foster interdisciplinary inquiry.

Note

1. Scholars identify the post-industrial context as possessing qualities such as competitiveness, uncertainty, and scarce resources (Cameron & Tschirhart, 1992) and globalization and managerialism (Becher & Trowler, 2001).

References

Altbach, P. (2008). The complex roles of universities in a period of globalization. In Global University Network for Innovation (Ed.), *Higher education in the world: New challenges and emerging roles for human and social development* (pp. 5–14). New York: Palgrave-McMillan.

Barnett, R. (2000). University knowledge in an age of supercomplexity. *Higher Education, 40*(4), 409–422.

Becher, T., & Trowler, P. (2001). *Academic tribes and territories: Intellectual enquiry and the culture of disciplines (2nd ed.)*. Buckingham: SRHE and Open University Press.

Birx, D., Anderson-Fletcher, E., & Whitney, E. (2013). Growing an emerging research university. *Journal of Research Administration, 44*(1), 11–36.

Brint, S. G., Turk-Bicakci, L., Proctor, K., & Murphy, S. P. (2009). Expanding the social frame of knowledge: Interdisciplinary, degree-granting fields in American colleges and universities, 1975-2000. *The Review of Higher Education, 32*(2), 155–183.

Bush, V. (1945). *Science: The endless frontier*. Washington, DC: United States Government Printing Office.

Cameron, K. S., & Tschirhart, M. (1992). Postindustrial environments and organizational effectiveness in colleges and universities. *The Journal of Higher Education, 63*(1), 87–108.

Clark, B. (1983). *The higher education system: Academic organization in a cross-national perspective*. Berkeley, CA: University of California Press.

Galison, P. (1992). *Big science: The growth of large scale research*. Palo Alto, CA: Stanford University Press.

Graff, H. (2017). *Undisciplining knowledge: Interdisciplinarity in the twentieth century*. Baltimore, MD: Johns Hopkins University Press.

Harris, M., & Holley, K. (2008). Constructing the interdisciplinary ivory tower: The planning of interdisciplinary spaces on university campuses. *Planning for Higher Education, 36*(3), 34–43.

Haynes, C., & Leonard, J. (2010). From surprise parties to mapmaking: Undergraduate journeys towards interdisciplinary understanding. *Journal of Higher Education, 81*(5), 645–666.

Holley, K. (2009). *Interdisciplinary challenges and opportunities in higher education (ASHE higher education report 35, 2)*. San Francisco, CA: Jossey-Bass.

Holley, K. (2009). Interdisciplinary strategies as transformative change in higher education. *Innovative Higher Education, 34*, 331–344.

Jacobs, J. A. (2014). *In defense of disciplines: Interdisciplinarity and specialization in the research university*. Chicago, IL: University of Chicago Press.

Jasanoff, S. (Ed.) (2004). *States Of knowledge: The co-production Of science and the social order*. New York, NY: Routledge.

Kellert, S. H. (2009). *Borrowed knowledge: Chaos theory and the challenge of learning across disciplines*. Chicago, IL: University of Chicago Press.

Kezar, A. J., Chambers, T. C., & Burkhardt, J. C. (Eds.). 2005). *Higher education for the public good: Emerging voices from a national movement*. San Francisco, CA: Jossey-Bass.

Klein, J. (2010). *Creating interdisciplinary campus cultures: A model for strength and sustainability*. San Francisco, CA: Jossey-Bass.

Lattuca, L. R. (2001). *Creating interdisciplinarity: Interdisciplinary research and teaching among college and university faculty.* Nashville, TN: Vanderbilt University Press.

Mansilla, V. B., & Duraisingh, E. (2007). Targeted assessment of students' interdisciplinary work: An empirically grounded framework proposed. *Journal of Higher Education, 78*(2), 215–237.

Mansilla, V. B., Duraisingh, E., Wolfe, C., & Haynes, C. (2009). Targeted assessment rubric: An empirically grounded rubric for interdisciplinary writing. *Journal of Higher Education, 80*(3), 334–353.

McPherson, P., Gobstein, H., & Shulenberger, D. (2010). *Forging a foundation for the future: Keeping public research universities strong.* Washington, DC: Association of Public and Land Grant Universities.

National Research Council (2012). *Research universities and the future of America.* Washington, DC: The National Academies Press.

National Science Board (2012). *Diminishing funding and rising expectations: Trends and challenges for public research universities.* Arlington, VA: National Science Foundation.

Parker, J., Samantrai, R., & Romero, M. (Eds.) (2010). *Interdisciplinarity and social justice: Revisioning academic accountability.* Albany, NY: State University of New York Press.

Rhoten, D., & Calhoun, C. (Eds.) (2011). *Knowledge matters: The public mission of the research university.* New York, NY: SSRC/Columbia University Press.

Rogers, E. (1988). The intellectual foundation and history of the agricultural extension model. *Science Communication, 9*(4), 492–510.

Palmer, C. (2001). *Work at the boundaries of science: Information and the interdisciplinary research process.* Norwell, MA: Kluwer Academic Publishers.

Sa, C. (2008). Interdisciplinary strategies in US research universities. *Higher Education, 55*, 537–552.

Slaughter, S., & Rhoades, G. (2010). *Academic capitalism and the new economy.* Baltimore, MD: The Johns Hopkins University Press.

Stehr, N., & Weingart, P. (Eds.). (2000). *Practising interdisciplinarity.* Toronto, Canada: University of Toronto Press.

Strober, M. H. (2011). *Interdisciplinary conversations: Challenging habits of thought.* Stanford, CA: Stanford University Press.

Vess, D. (2001). Exploration in interdisciplinary teaching and learning: A study of learning outcomes in an interdisciplinary fine arts course. *Inventio: Creative Thinking about Teaching and Learning 3*(1).

9 Public Research Universities in the Metro Nation

Nancy L. Zimpher, Wim Wiewel, and Robert J. Jones

Today's metropolitan areas are hotbeds of innovation. They form the social, mechanical ecosystems that grow cutting-edge industries and technologies, creating the foundation for strong regional economies and offer a high quality of life. Now, for the first time in recorded history, more than half the world's population resides in metropolitan areas. A century ago, there were just 16 metro areas in the world with more than one million people. Today, there are more than 450. In the United States, 65 percent of its continually diversifying population now lives in the nation's hundred largest metro areas (Berube, 2007). In 24 states, more than 75 percent of the population calls some part of a metro area home. As the world's population is expected to exceed 5 billion in the next 20 years, the percentage of people living in metropolitan areas is expected to continue to grow (Katz & Bradley, 2014).

In this chapter, we examine how higher education's structure, culture, and policies need to be recast to address this metrofication phenomenon. The phenomenon can be best characterized as a syllogistic cycle whereby the metrofication is related to innovation, innovation is related to higher education, higher education is related to quality of life, and, to bring it full circle, quality of life is related to the unfurling revitalization of cities and metros across the country. Bearing this in mind, here we explore two questions: *How are public research universities changing to meet the complex needs and challenges of today's cities and metros? And, looking to the future, what specific actions must universities take to fulfill their commitments to our increasingly diverse citizenry and to strengthen our communities, regions, and the nation as a whole?*

The Magnetism of Metros

Metropolitan areas, or metros, are high-population geographical regions that include one or more cities together with their surrounding townships, suburbs, and exurbs. Unlike cities, metros are not defined by the governance of an overarching administrative body. Rather, with population growth and the suburban sprawl that has occurred over the last half

DOI: 10.4324/9781315110523-10

century, shared industry and infrastructure have knit together metro areas that are inter-reliant, geographically distinguishable, and complex entities unto themselves. Today, in 47 of the 50 states, the majority of the state's economy is generated by its metropolitan areas, and metros are now home to more than eight in ten American jobs (Berube, 2007; Katz & Bradley, 2014).

There is a symbiotic connection between cities and innovation. Innovation hubs take root in cities because innovative thinkers thrive on the energy and ideas of other innovative thinkers. Their interaction sparks creativity and requires environments where they can easily interact, mix, and mingle, allowing, as Bruce Katz and Jennifer Bradley (2014) observe in *The Metropolitan Revolution*, "knowledge to be transferred between, within, and across clusters, firms, workers, and supporting institutions, thereby enabling the creation of new ideas that fuel even greater economic activity and growth" (p.114). The metro dynamic is an idea fomenter. Importantly, metros also have the range of services and amenities that both meet basic daily needs and create a high quality of life. Concentrations of services and amenities have traditionally clustered together in downtowns, and as people are flocking back to cities from far flung culs-de-sac and island-like office parks to live and work, these concentrations are taking on renewed importance. Walkable, bikeable neighborhoods with easy access to mass transit—places that shuffle together working, thinking, creating, and living spaces with amenities and outlets for entertainment—are increasingly becoming the models for how the most successful and vibrant American cities will look as we step into the future.

Metros' density and magnetism are associated with more creativity and a better ability to invent new ways of working. New work earns significantly higher wages than similar work in old jobs for at least the first few years after a new kind of job is created (Moretti, 2012). In 2000, for example, new work included jobs like IT manager, Web administrator, information systems security officer, and biomedical engineer, to name a few—all jobs that require a level of education and training above what is currently achieved in high school. Between 5 and 8 percent of American workers are engaged in new work at any time, and the number is higher in cities that have a high density of college graduates and a diverse set of industries (Moretti, 2012).

The Innovation Economy

Innovation-driven fields are the force behind the 21st century economy and global competitiveness and hold the most promise for good-paying jobs. The U.S. Census Bureau (2011) tracked and tabulated job-growth projections for the 10-year period between 2008 and 2018, concluding that the fastest and largest job growth in the United States is occurring at either end of the wage spectrum—a dynamic of extremes that is the force behind the widening income gap in the United States. Of relevance to this discussion is the correlation between income and education. The disparity in the income gap is strongly tied to education levels and the related skill sets people bring with them to the job market in their metaphorical tool kits.

The data here show that the jobs that pay the highest wages in the fastest- and largest-growing fields are jobs that require post-secondary education and training, especially in innovation fields related to science, technology, engineering, and mathematics, a broad group of disciplines that we have come to collectively known as STEM. So it follows that strong STEM education is critical to American students being prepared for these kinds of jobs in adulthood, and are the areas where students have been falling short globally over the last many decades, just as the need for excellent advanced STEM education has been ramping up.

A better-educated metropolitan workforce tends to be more productive and command higher salaries, benefiting not only highly educated people, but also workers of varying skills throughout the metropolitan area. Recent investigation into the relationship between innovation jobs and their communities indicates that for each new high-tech job in a city, *five* additional local jobs are ultimately created outside of the high-tech sector (Moretti, 2012). An increase in the number of other college graduates in the same city results in slightly higher salaries among their similarly educated peers. Inversely, a shortage of educated workers in a metropolitan area leads to higher unemployment—jobless rates are 2 percent points higher in metros with too few educated workers to meet demand (Katz & Bradley, 2014).

Educated workers then are not just creating jobs for themselves and their similarly highly educated peers: less educated and younger people are more likely to be working, and are earning comparatively higher wages, if they live in metropolitan areas with a narrower education gap (Katz & Bradley, 2014). What this means is that wage differences and quality of life in the United States have as much, or possibly more, to do with geography than with career choice or social class (Moretti, 2012). That means that if high school graduates want to earn a middle-class living or better, they will need to increase their level of educational attainment. However, it also helps to live where the jobs are, and those jobs are increasingly in city centers and well-interconnected metros.

Public Research Universities in the Metro Nation

The top 100 metro areas in the United States are home to 67 percent of the nation's major research universities, most commonly located in their central cities. These same areas account for more than three-quarters of all knowledge-economy jobs in the U.S. and are home to 72 percent of adults with a post-secondary degree and 75 percent of those with a graduate degree (Berube, 2007). Of the top 100 research universities in the world, 50 are American, and more than half of those are public (Academic Ranking of World Universities, 2016). Seventy-three percent of all undergraduate students in the U.S. attend public universities and community colleges (Yudof & Callaghan, 2012).

The importance of research universities to the American economy, and by extension the American standard of living and quality of life, cannot be overstated. Innovation in scientific and technological research has been and is projected to continue being the strongest driver of economic growth and new industries and jobs both in the United States and globally, and our nation's research universities are the primary source of the new knowledge and trained talent driving innovation (Wesser, 2013). America's public research universities, in particular, conduct most of the nation's academic research (62 percent) and produce the majority of its scientists, engineers, doctors, teachers, and other learned professionals (70 percent) (Duderstadt, 2012). The majority of these universities are located in urban centers, and these universities have been found to be highly correlated to the development of the nation's leading biotech clusters (Katz & Bradley, 2014).

Given this growing migration to cities, coupled with the fact that the STEM fields will dominate job opportunities in metropolitan areas, we are likely to see a growing income gap between those who complete a higher education degree and those who do not. Today, in the 100 largest metro areas in the U.S., 43 percent of job openings require at least a bachelor's degree, but only 32 percent of adults over age 25 have earned one (Rothwell, 2012). Trend data reveal that the percentage of employment opportunities that will require a college degree will continue to increase over the next decade (Carnevale, Smith, & Strohl, 2013). Individuals without access to a college degree will be at a disadvantage for maintaining or even attaining a middle-class life. Universities, therefore, must find ways to bring more and better equilibrium to the new urban society.

It goes without saying that colleges and universities are in the business of not only preparing the next generation of adults for the workforce, but also training students to become knowledgeable problem-solvers and thinkers. Higher education institutions are anchor institutions that function like vital organs in their regions, playing important parts of what makes their communities more prosperous, competitive, creative, and connected. But universities themselves alone do not create innovation clusters or successful cities (Katz & Bradley, 2014). They must be part of a community-development ecosystem that brings together influential institutions that shape the economic, social, cultural, and political vibrancy of the metropolitan region.

Successful community-development ecosystems are built on the cultivation of "innovation hubs" (Moretti, 2012). Today, there are only about a dozen such hubs in the United States. For now, they are not tied to a reliance on natural resources, factories, or even universities themselves. Rather, as Enrico Moretti (2012) argues, it is probable that innovation hubs are born out of the presence of one of a few "academic stars," who by virtue of their genius, productivity, and cutting-edge nature of their work create a pull that attracts other innovation workers. In the places where these hubs are being established, public research universities are redesigning their academic programs to satisfy STEM-centric nature of the world's job market and are investing in cutting-edge lab equipment and technology, such as new virtual reality labs. In this regard, such universities become the anchors for creating the conditions that build economic opportunities for those within the metro region.

What more can public research universities do to expand opportunity and access and improve social and economic outcomes for those within metro region and across the United States as a whole?

Making and Meeting Our Commitments: Engaging with Metros in the 21st Century

The complexity of our culture means that there are no easy solutions to our education and workforce challenges. However, with intentional effort and genuine purpose, public research universities can improve student outcomes, such as retention and completion rates, and help more workers in the metro nation achieve gainful employment after graduation. Specifically, here we offer action steps that public universities can take to strengthen their relationships with their regions, supporting the development of innovation hubs that promote the economic health and vibrancy of metropolitan regions. In each of the three sections below we offer recommendations and examples learned from our leadership positions at The State University of New York (SUNY) and Portland State University (PSU) that we have found to be successful, or which are promising or necessary to ensure the strength of public research universities in an era of growing metros.

Expand Learning Options to Serve a Diversifying Population

Income disparity cannot equal opportunity disparity, and most certainly not when it comes to access to the kind of high-quality education that prepares students to enter the workforce and become creative, contributing adults. The expanded employment and cultural opportunities that metro regions provide attract diverse populations. Public research universities need to consider the changing nature of the student body and how to best serve a more diverse student population.

Between 2000 and 2010, the total population in the United States grew by nearly 10 percent, climbing from 281.4 million to 308.7 million. During that same time, the Hispanic population grew by 42 percent to represent 50.5 million people of Hispanic origin living in the United States. This huge upshot accounts for more than half of the overall total population increase in the U.S. during the first decade of this century (Ennis, Rios-Vargas, & Albert, 2011). At the same time, the black population, including those who consider themselves of mixed race, grew by 15 percent to represent 42 million Americans. This group now represents 14 percent of the overall population (Rastogi, Johnson, Hoeffel, & Drewery, 2011). To compare, the non-Hispanic white segment of the population, which is overall still the largest group in America, grew by only 1 percent during that same time (Humes, Jones, & Ramirez, 2011). Clearly, the face of the nation is changing.

This population growth and diversification is most prominent in metropolitan regions. As the demands of the workforce become more complex, the limitations of today's educational systems become more apparent. Too few minority and low-income students enroll in or complete college, whether two- or four-year, and this is one of the factors driving the widening income and quality-of-life divide. Public universities, in particular, have a responsibility to keep higher education within reach for all, and therefore, they need to be proactive in ensuring that these students achieve educational success. This means working in sync with the K-12 sector to ensure college or career readiness and decrease the need for remediation in college, given that better preparation for college is correlated with greater college student persistence and retention (Pascarella & Terenzini, 2005).

The SUNY has sought to address the demographic shifts in its system. SUNY is the largest comprehensive university system in the nation. With 64 schools, including research universities, liberal arts colleges, specialized and technical colleges, health science centers, land-grant colleges and community colleges, the university currently enrolls more than 463,000 students, employs 88,000 faculty and staff, and offers more than 7,500 degree and certificate programs. From its founding, and at its core, SUNY has always been shaped by its responsibility to serve the whole of New York, every resident from every background and walk of life, one of the most ethnically and racially diverse states in the country.

To better meet that responsibility and up the ante like never before, in 2010 SUNY created and launched a new strategic plan, *The Power of SUNY.* Nurturing the state's and university's diverse composition is a driving force behind each of the plan's "Six Big Ideas," which run from SUNY positioning itself to be the state's leader in building a healthier, more energy-smart, and entrepreneurial New York; SUNY doing its part to mend the leaks in the state's education pipeline, from cradle-to-career (C2C); and SUNY actively engaging with both local and global communities to enrich lives at every level.

Toward this end, in September 2015, the SUNY Board of Trustees passed a Diversity, Equity, and Inclusion policy that is among the most aggressive in the nation. The policy called for each of SUNY's

64 institutions and our System headquarters to put in place a diversity and inclusion plan that addresses recruitment, retention, campus climate, and more. Central to the plans: Every campus must have a designated chief diversity officer, every campus must offer cultural competency training, and every campus will report annually on their progress, tied to campus leadership evaluation. To ensure the efficacy of this new policy, dedicated faculty researchers continually support our chief diversity officer network and evaluate the policy.

Another of SUNY's many programs or approaches to ensuring brad access is the Educational Opportunity Program (EOP), which marked its 50th year in 2017. This is a statewide SUNY program that provides admission and intensive support services for economically and educationally disadvantaged students and has been a highly successful model and pipeline for underserved populations. The University at Albany, for example, has seen tremendous benefits from this program, which boasts significantly higher first-to-second year retention (92 percent) and a higher six-year graduation rate (76 percent) than the overall student body. Because of the success of this program, SUNY was able to get an additional $4.8 million in the state budget for EOP, which allowed UAlbany to expand its program by 50 students in 2015–2016. The University has also worked to replicate EOP's best practices in campus-wide programs, focusing on the successful strategies of mentorship, enhanced faculty advising, and community building.

At PSU efforts to serve the diversifying population of the Portland metropolitan area have been particularly interesting because for so long the city of Portland and the state of Oregon have been the least diverse and racially "whitest" major city and state, respectively, in the United States. However, since the 1990s, the Latino population has been growing rapidly, now making up at least 11 percent of the state's population, and over 20 percent of the Portland area's public school population. In response, PSU created a Taskforce on Latino Student Success in 2008 and has been implementing key recommendations since then. Among the key actions have been: the hiring of bilingual recruitment, admissions, and financial aid staff to help families understand the college matriculation process; reaching out to middle school students, community organizations, and other intermediaries; and creating a "Casa Latina" dedicated space on campus. As a result, Latino enrollment at PSU has doubled to 8 percent of the student body.

Ensure Affordability

Re-envisioning the policies, structures, and the institutional culture is also key to ensuring to serving a diverse student population. Critical to this ensure college affordability. Nationally, per-student funding from the state has fallen more than 15 percent from where it was in the late 1980s, resulting in higher tuition and fees for students. In essence, the cost of education has shifted from the state to the students, creating an undue hardship to many students and their families. With this funding shift has come a growing marginalization for a widening base of people with limited income, in essence putting college education and post-secondary training out of reach. While public research universities—the institutions with primary responsibilities for ensuring broad access to education—have experienced declining funding, their private research university counterparts have enjoyed real, per student funding increases as their revenues from both tuition and private giving have greatly exceeded those of the public institutions (Schulenburger, 2012). Although public research universities receive about 62 percent of all federally awarded research grants (up from the 57 percent level of the late 1970s.[1]), declining state funding has meant that "public research universities today pay faculty more than 20 percent less than private universities (a decline from a position of near parity in the 1970s), have leaner instructional staffs, and are attracting students with lower SAT scores" (Schulenburger, 2012, p. 80).

Slashes in state funding over the last decade mean that leaders of public universities must look for new ways to keep their institutions viable. Experts and scholars of higher education unanimously and aggressively call for the return of state support and lay out the denouement of what the persisting decline in support will look like for the not-too-distant future United States (Fogel & Malson-Huddle, 2012). We are ardent supporters of the "new national higher education compact" that Mark Yudof and Caitlin Callaghan proposed in *Precipice or Crossroads?* They present a four-part prescription to maintaining education funding and quality that involves establishing a stable new dynamic between public university leadership, private funders, and critical state and federal support. They recommend that public universities

> ...should look at their operations with a "private" sensibility. They should establish realistic priorities, eliminate weak programs, adopt money-saving Internet technology services, and aggressively reduce waste.
>
> At the same time, state governments should rededicate themselves to supporting these universities' core functions, not least because core functions will probably never get enough from private sources.
>
> And if and when the federal government does begin to contribute in some way to core costs, a mechanism must be put in place to ensure that states do not treat the federal funding stream as an opportunity to disinvest even further in the institutions.
>
> Most importantly, by implementing this compact we would demonstrate—at a national level—a public commitment to, and understanding of, these universities' societal value (Yudof & Callaghan, 2012, p. 75).

In line with this, SUNY instituted a rational tuition program that allows students and their families to plan for the cost of their education over the course of 5 years. Historically, one of the biggest and most stubborn challenges SUNY faced for decades was that its tuition-setting ability was tied to the New York State Legislature's budget practices. When SUNY had been allowed to raise tuition in the past, it was sporadic and dealt an unexpected blow to students and their families. In the University's 60-year history, the State allowed the University to raise tuition only thirteen times—the smallest of these increases was 7 percent (2009–2010), and the highest was 43 percent (1991–1992). Seventeen times since 1963, a first-year student entered SUNY and during his or her college career never had to pay a tuition increase; 19 entering classes saw one tuition increase; eight entering classes saw two tuition increases; and the class entering in 1989–1990 saw three tuition increases. The process was anything but fair.

In June 2011, through rallying the support of the student body, faculty, community stakeholders, legislators, and a critical partner in New York's Governor Andrew Cuomo, SUNY finally accomplished what some maintained was impossible. The university secured legislation that: (1) creates a fair and predictable tuition plan; (2) provides SUNY with a reliable revenue source to maintain education quality; and (3) includes a maintenance-of-effort assurance from the State. The legislation also included provisions that strengthen the academic programs of the University Centers and positions SUNY to be a leading catalyst for job growth throughout the state. With this policy in place, SUNY's annual tuition remains the lowest among all state university systems in the northeast and in the lowest quartile of all such public institutions of higher learning in the country. This legislation was an intentional effort to address the growing dilemma of how to maintain access for students across the economic spectrum in an era of scarce and diminishing resources.

In an era defined by resource scarcity, sound planning and vision are more important than ever to public higher education. With budget cuts to SUNY exceeding $1.5 billion in recent years, SUNY advocated to restructure the University's budgeting process. To begin modeling a new way forward, the university created a budget task force made up of campus presidents, provosts, and other administrators and gave them a two-fold charge: develop proposals to absorb cuts, and create a long-term approach to financial management that aligns with the strategic plan. The result is SUNY's Campus Alliance Networks, a shared services initiative that represents a new commitment on SUNY's part to eliminate duplicative and unnecessary expenses, streamlining services, making the most of the fact that SUNY is a system and could work better as thus, all with the idea of better serving students.

SUNY's shared services goal from the outset was to save $100 million over three years and reinvest those dollars in expanding academic and student services at SUNY campuses, adding faculty positions, increasing offerings of courses required for degree completion, and a continual reduction in time to degree. SUNY met its shared services goal in advance of its three-year deadline; by January 2015 the system had exceeded its goal and continues to save using shared-services measures.

Maintaining affordability has been a problem in Oregon also because of the very large reductions in public funding that even preceded the 2008 Great Recession. The reductions and overall budget crisis had become worse since then. In the mid-1990s, Oregon limited property tax increases and mandated that the State pay more for K-12 education. In addition, voters approved several mandatory sentencing referenda, which required significant investment in the criminal justice system. As a result, Oregon's support for higher education per student ranks around 45th–48th among the states. The state's universities have had to raise tuition in response, although legislative constraints have moderated this somewhat. At about $8,000 per year for tuition and fees for a full-time undergraduate, Oregon ranks about in the middle of states. Adding together the state support and tuition, Oregon ranks 49th in the nation (ahead of only Colorado), in the amount of funding available per student.

While students and their families understandably care most about tuition, the low level of total available funding also means there is little institutional financial aid, and fewer resources available to advise, tutor, improve faculty-student ratios, and do all the other things that increase the likelihood of student success. For example, the Oregon Opportunity Grant, the main state financial aid program, has been consistently underfunded and serves less than half the students that the program was intended to serve.

This dilemma has led to creative ideas, which so far have not yet been implemented. One that received considerable attention is "Pay it Forward," where students would pay no tuition, in exchange for paying a tax on their salary after graduation. Oregon is currently developing a pilot project to try this with a group of about a thousand students. It is clear, however, that the program will require a very large upfront investment, and there are concerns that only those pursuing careers in lower-wage fields will choose to participate, casting doubt on the fiscal viability of the idea.

Like all universities, PSU engages in a variety of other efforts to reduce costs and enhance revenues. The University began an Academic Program Prioritization project; is increasing its online offerings and recruiting more out-of-state students; and through repeated rounds of budget reductions is eliminating all activities that do not directly contribute to student success. In addition, all Oregon universities are collaborating on efforts to increase state funding in the next few legislative sessions. Without such renewed state funding, affordability will continue to decrease, and efforts to diversify the student body will not succeed.

Develop Platforms for Effective Online Learning

Accelerating advancement in communication technology is perhaps the largest boon to accessibility in education since the passage of the G.I. Bill. Moving forward, public research universities must adapt to include a strong online learning component to their offerings. The addition of such programming introduces an unprecedented level of flexibility and greater accessibility for students, allowing students to engage in the educational process on their own terms as necessary and appropriate. This increased "anytime" access means universities have to adjust and change to take an added step to help speed student completion. Quicker completion provides students with an effective way of cutting college costs.

Online learning has sparked a debate about the quality of the education it offers. Critics are concerned that the quality of the instruction can't possibly be as good as face-to-face interaction, and they also worry that speeding up college and making it cheaper means dumbing it down, that the value of a degree earned this way means less. We argue that online learning must become an important piece of the puzzle, not the whole picture, as some critics of the medium fear. Online courses will not supplant the campus or classroom experience, but they will be a strong supplement, one that enhances flexibility for students and adult learners who are reaching for the next rung on that ladder, and who also have real-life commitments and constraints that make pursuing a degree or certificate that much more challenging: jobs, children, aging parents, financial constraints, community ties—all very real factors that limit access to traditional higher education.

The relative newness of online learning is creating a new dynamic between faculty and students, and it is critical that universities pay special attention to ensuring that this dynamic is a productive one. Perhaps the most essential aspect of creating and maintaining truly useful and excellent online offerings is engaging the best faculty. Online learning must not be synonymous with decreased quality: this is a new, additional learning application, not an ersatz one. But seasoned faculty who have been in the classroom for years or decades, however skilled in classroom instruction and respected in their fields, will not necessarily be naturals in translating their specialties and teaching styles to an online environment. The dilemmas for public research universities in particular is to optimize their faculty members' capacities to teach with the new technologies and various modes of online learning.

Universities must take intentional, bold steps to hone faculty skills in online course creation and delivery in order to ensure that such courses offer students an enriching experience. At SUNY, for instance, the University is creating a Center for Online Teaching Excellence with the input of more than 40 faculty and staff members from across the system, including researchers, instructional designers, and online educators. The purpose of the Center is to

- engage and connect a community of online education experts;
- encourage scholarship in online teaching and learning practices to meet the needs of today's diverse learners, and pursue research-driven innovations that increase online teaching and learning effectiveness;
- provide distinctive and comprehensive development opportunities to faculty directly and in conjunction with their home campuses; and
- support faculty with resources needed for course development and enhancement in conjunction with their home campuses.

As part of this initiative, SUNY is also developing what we call a "scale-up lab" that provides an outlet for faculty to experiment with and pilot innovative learning practices.

Similarly to SUNY, PSU is increasing its online offerings, and doing so deeply integrated with its current curricular offerings. PSU does not see online learning as a way to reach far-flung markets. Rather, online learning is designed to enhance PSU's traditional commitment to older and returning students, while continuing to build on PSU's strength in community engagement. In 2012, PSU kicked off a campaign to "reTHINK PSU," with the goal of producing more graduates at the same or higher quality at the same or lower cost by using technology and community engagement. The keystone of the campaign is the Provost's Challenge, which solicited proposals for a total of $3 million in one-time funding to develop online courses or student assistance processes. Only teams could submit, and almost one-third of our faculty *and* staff were involved in at least one of the 165 proposals. We used crowdsourcing to comment on, enhance, and combine proposals and ultimately funded the 25 strongest ones. They range from an automated process for changing or affirming a student's major, to a fully only bachelor of social work. Most projects, however, are focused on creating flexible degrees that combine classroom learning with online capabilities. PSU created a new Office for Academic Innovation to assist the projects and provide close project management to ensure success.

On the whole, PSU sees its niche as continuing to serve our traditional geographic market—two-thirds of our students come from the Portland region. To do this well, the University must allow its students to spend less time on campus, and more time on their jobs and with their families. At the same time, students want and need the personal contact that can only happen in a classroom and in interaction with faculty and other students, as well as through placements and projects with local business, community organizations, schools, and units of government. Online technologies, if done right, can replace some amount of classroom learning, and free up time for interactional activities. PSU is still in the experimental phase, and it intends to continue investing in projects to refine the approach.

Students engaged in online learning also need support. As universities develop their online offerings, they need to design more than courses—the interaction between student and school needs to be as dynamic as ever. In order to ensure this, a university's online presence would do well to include a live round-the-clock and easily accessible "help desk" with tutoring, mentoring, degree planning, and advisement services, as well as financial aid information.

Another critical aspect of online offerings must be that they are aligned with workforce needs. In New York, for instance, there are currently 6.9 million adults with high school diplomas or General Education Developments (GEDs) but no college education. Meanwhile, as was suggested previously, the percentage of jobs that will require a college degree will increase substantially in the coming years. In New York, it is expected that by 2025, 60 percent of job opportunities will require at least a bachelor's degree, and this requirement will be most pronounced in the state's metro regions. There is a lot of ground to make up in this regard, and this is where online learning can prove effective in increasing student access to higher education and preparing metro residents for full employment.

Expand Co-Operative Education

The workforce, as we can see, is increasingly technology reliant and specialized, and will only become more so. That said, the best universities will have come to understand that immersing students in practical experiences in their chosen fields is among the best ways to prepare them for success after college. Today, the majority of college students—as many as 80 percent—work while enrolled in classes. For many students, the need to balance school with work is a serious challenge to completing their degrees in a timely manner. Co-operative education initiatives, however, give students the chance to marry their need to earn income while enrolled in college with work experience applicable to their fields of study, which in turn can help them be better prepared and more employable following graduation. This dynamic is considered a win–win by students and employers: students get the experience (and financial resources) they need while businesses are infused with fresh, eager, experienced talent.

In New York, some of SUNY's co-op partners include notable companies such as Global Foundries, General Electric, IBM, Motorola, and Chevron, to name a few. These companies not only play influential roles in metro regions, but they also offer a wide range of future employment opportunities. In fact, because the win–win is so strong and employers are often pleased with the students' performance, 60 percent of participating co-op students are offered positions by the employers for which they worked while enrolled in the program (Koc, Koncz, Tsang, & Longenberger, 2014).

Obviously, co-op works best in areas with a high density of business and employment options, i.e., cities and metros. And while skilled graduates are among the most mobile people in the world, strong co-op programs offer a promising way to retain home-grown talent and make local, public good on the return on education investment.

In New York State in 2015, Governor Andrew M. Cuomo called on SUNY to require experiential learning of all students to receive a degree. SUNY's Board of Trustees quickly responded with a resolution stating that SUNY would develop a plan to make approved applied learning activities available to SUNY students enrolled in the 2016–2017 academic year.

To coordinate this significant undertaking, SUNY's system provost established an Applied Learning Steering Committee, which combined campus-level quality assurance standards and principles of good practice from the National Society of Experiential Education to form criteria for determining approved applied learning activities. At the time of this writing, this is still a work in progress, but great headway has been made. In 2017, every SUNY student has the opportunity to engage in a campus-approved applied learning activity before they graduate. Through SUNY, there are now nearly 9,500 approved applied learning opportunities for the system's 460,000 students.

One goal for universities should be to increase the "stickiness" of their local college campuses—that is, strategically collaborate with local and state governments and the private sector to create better alignment between programs at high schools, colleges and universities, and local workforce needs. This sort of collaboration takes time and trust building. C2C collective impact approaches are proving to be one way to not only build community-wide trust, but to set common goals, determine desired outcomes, and meet needs of both students and the local workforce.

Drive Collective Impact From Cradle-to-Career

Education is the single best antidote to poverty that any society has. It is the best means, and perhaps the only real means, of lifting society up in the manner of the well-worn aphorism, "a rising tide lifts all boats." But the most stubborn obstacle to improving education outcomes is poverty itself. No new or advanced higher education learning options—no online courses or degrees pursued, no co-op opportunities—matter if students aren't prepared to take on the work when they arrive at college.

Traditionally, there has been a gulf between K-12 and higher education, as though one had little or nothing to do with the other, as though there is not a continuum between the two. It is only rather recently that this disconnect is getting the close attention it is due, and more universities are doing their part to actively partner with their regional K-12 counterparts to ensure that students meet important developmental benchmarks every step of the way, from before kindergarten even, so that they are equipped to succeed in college and beyond.

As was suggested in the previous section, one of America's most pressing challenges that is likely to become even more prominent in the near future, lies in ensuring that the large and growing groups of people who have been traditionally underserved by education institutions are prepared for the workforce. This means that they need to become empowered to make choices about their futures and that they are equipped to set and meet life goals. Impoverished conditions in homes, schools, and communities unequivocally hobble children's abilities to develop and contribute to society when they become adults. So the challenge, then, is this: How can public research universities work to address the negative effects of poverty, neutralizing or eradicating them wherever possible, so that everyone, regardless of socioeconomic background, has access to the kinds of high-quality education and support that make a *real* difference in their lives? What do public research universities need to do to give everyone a chance to earn a better living and have a better life? How do these institutions reliably move the dial on those goals, and do it in a sustainable way?

Beginning in the early 1970s and until very recently, high school graduation rates in the United States declined or plateaued, the result of what is often referred to as a leaking education pipeline, an education system riddled with holes and pitfalls through which too many students too easily fall. And once these students are out of the system, their chances of recouping opportunities and options diminish sharply.

Build Civic Infrastructures

The collective-impact-driven C2C approach to improving education outcomes, best exemplified by the work being led by StriveTogether and its National Cradle to Career Network, is designed to serve every student in every respect. The approach provides a roadmap for how community stakeholders from across sectors can come together and look closely at the specific needs of students and future students and then target those needs with services, ensuring kids have what they need to succeed in school and that they are motivated and prepared to continue on to college. Each of the universities or systems we currently head, and some we previously served, is actively engaged as leaders in some stage of the creation of a local C2C.

The preponderance of data related to child wellbeing, cognitive development, academic success, educational attainment, skill building, employment, job satisfaction, and overall health and happiness, taken together, point to the fact that these outcomes are intimately related. What happens every step of the way in a person's life, positive and negative, and most especially in childhood, has a cumulative effect and strongly influences outcomes in adulthood. The best outcomes occur when children receive consistent positive support, both academic and social-emotional, from before birth and until adulthood (Campbell, 2009).

The problem, then, with too-low college enrollment or completion or even high school graduation, does not start in high school. The origins of too-low success rates can be traced back to the very beginning of a child's life. Not enough Americans are graduating from high school today (or graduating prepared for college or a career) because many of these students did not enter kindergarten ready to learn. These children spend the rest of their K-12 lives needing to catch-up, and if they attend schools that are not equipped to truly help them in all the ways they need helping, with both academic and social-emotional support, they will not reliably meet important developmental benchmarks. Simply put, not enough students are laying the solid groundwork in cognitive development—a process that begins in infancy—to allow them to develop the skills and abilities they will need as adults.

A college degree is not a guarantee of success, but it opens doors that otherwise would be bolted shut. It offers exposure to experiences that are not necessarily more valuable than "life experiences" had out in the world in the formative sense, but which are not likely to be had otherwise outside the arena of higher education—on a campus, in a classroom, through an internship, or online, if the circumstances are right. There are self-made people, autodidacts who are beyond bright and self-directed, but here we are discussing the educational needs of everyone else—most people.

Today, if a child is to have a real chance at becoming a successful adult, his or her learning and cognitive development need to be nurtured and encouraged beginning in her or his earliest years—at home and well before they enter school—and then consistently and systematically supported all along the education pipeline. If continuous, coordinated, high-quality support is what it takes to effectively prepare children to grow into functional, successful adults today, the challenge before us then is two-fold: First, we need to devise systems that ensure that *all* children, regardless of circumstances or background, have access to the right kinds of opportunities and support for learning *from cradle to career*. And second, we need to ensure that these systems are reliably sustainable across the long haul.

PSU chose to become involved in this issue for a variety of reasons. In close collaboration with PSU's dean of education, the Portland mayor, the central county's board chair, and the superintendent of the largest school district in the region, PSU took the lead in creating a strong county-wide C2C initiative. PSU conducted the initial research that helped identify key metrics of success, after which an existing nonprofit organization was transformed to take on the role of "backbone" organization. All Hands Raised (the former Portland Public Schools Foundation) has now firmly established itself as the convener for C2C work in the six school districts of the county, managing a multitude of projects and interventions all aimed at creating collective impact through the work of the schools, social service organizations, businesses, local government, and multiple higher education institutions. The effort is beginning to result in earlier and higher rates of enrollment in kindergarten; improved attendance in ninth grade; and greater attention to issues of equity throughout the educational system. It has also greatly enhanced PSU's reputation as a truly engaged institution that is collaborative and willing to share the credit.

The University at Albany, along with SUNY System Administration, has been instrumental in the launch and support of a C2C partnership, The Albany Promise, now serving as the backbone organization for the partnership. UAlbany provides office space, staff support, convening capacity, and research and data analysis. The Albany Promise works closely with the City School District of Albany, the City of Albany, and a wide range of community stakeholders to improve educational outcomes in Albany's public schools. Given that the student population in the Capital Region is immensely mobile between the three urban districts in the region (Albany, Schenectady, and Troy), the partnership is exploring the possibility of expanding the partnership to the regional level.

Lead by Example

It is a well-known sentence, and one commonly, though incorrectly, attributed to Charles Darwin: "It is not the strongest of the species that survives, nor the most intelligent, but the one most responsive to change." These words actually belong to Leon C. Megginson, an expert, not in biology, but management, and a longtime faculty member at Louisiana State University (Megginson, 1963).

Megginson's words, of course, echo Darwin's theory, and in doing so provide useful advice to university leaders today. Institutions and systems that continually adapt to meet the needs of the increasingly complex, changing world are those that stand to flourish. That flourishing is measured not only by institutions' internal health—its graduation rates, headcounts, endowments, reputations—but by the success of its service to the community, how fully and efficiently universities prepare the workforce and provide training and tools that empower students to build successful lives and engage with, and give back to, their communities.

Leadership at future public research universities takes a specific skill set. It takes dynamism, extroversion, and mastery of not only an academic field or administration, but visionary economic development and an understanding of placemaking, of what makes communities attractive, strong, and vibrant. Because universities are themselves diverse entities—with their ranges of fields of departments and specialties; their function as job creators and preparers; their physical plant—their reach into the community, and therefore responsibility to the community is broader than other anchor institutions that might have just one function. Future urban universities require as their heads leaders who are conveners, who are active in their communities beyond their campuses.

Looking to the Future

Public research universities of the future will have to expand their learning options to guarantee access and completion to a diverse, often economically and educationally disadvantaged population. They also must find creative ways to bridge the divide between the university education and industry by building civic infrastructure for C2C pipeline, developing co-operative education, and building a platform for effective online learning. Public research universities, as stable anchor institutions with long historical roots in the community, are especially positioned and equipped to contribute to the overall betterment of society. In fact, they have a special responsibility to society to do so. As producers of skilled human capital and innovation and sources of jobs, public research universities must expand their visions of their roles in their regions and continually strive to make good on meeting society's needs.

These institutions must find ways to shift the policies, infrastructure, and culture so that they can best respond to increased metrification and fully address the needs of a rapidly evolving workforce and changing student demographics. Our nation is confronting the serious dilemma of a woefully underprepared workforce, which if not attended to, will continue to produce greater disparities between economic classes. Through intentional attentiveness to expanding learning options, applying strategic institutional leadership for change, and developing innovative C2C programs, public research universities can improve students' academic success preparation for employment that will allow them to thrive in America's metro nation.

The Association of American Universities defines the purpose of the American research university simply enough: to ask questions and solve problems. And by combining cutting-edge research with undergraduate and graduate education, America's research universities are training new generations of leaders in all fields (Association of American Universities, n.d.).

Note

1. University-based research and development funding is primarily supplied by six agencies of the federal government: the National Institutes of Health, National Science Foundation, Department of Defense, National Aeronautics and Space Administration, Department of Energy, and Department of Agriculture.

References

Academic Ranking of World Universities. (2016). *Academic Ranking of World Universities 2013 [Data file].* Retrieved from http://www.shanghairanking.com/ARWU2013.html

Association of American Universities. (2014). "About Research Universities," https://www.aau.edu/ (accessed Feb. 25, 2014).

Berube, A. (2007). *MetroNation: How U.S. Metropolitan areas fuel American prosperity. Brookings Institution.* Retrieved from https://www.brookings.edu/wpcontent/uploads/2016/06/MetroNationbp.pdf

Campbell, D. E., (2009, October) Civic engagement and education: An empirical test of the sorting model [Abstract]. *American Journal of Political Science. 53*(4). 771–786. Retrieved from http://rooneycenter.nd.edu/assets/12026/sorting.pdf

Carnevale, A. P., Smith, N., & Strohl, J. (2013). Recovery: Job growth and education requirements through 2020. *Georgetown Public Policy Institute: Center of Education and the Workforce.* Retrieved from http://www.columbiagreeneworks.org/Recovery2020.pdf

Duderstadt, J. J. (2012). Creating the future: The promise of public research universities for america. In M. Fogel, & E. Malson-Huddle (Eds.), *Precipice or crossroads?: Where America's great public universities stand and where they are going midway through their second century (221–240).* Albany: State University of New York Press.

Ennis, S., Rios-Vargas, M., & Albert, N. (2011). The Hispanic Population: 2010. *U.S. Census Bureau.* Retrieved from http://www.census.gov/prod/cen2010/briefs/c2010br-04.pdf

Fogel, D. M., & Malson-Huddle, E. (Eds.). (2012). *Precipice or crossroads?: Where America's great public universities stand and where they are going midway through their second century.* Albany: State University of New York Press.

Humes, K., Jones, A. S., & Ramirez, R. R. (2011) Overview of Race and Hispanic Origin: 2010. *U.S. Census Bureau.* Retrieved from http://www.census.gov/prod/cen2010/briefs/c2010br-02.pdf

U.S. Census Bureau. (2011, August). Statistical Abstract of the United States: 2012. Retrieved from http://www.census.gov/compendia/statab/2012/tables/12s0618.pdf

Katz, B., & Bradley, J. (2014). *The metropolitan revolution: How cities and metros are fixing our broken political and fragile economy.* Washington, DC: Brookings Institution Press.

Koc, E. W., Koncz, A., Tsang, K. C., & Longenberger, A. (2014). 2014 Internship and Co-Op Survey. National Association of Colleges and Employers. Retrieved from http://www.naceweb.org/uploadedfiles/content/static-assets/downloads/executive-summary/2014-internship-co-op-survey-executive-summary.pdf

Megginson, L. C., Lessons from Europe for American business. *Southwestern Social Science Quarterly. 44*(1). (1963): 4. Retrieved from the Darwin Correspondence Project, http://www.darwinproject.ac.uk/six-things-darwin-never-said

Moretti, E. (2012). *The new geography of jobs.* New York: Mariner Books.

Pascarella, E. T., & Terenzini, P. T. (2005). *How college affects students.* San Francisco: Jossey-Bass.

Rastogi, S., Johnson, T. D., Hoeffel, E. M., & Drewery, M. P. Jr. (2011). The Black Population: 2010. *U.S. Census Bureau*. Retrieved from http://www.census.gov/prod/cen2010/briefs/c2010br-06.pdf

Rothwell, J. (2012). Education, Job Openings, and Unemployment in Metropolitan America. *Brookings Institution*. Retrieved from https://www.brookings.edu/research/education-job-openings-and-unemployment-in-metropolitan-america/

Schulenburger, D. E. (2012). Challenges to viability and sustainability: Public funding, tuition, college costs, and affordability. In D. M. Fogel, & E. Malson-Huddle (Eds.), Vol. 80. *Precipice or crossroads?: Where America's great public universities stand and where they are going midway through their second century*. Albany: State University of New York Press.

Wesser, C. W. (Ed.). (2013). *Best Practices in state and regional innovation initiatives: Competing in the 21st century*. Washington, DC: The National Academies Press.

Yudof, M., & Callaghan, C. (2012). Commitments: Enhancing the public purposes and outcomes of public higher education. In D. M. Fogel, & E. Malson-Huddle (Eds.), *Precipice or crossroads?: Where America's great public universities stand and where they are going midway through their second century*. (63–78). Albany: State University of New York Press.

10 Diversity

An Investment in Democracy and Academic Excellence

Heidi Lasley Barajas and Caryn McTighe Musil

A resurgence of an old and discredited dichotomy is seeping surreptitious back into national discussions about higher education. It falsely suggests one must choose either diversity *or* excellence (Alon & Tienda, 2007; Posselt, Ozan, Bielby, & Bastedo, 2012). Especially troubling is that this misconception influences policies and practices in public research universities on which the states and the nation rely to advance knowledge, prepare students for the contemporary global workplace, build strong communities, and address pressing complex problems. Taxpayers invest in public research universities. These citizens deserve to have public universities invest in them too. The evidence is irrefutable: academic excellence is not possible without diversity (Asumah, Nagel, & Rosengarten, 2016; Ghosh, 2012; Gurin, Dey, Hurtado, & Gurin, 2002). The very heart of intellectual inquiry demands a diversity of ideas and experiences. Likewise, profound and deep exclusions undermine the opportunity to educate every student to ensure America as a nation thrives. Public research universities, one of society's most prized opportunities, treasure providing valuable and unique opportunities for personal and societal advancement. If they do not include diverse students, they misshape America's future and miss-educate all students. Without diversity, students are deprived of essential sources of knowledge, underprepared for the modern workplace, and ill equipped to be a constructive force in diverse countries like the U.S. and in the global context in which they will work and live.

Research and practice accumulated over the past 25 years should cause public research universities and others to embrace diversity as higher education's most powerful high impact practice (HIP). Diversity has proven again and again to be a positive means of accelerating public research universities' core goals of producing knowledge, engaging students in their learning, and fostering a commitment to democratic ideals of equality, social justice, and the public good.

Colleges are one of the few places where privilege and disadvantage can be analyzed along with how systems operate to sustain them in society at large. Current policies that adopt traditional definitions of merit without

DOI: 10.4324/9781315110523-11

questioning how they reflect and re-inscribe legacies of stratifications and inequalities put academic excellence at risk and abandon the important civic mission of higher education. Nowhere is this felt more keenly than at public research universities, especially the elite ones. It is critical that institutional leaders work to establish constructive and creative means to disrupt the effects of privilege and disadvantage. This requires a complex and deep analysis of how institutions currently work and for whom. Participants on multiple levels of leadership in higher education institutions must be willing to take on this challenge. Public research universities cannot move productively into the future without seriously understanding the implicit bias of individuals, and the institutional racism and sexism rampant in our current institutions, often unconscious and too often unchecked.

Why Public Research Universities Need Diversity and How Diversity is at Risk

We live in a multicultural world that is stratified in every imaginable way. Issues of race, class, gender, disability and the intersection of these larger social issues continue to be prevalent and perhaps are inevitable. Such issues establish privilege and disadvantage at an individual and systemic level. Inherited stratifications have given some students unequal access to cherished spots at selective public research institutions. However, as Takaki (1990) suggests, the 21st century provides an opportunity to re-imagine public research universities:

> The prospects for American race relations in the coming century do not seem sanguine. A mood of pessimism pervades the debate among intellectuals and policymakers over such issues as welfare and affirmative action. Racial tensions and conflicts continue to deepen racial divisions...imagine what kind of society we could have in the next century...
>
> (p. 309)

Sylvia Hurtado (2007) states, "It is time to renew the promise of American higher education in advancing social progress, end America's discomfort with race and social difference, and deal directly with many of the issues of inequality present in everyday life" (p. 186).

Higher education institutions of the future must be willing to concede that inequality cannot be met through traditional definitions of merit. It is critical to establish means through which to mitigate the effects of privilege and disadvantage. Why? Because access to public research institutions is one way to disrupt legacies of exclusion and is "at the core of twenty-first-century America's understanding of itself as democratically legitimate" (*Grutter v. Bollinger*, 2003). The educational benefits of diversity in general are crucial to "a long-term effort to transform undergraduate education, which will prepare the next generation of citizens for a multicultural society" (Hurtado, 2007, p. 186). The benefits of diversity are also a challenge to "the theoretical foundation for the claim that 'anti-preference' initiatives produce colorblindness and race neutrality" (Carbado & Harris, 2008, p. 1152). However, perceptions and practices focused on diversity provide a cautionary tale that includes assumptions about how diversity, learning, and the civic–social mission in higher education may or may not be linked. Intentionally and clearly linking these three goals must be a central part of transformation if the learning and civic and social goals of higher education are to be realized.

Despite the persistence of barriers to higher education for some, there has been progress in the racial diversification on college campuses. We are, however, drifting away from the progress we have made in demographic diversity. One reason is declining State support for public institutions. As a result, higher education has attempted to tighten the proverbial belt in administrative and programmatic areas. At the same time, more publics (including land-grant institutions) are seeking better rankings through what Carnevale (2012) refers to as "the great sorting." For Carnevale, higher education offers opportunity but also increases the reproduction of economic privilege, increasing both quality and inequality by "matching the most advantaged students with the most selective institutions" (p. 1). Participants on multiple levels of leadership in higher education must be willing to identify latent consequences that chasing higher rankings produces (Dalton & Crosby, 2015). Part of a strong undergraduate picture is students being retained and graduating in four years. However, increasing numbers of institutions make decisions based on the assumption that character, capacity, and hard work required for students to succeed academically can only be demonstrated through high standardized test scores and weighted grade point averages obtained through special K-12 options available primarily to economically privileged students. These assumptions drive practices such as buying National Merit Scholars and continually raising the required standardized test score for admission.

In a 2012 address to the Association for Public and Land-grant Universities (APLU), Bill Gates commented that the mistake higher education makes in trying to increase students in STEM is the practice of "creaming." This practice does not increase the number of students in STEM, but simply moves the most qualified students around. Gates suggested that to actually increase the number of qualified students, we should engage the second quintile of students who, with some support, could become a new cohort of high achieving STEM students. There is a trade-off in this kind of thinking. Since institutions are ranked both by the student profiles of admitted students and time to degree completion, some give and take would be required. Nonetheless, such a practice would grant more flexibility for admissions offices to recruit, and society would benefit by increasing the number of qualified candidates for the workforce. Most important, expanded spaces would be available for students who are qualified, but perhaps do not have the most privileged background.

Higher education is also finding that new or highly advertised admissions practices and policies as well as continued legal actions associated with admissions impact students' perceptions and application patterns. Hoxby and Avery (2012) found that the majority of high-achieving low-income students do not apply to selective institutions. Exacerbating the problem, institutions are not looking for them. The combined result is referred to as undermatching. Bastedo and Flaster (2014) believe there are flaws in the assumptions behind undermatching. For example, they assert that the research relies on patterns based on high school grades and American College Testing (ACT) or Scholastic Aptitude Teasting (SAT) scores which do not take into account admissions policies favoring holistic review. In the end, the authors doubt that reliance on the current educational meritocratic model can actually reduce the gap. Bastedo and Flaster make excellent points. However, public research institutions today continue to be driven by an average ACT/SAT ranking goal whether it can reduce the gap or not, and continue to consider an average ACT/SAT ranking regardless of holistic review. Undermatching, although not a magic bullet is an important idea. Harper and Williams, Jr. (2014) report, for instance, explores qualities that help black and Latino males succeed in high school. Many high achieving blacks and Latinos in Harper's study did not know they would be attractive candidates for admission to elite colleges.

As institutions balance ranking goals for ACT/SAT scores, so goes the process in terms of financial need. Attention was brought to the balance between need-blind and need-aware admissions practices when George Washington University had to correct a statement on their website, which stated that requests for "financial aid do not affect admissions decisions" (Jaschik, 2013, p. 1). There is a balance and a challenge to both practices. When financial aid runs out, institutions do admit wealthier students over low-income students. Combining this practice with institutional increases in ACT/SAT scores may have unintended consequences. Institutional data from the University of Minnesota, for example, estimates that 60 percent of the 2012 admitted freshman class came from families with incomes of $110,000 or more and that this percentage continued to increase over the next 2 years. For many, the concern is not the practice as much as transparency about the practice. However, the impact on diversity is clear. A recent study by Goodman, Hurwitz, and Smith (2015) found that minimum thresholds for SAT scores send many students to 2-year institutions rather than 4-year institutions. The group most impacted is low-income students. For low-income students, enrollment in a 4-year institution increased the likelihood of earning a bachelor's degree by 50 percent points. When we consider the collective impact of concerns about ranking, undermatching, and need-aware admissions policies, public research institutions seem to be drifting away from earlier progress in increasing demographic diversity.

New Elitism Through Ranking Related to Anti-Affirmative Action Fear

The policies and practices related to the drive for higher rankings, financial aid limitations, and undermatching contribute to growing inequality. More than that, selective institutions like public research institutions are intentionally or not, creating a new elitism. Elitism and inequality are often linked when discussing admissions practices related to legacy admissions, the priority given to children of institutional alums. In addition, educational institutions in competition for high profile students are now offering social amenities that increase the visibility of inequality once students are matriculated. One example is housing. In the past, students who had the means to live on campus (or those who benefited from financial aid that allowed them to live on campus) could opt for a dorm or a minimal off-campus apartment. The last several years has seen an increase in families purchasing apartments or condominiums close to campus rather than paying for on-campus dormitory living. New campus housing and off-campus housing advertise condo-like options. The new elite student has the opportunity not to live like a student, but to live at such a scale while a student that often outpaces employees on campus. Most important, students who can afford to attend without financial aid are provided the means to be even more elite by providing more opportunities and amenities that appeal to elite students. Selective institutions also begin to define qualified through an elite lens. Contributing to this phenomenon is the ongoing debate over affirmative action.

Public research universities have both learned and not learned from *Grutter v. Bollinger*, a case selectively cultivated to affect exactly this sector in higher education. Legal assaults have produced an understandable but dangerous cautiousness in higher education institutions. Anti-affirmative action legislation and rulings only affect selective admissions schools like public research institutions. Yet, institutions too often censor themselves before they need to, abort inventive ways to make their institutions more inclusive, and resort to old and unreliable means of determining who can succeed in a given school. The passing of anti-preference laws in California (1996), Washington (1998), and Michigan (2006) has also resulted in challenges to those laws. For example, evidence showed that students of color were "disproportionately disadvantaged by lack of access to Advanced Placement (AP) classes…[and] that AP classes had become a *de facto* admission requirement" (Miksch, 2008, p. 112). Other challenges included lack of textbooks, qualified teachers, or no teachers. Miksch notes that challenges were not directed at anti-preference laws, but were focused on challenging the "presuppositions under-girding initiatives that end race-based affirmative action in college admissions. That is the notion that grades, rigor of high school curriculum, standardized test scores, and other so-called academic indicators are race neutral and measure merit" (p. 113).

Carbado and Harris (2008) also address assumptions in college admissions related to anti-preference laws. Focusing on the personal statement, they argue that race cannot be removed from the admission process. They challenge the assumption that "prohibiting explicit references to race in the context of admissions does not make admissions processes race neutral. On the contrary, racial prohibition installs what they call a new racial preference'" (p. 1138). For example, an applicant that is required by anti-preference law to exclude references to race in a personal statement may feel compelled to suppress racial identity or even to take on the idea that race does not matter. Doing so would constrain self-expression, generally thought of as crucial to a personal statement. In this situation, the law has not eliminated race in admissions or made the process race-neutral or colorblind. Instead, the law has merely provided a preference for those who would not include race as an essential part of a personal statement. (Carbado & Harris, 2008).

The issue for higher education is not that the debate exists. The issue is that we do not challenge decisions or work within what the law actually allows. Since the anti-preference debate began, many of us have watched selective institutions like public research universities make fear-based decisions under the threat of a lawsuit challenging the use of affirmative action. What we need is more imagination, not less; more courageous affirmation of core values, not cowering hesitancy; evidence-based systems that show how the multiple aims of education can be honored, not safe uncontroversial ones. If higher education leaders at elite institutions work from a place of fear, what do we expect of the students, staff and faculty when faced with controversial topics in their research, teaching/learning, and engagement?

Courageous thinking that understands the strength of diversity as an integrated part of higher education rather than a problem to be solved does exist. Courage may be subtler than we think. For example, Bensimon (2005) found that in higher education institutions we tend to talk more about deficit and diversity than about equity even though the changes required for student success are better addressed through the discourse of equity. Bensimon challenges us in two ways. First, she moves from a discussion of equality to equity. Second, she focuses on individual equity thinking and cognitive frames that link to decision-making in higher education institutions. This is why, for example, higher education leaders may have:

> Positive attitudes toward increasing minority student participation in higher education, but they are inclined to attribute differences in educational outcomes for black, Hispanic, and Native American Students, such as lower rates of retention or degree completion to

> cultural stereotypes, inadequate socialization or lack of motivation and initiative on the part of the students.
>
> (p. 102)

Bensimon concludes that leadership that is equity-minded is less likely to attribute disparities in student outcomes to student deficits, and will take into account their own roles and decisions related to those outcomes. That is courageous thinking. Such a shift in approach will have significant positive consequences at public research universities. A related effort is the Student Achievement Measure (SAM) project that provides a different method for tracking student progress to degree completion. Currently, rankings on degree completion only include the paths of new high school students that enter postsecondary institutions and remain in that institution. SAM reports aggregate outcomes for a group of students who start at a college or university at the same time, and report not just the percentage of students who graduate from their first institution, but also the percentage of students who continue to work toward a degree as well as those who transfer to other institutions. Creating this method of measure changes what we know about graduation rates and challenges the current outcomes that are only a snapshot of one group of postsecondary students. Creating a new measure that is inclusive is courageous thinking.

Other kinds of courageous thinking are seen in Tienda's (2013) challenge for educational institutions to intentionally link or include diversity within university missions. Tienda challenges higher education's "strategies and practices that promote meaningful social and academic interactions" by questioning whether higher education is "harnessing the educational benefits of diversity, or is social and cultural heterogeneity largely symbolic?" (p. 468). Although legal decisions such as *Grutter v. Bollinger* (2003) have brought attention to the benefits of a diverse student body on campus and in the workplace, such efforts are a first step in the work of integrating the benefits of diversity (Tienda, 2013; Hurtado, 2007). When integrated, diversity can be a mechanism that supports the goals of higher education and moves the discourse toward equity. For Tienda, higher education leadership must leverage diversity through "curricular and cocurricular practices that purposefully activate the coalition-building system" (p. 472). Hurtado (2007) argues that although higher education has launched substantial initiatives related to diversity, civic engagement, and a more cohesive undergraduate education, these efforts are not yet coordinated across areas that often have common goals. Linking or integrating diversity with other related areas such as civic engagement and undergraduate education can improve institutional practices while providing an intentional frame for using limited resources more effectively. If we do not integrate diversity across common goals, focused work on access and success for diverse students will continue to be subjected to further attacks by anti-preference thinking.

Connecting Diversity and Civic Engagement to Retention and Graduation

One of the most persuasive reasons for coupling diversity with civic engagement at public research institutions is the emerging evidence of the link between civic engagement and retention. There is an insistent drumbeat to raise college completion rates for numerous reasons. Employers warn that the contemporary, fast-changing workplace requires educated workers adept at invention, adaptation, and teamwork. It is also hard to compete in a global economy when the US has slipped in the education ranking from 1st to 14th according to the Organization for Economic Cooperation and Development (2012). Since educational levels correlate with future economic earnings, a college degree is a pathway out of poverty and a means of remediating the growing economic inequality that threatens to undermine political and social stability. As trendsetters, public research universities could play an influential role; however, too few who argue for increasing completion rates realize that investing in civic learning opportunities in college will help achieve that goal. For example, The National Taskforce on Civic Learning and Democratic Engagement (2012) found there were multiple scholars whose research found that "student participation in service-learning...correlate[s] with outcomes that contribute to increased retention and completion rates" (p. 12). In their examination of existing research, Cress, Burack, Giles Jr., Elkins, and Stevens (2010) asserted, "College students who participate in civic engagement learning activities not only earn higher grade point averages but also have higher retention rates and are more likely to complete their college degree" (p. 1). Given the connection between college success and civic engagement activities, increasing the retention and graduation rate at public research institutions would serve the students' and the nation's economic, social, and political future.

The University of Michigan has developed a nationally recognized program designed to blend student success with leadership development and preparation for being social responsible citizens. They have combined a commitment to community service, diversity and academic success in a program called The Michigan Community Scholars Program (MCSP), which began in 1999. Designed as a residential living and learning experience for a multicultural group of first-year students, this nationally lauded program includes a focus on intercultural understanding and dialogue, seminar courses, community-based service-learning courses, and an array of volunteer service leadership opportunities. In addition, they have designated staff to support students' successful transition from high school to college and presume that all students can and will succeed academically. Statistics bear out the presumption. They have retained 100 percent of first-year underrepresented students of color and close to that number for all first-year students. Of MCSP student leaders, 98 percent graduate.

Finally, MCSP students are more racially diverse than the student body as a whole (Michigan Community of Scholars Program, n.d.). Investing in civic learning opportunities, then, not only raises the bar for educating responsible, engaged citizens, it raises the retention rate for all students, but especially for at risk students.

Diversity as a High Impact Educational and Civic Practice

George Kuh (2008) published a groundbreaking monograph identifying and measuring activities students engaged with that increased their success in college. These activities are referred to as HIPs. HIPs are essentially high student engagement practices that include service-learning, learning communities, study abroad, capstone courses and projects, internships, diversity and global learning, first-year seminars, a common intellectual experience, undergraduate research, and writing-intensive courses. Kuh's volume offered four important pieces of evidence. First, civic-oriented practices like service-learning had the greatest impact on student learning over any of the other ten practices cited. This evidence has only continued to grow stronger, underscoring the fact that civic engagement contributes both to student overall achievement and retention. This has special resonance for public research institutions.

Second, Kuh's (2008) data showed that while *all students benefitted in their academic acceleration* by having access to high-impact practices, *underserved students benefitted even more*. In fact, these practices help close the achievement gaps that are often traced to poor school systems that were not preparing many first-generation students and students of color to be college ready. In a summary of Kuh's HIP findings, Finley and McNair (2013) explained, "*High-Impact Educational Practices* showed that Hispanic and black students who engage in high-impact practices demonstrate greater gains in their first-year GPAs and a higher probability of first-to-second-year retention, respectively" (p. 2). Kuh described these practices as having a compensatory effect, which echoes Bensimon's (2005) equity effect. Such findings should encourage public research universities to be even more courageous about attracting a diverse pool of students.

Third, Kuh (2008) affirmed that diversity and global learning were in and of themselves HIPs. He defines these as:

> Courses and programs that help students explore cultures, life experiences, and worldviews different from their own. These studies—which may address U.S. diversity, world cultures, or both—often explore 'difficult differences' such as racial, ethnic, and gender inequality, or continuing struggles around the globe for human rights, freedom, and power.
>
> (p. 10)

Kuh has also consistently argued that all the high-impact practices were improved when diversity was a component. Diversity helps higher education achieve academic excellence both through the study of diverse sources, histories, and perspectives and through the physical engagement with diverse people in a variety of settings both in and out of class, and on and off campus. Compelling research suggests that colleges and universities that provide access to diverse students at public research institutions are investing in America's economic, social, and political future. All students are beneficiaries.

But just who has access to HIPs? Public research institutions in particular need to monitor this data. Finley and McNair (2013) explained that white students "engage in significantly more high-impact practices than Asian American and Hispanic students" (p. 8), and "students who were first-generation students engaged in significantly fewer high-impact practices than students who were not first generation" (p. 3). Interestingly, transfer students in their sample "engaged in significantly more high-impact practices than non-transfer students" (p. 3). But like Kuh's (2008) earlier study, Finley and McNair's study also found that if underserved students did participate in high-impact practices, they made greater gains in general education, practical competence, and personal and social development than those who did not participate. Moreover, the number of high-impact practices had a dramatic effect on learning outcomes. In 2008, Kuh had recommended that every student have two high-impact practices. By 2013, Finley and McNair found that when students had 56 high-impact experiences, they could increase their learning outcomes by anywhere from 19 to 24 points. For public research universities where the stakes are so high to accept and graduate more representative student bodies, this research should shift curricular designs.

When comparisons were made within groups, Finley and McNair's (2013) results were even more revealing. First-generation students who had 1-2 HIPs boosted their deep learning gains and self-reported gains over those with no HIPs by 11 percent (p. 12). If they had 5-6 HIPs, they boosted their learning by 35 percent (p. 12). Transfer students with 1-2 HIPs boosted their learning 14 percent over those with no HIPs, and if they had 5-6 HIPs, they boosted their learning by 40 percent (p. 12). A similar pattern of doubling, tripling, and for Asian Americans even quadrupling their gains by taking 5-6 HIPs was repeated when comparing gains within racial and ethnic group categories (p. 13). White students had a 37 percent gain over their counterparts who had taken no HIPs; and African Americans and Hispanics got a hefty boost in deep approaches to learning and self-reported gains over their racial counterparts by 27 percent and 26 percent, respectively (p. 13). Finley and McNair concluded from their study, "The evidence that high-impact practices provide distinctive and compelling benefits for multiple groups of students, including those who have been traditionally underserved in higher education, illustrates what might best be referred to as the 'equity effects' of high-impact practices" (p. 18).

Diversity also functions as a kind of high-octane fuel in other types of high-impact practices. First-year seminars are adopted widely now at public research institutions because they cultivate an immediate sense of belonging. They have very positive outcomes, including student persistence, higher graduation rates, more faculty interaction, and more involvement in campus activities (Brownell & Swaner, 2010). Some of these outcomes correlate with retention, but without diversity, the civic outcomes of first-year seminars are depressed. Engberg and Mayhew (2007) demonstrate that first-year seminars with an emphasis on diversity showed more growth in commitment to social justice and multicultural awareness than a first-year communication class or engineering course.

Learning Communities with their linked courses and intense cohort development are difficult to construct without diversity emerging as a defining element. They also help counter-balance large lecture classes commonly found at public research universities. It is no surprise that they have "*non-civic specific outcomes* like student persistence, higher grades, more faculty and peer interaction, and growth in academic self-confidence" (Brownell & Swaner, 2010, pp. 14–19). They also have significant *civic outcomes* like building a sense of community and "social space," personal and social development in terms of understanding self and others different from oneself; more openness to new ideas; more likely to participate in diversity-related activities; and higher rates of civic engagement. These civic ends are especially relevant for institutions expected to deliver on cultivating the public trust.

Intergroup dialogue, identified as a high-impact civic practice by National Task Force on Civic Learning and Democratic Engagement (2012), uses diversity as the rationale for the course design. Its civic outcomes were remarkable and held across a multi-university study involving 52 different comparable intergroup dialogue courses on race and gender taught principally at research institutions (Gurin, Nagada, & Sorensen, 2011). Their compilation included: greater increases in understanding race, gender, and income inequality; intergroup empathy and motivation to bridge differences; commitment to post-college social and political action; greater increases in the efficacy and frequency of their intergroup action during college; cognitive openness and positivity in intergroup situations.

As mentioned earlier, service-learning continues to be the leader across all the other high-impact practices in terms of the effect and range of its outcomes. As a pedagogy, it mirrors the public purposes of public research universities. The *non-civic specific outcomes* include persistence and graduation; higher grades; more faculty and peer interaction; deeper understanding of subject matter and social issues; higher satisfaction in learning experiences; and working harder (Brownell & Swaner, 2010). But Brownell and Swaner include a wide range of *civic outcomes*: applying knowledge to real world problems, recognizing there are needs in communities, reducing stereotyping, gaining greater tolerance, enhancing a sense of personal efficacy, and awareness of the world. The National Task Force on Civic Learning and Democratic Engagement (2012) cites additional kinds of civic outcomes generated: increasing a sense of social responsibility, working well with others, critical consciousness and action, and exploring intersection of identity and privilege.

Researchers speculate that one explanation for service-learning's continuing higher yield on academic and civic outcomes is a result of students being removed from their comfort zone and engaging with people who differ from them. In addition, service-learning usually involves working across differences to achieve a common end. Knowledge in such settings is therefore effortful, not effortless. Commonplace assumptions are challenged. Disequilibrium generates new questions and new insights. Jacoby (2015) argued that through reflection, students are expected to ponder, compare, analyze, and question.

Diversity and Democratic Outcomes

Hurtado (2003) summarizes her findings from her pioneering work in the 1990s at ten large public research universities. She explained, "Campus practices that facilitate student interaction with diversity promote development of cognitive, social and democratic skills" (p. iii). The link between diversity and civic engagement surfaced in another study that found, "Taking a diversity course in the first two years of college is...associated with the likelihood of voting in federal or state elections" (Hurtado, 2007, p. 192). Braskamp and Engberg (2011) found that students enrolled in diversity coursework showed an "acceptance of multiple perspectives in their thinking and knowing" and "demonstrated a strong preference toward cross-cultural interaction and making a difference in society" (p. 3).

Hurtado and her colleagues have created a new instrument called the Diverse Learning Environments (DLE) Survey (https://www.heri.ucla.edu/dleoverview.php). Recognizing the interconnection between diversity and democracy, the DLE can reveal for campuses how a DLE contributes to six outcomes that correspond with those identified in the Civic Learning Spiral developed by an AAC&U Working Group (Musil, 2009): social agency; pluralistic orientation and critical consciousness and action; integration of learning; and civic engagement in public forums and political engagement. Hurtado, Ruiz, and Whang (2012) focused their investigation on the impact of diversity within the curriculum rather than the diversity of students themselves, and unearthed evidence of how an inclusive curriculum correlates with a "pluralist orientation...students' perspective-taking, tolerance of different beliefs, openness to having their views challenged, ability to negotiate controversial issues, and ability to work cooperatively with diverse people" (p. 11). They concluded:

> The more courses students took that included opportunities to study and serve communities in need…materials or readings about race/ethnicity, or opportunities for intensive dialogue between students with different backgrounds and beliefs, the more confident students were in their skills for living and working in a diverse society.
>
> (p. 12)

This is good news for public research institutions charged to produce not just knowledgeable employees but also responsible, civic-minded graduates.

Researchers attest that engaging out of class within a multicultural student body also contributes to students' civic and intellectual learning. Only in the last three decades has such a diverse student body become the norm on some campuses. In such cases,

> higher education can serve…as one of the defining sites for learning and practicing democratic and civic responsibilities in large part because it now includes a wider range of students—across class and color, religion and gender, nationality and age—than ever before in our history…where it is possible not only to theorize about what education for democratic citizenship might require in a diverse society, but also to rehearse that citizenship daily in the fertile, roiling context of pedagogic inquiry and hands-on experiences.
>
> (National Task Force on Civic Learning and Democratic Engagement, p. 2)

Hurtado et al. (2012) explain further:

> Our analysis confirms that the more students reported engaging with others of different racial/ethnic groups (such as meaningful discussions about race, or intellectual discussions outside of class), the higher their scores or change on all six civic outcomes. Student participation in racial/ethnic student organizations is also significantly related to positive changes in students' social agency and political engagement, and higher scores on civic engagement in public forums.
>
> (p. 12)

Such out-of-class intercultural experiences are dependent on having a diverse student population. At public research institutions, that forward motion has been stymied by legal attacks and admissions relying too heavily on indicators like standardized tests, AP courses, and high performing high schools. Such filters diminish rather than expand access for promising students who would otherwise succeed at public institutions. Expanding students' imagination and knowledge about the realities of different people's lives leads, as research tells us, to lifelong commitments to strive as citizens for greater equality and opportunities and for intervening in the face of racism, sexism, homophobia, and other forms of discrimination. Such capacities contribute to the flourishing of a diverse democracy. Public research institutions have a stake in investing in these civic-inducing practices.

Diversity and Academic Excellence

We end our chapter where we began: with a reminder that evidence increasingly points to diversity as a vehicle for expanding sources of knowledge and modes of inquiry. As higher education has introduced more inclusive curricula, areas of investigation, and authorities, all of this new scholarship has had profound influences on students and faculty. It tests accepted norms, challenges long accepted paradigms, redefines historical periods, and opens up entirely new subjects of study. Diversity pushes students to question, increases their powers of discernment, and fosters taking the perspectives of others seriously. Diversity is, then, a way of understanding and interpreting the world. As the earlier part of this chapter made clear, diversity is about real people—the students who are shut out or welcomed into public research institutions, the faculty who are recruited or overlooked, and the administrators who are promoted or driven out by a hostile environment. Too often underprepared students are mistakenly seen as "the problem" because some assume they cannot succeed. However, there is an understudied group of students at risk as well: those who are fearful, ignorant, or unaccustomed to diversity. These students risk being woefully underprepared to live, work, and build a socially cohesive society with others unless public research institutions construct positive learning environments for them. Diversity is essential to that learning.

Diversity Re-Envisioned in the Public Research University

Public research institutions have a unique opportunity to exercise their influential role in improving the quality of human lives and the sustainability of the planet. Achieving both will require deep engagement with others across profound differences replete with innovative alternatives. The paradigm of the ivory tower as isolated from the world and its urgent questions is no longer a viable blueprint for the future in a fluid, interconnected, and interdependent world. As we re-envision the public research university, it will be critical to tap the powerful evidence that diversity promotes intellectual excellence and enhances a lifelong commitment to the public good whether in one's home community, at one's workplace, or in the global community.

Diversity, then, helps insure the intellectually rich and rigorous future of public research institutions and the contribution such institutions—if diverse—can make to the larger world. It is therefore no time to renege on the promise of equitable opportunity or to retreat from the forward progress towards greater inclusion fought for by so many for so long. The courageous-thinking poet and writer Gloria Anzaldua describes what to do when one is at a crossroads:

> Qué hacer de aquí y cómo? (*What to do from here and how?*) Basta de gritar contra el viento—toda palabra es ruido si no está acción. (*Enough of shouting against the wind—all words are noise if not accompanied with action*).
>
> (Moraga & Anzaldua, 1983. Forward.)

What are some of the concrete actions research universities could take in the future instead of just "shouting against the wind"? The re-envisioned public university will need to disrupt the historic and current rampant inequalities and stratifications that like medieval times determine a person's future status by the rank into which he or she was born. To do that, public research universities will need to be driven by rankings not built on exclusivity but on how well they are educating a diverse student body that represents America's future, not its past. We will abandon legacy admissions that only recreate old divisions. Instead, we will invent more accurate and opportunity-oriented admission standards which do not rely heavily on AP courses, high performing high schools, or standardized tests, none of which is race neutral and all of which reveal high incomes more than high individual achievements. We will also need to aggressively invent ways of identifying students of promise and talent who will never dream of applying on their own. This search for hidden excellence will be coupled with raising and allocating more funds for financial aid to increase need-blind admissions.

In public research universities that embrace and invest in diversity, these kinds of bold actions mean leaders at public research institutions will cease to operate from a place of fear and dangerous cautiousness spurred by anti-affirmative action activists. Instead, by espousing equity-minded leadership, they will be emboldened to reach out to the millions of students across racial, ethnic, gender, and economic divides hungry for education and opportunity and ready to learn in the best educational environment. The evidence about how effective high-impact practices can be in closing much of the initial achievement gaps derived principally from under-resourced schools and economic deprivations offer a clear option for public research universities. Effective leaders of these institutions will need to lead public research universities to build such practices into their curriculum and co-curriculum, incentivize faculty and student investment in such practices, and make them so pervasive that all students, not just honors students, will have access to high-impact practices repeatedly over their four years. Campus practices will be governed by understanding the resonance between diversity, student retention, academic success, graduation, and engagement through work done collectively with others to address pressing problems. Leaders at public research institutions will, then, give priority to civic learning and democratic engagement in curricular designs, faculty scholarship, co-curricular activities, and global experiences. Every major will help students explore the public consequences and ethical questions common to their chosen fields. Public research institutions will also take the lead in nurturing robust, generative campus/community partnerships as a new arena for deep learning, scholarship, and collective practice in working across differences to achieve shared goals.

It is time to reinvest in diversity not divest from it. Diversity is what we have in common on this planet; it is the very reality of everyday life and a source of renewal and invention. Despite gated communities, zip codes that align with income, and wars fought over geographic and religious boundaries, human beings today are not so much autonomous as connected, not self-sufficient but interdependent. Each person therefore needs to feel accountable for what is happening down the street, south of the border, or across the sea. Public research institutions are incubators where students can learn what it means to live productively and constructively in such a world and use their talents to solve the daunting environmental, political, economic, religious, and social problems that threaten our shared futures. Collaboration, invention, shared knowledge, unified political will, spiritual resilience, and a commitment to the public good—all of these will be needed if we are to collectively construct a future in which everyone and everything flourishes. Public research institutions should do what they do so well—imagine what has not been invented, invest in possibilities, advance knowledge, involve everyone, and contribute to the well-being of the public. "Caminante, no hay puentes, se hace puentes al andar. (*Voyager, there are no bridges, one builds them as one walks*)." (Moraga & Anzaldua, 1983).

References

Alon, S., & Tienda, M. (2007). Diversity, opportunity, and the shifting meritocracy in higher education. *American Sociological Review, 72*(4), 487–511.

Asumah, S., Nagel, M., & Rosengarten, L. (2016). Two: New trends in diversity leadership and inclusive excellence. *Wagadu: A Journal of Transnational Women's and Gender Studies, 15*, 140–161.

Bastedo, M. N., & Flaster, A. (2014). Conceptual and methodological problems in research in college undermatch. *Educational Researcher, 43*(2), 93–99. doi: 10.3102/0013189X14523039.

Bensimon, E. M. (2005). Closing the achievement gap in higher education: An organizational learning perspective. *New Directions for Higher Education*, 131, 99–111. doi: 10.1002/he.190

Braskamp, L. A., & Engberg, M. E. (2011). How colleges can influence the development of a global perspective. *Liberal Education, 97*(3/4), 34–39.

Brownell, J. E., & Swaner, L. (2010). Five high-impact practices: Research on learning outcomes, completion, and quality. *Peer Review, 14*(3), 29.

Carbado, D. W., & Harris, C. I. (2008). The new racial preference. *California Law Review, 96*(5), 1139–1214.

Carnevale, A. P. (2012, July 2). The great sorting. *The Chronicle of Higher Education.* Retrieved from http://www.chronicle.com/article/The-Great-Sorting/132635

Cress, C. M., Burack, C., Giles, D. E. Jr., Elkins, J., & Stevens, M. C. (2010). *A promising connection: Increasing access and success through civic engagement.* Boston: Campus Compact. Retrieved from http://www.compact.org/wp-content/uploads/2009/01/A-Promising-Connection-corrected.pdf

Dalton, J. C., & Crosby, P. C. (2015). Widening income inequalities: Higher education's role in serving low income students. *Journal of College and Character, 16*(1), 1–8. doi: http://dx.doi.org.ezp3.lib.umn.edu/10.1080/2194587X.2014.992914.

Engberg, M. E., & Mayhew, M. J. (2007). The influence of first-year "success" courses on student learning and democratic outcomes. *Journal of College Student Development, 48*(3), 241–258.

Finley, A., & McNair, T. (2013). *Assessing underserved students' engagement in high-impact practices.* Washington, DC: Association of American Colleges and Universities. Retrieved from https://leapconnections.aacu.org/system/files/assessinghipsmcnairfinley_0.pdf

Ghosh, R. (2012). Diversity and excellence in higher education: Is there a conflict? *Comparative Education Review, 56*(3), 349–365. doi: 10.1086/666545.

Goodman, J., Hurwitz, M., & Smith, J. (2015). *College access, initial college choice and degree completion.* National Bureau of Economic Research. Working paper 20996 http://www.nber.org/papers/w20996

Grutter v. Bollinger, 539 U.S. 306 (2003). https://www.loc.gov/item/usrep539306/

Gurin, P., Dey, E. L., Hurtado, S., & Gurin, G. (2002). Diversity and higher education: Theory and impact on educational outcomes. *Harvard Educational Review, 72*(3), 330–366.

Gurin, P., Nagada, B., & Sorensen, N. (2011). Intergroup dialogue: Education for a broad conception of civic engagement. *Liberal Education, 97*(2), 46–53.

Harper, S. R., & Williams, C. D. Jr (2014). Succeeding in the city: A report from the New York City Black and Latino male high school achievement study. *Center for the Study of Race and Equity in Education.* Retrieved from https://www.gse.upenn.edu/equity/sites/gse.upenn.edu.equity/files/publications/Harper_and_Associates_2014.pdf

Hoxby, C. M., & Avery, C. (2012). The missing "one-offs": The hidden supply of high-achieving, low-income students. *Brookings Papers on Economic Activity*, (1), 1–65. Retrieved from http://www.nber.org/papers/w18586.pdf

Hurtado, S. (2003). Preparing college students for a diverse democracy. *Final report to the US department of education, office of educational research and improvement, field initiated studies program.* University of Michigan: Charting the Future of College Affirmative Action.

Hurtado, S. (2007). Linking diversity with the educational and civic missions of higher education. *Review of Higher Education, 30*(2), 185–196.

Hurtado, S., Ruiz, A., & Whang, H. (2012). Advancing and assessing civic learning: New results from the diverse learning environments survey. *Diversity & Democracy, 15*(3), 10–12.

Jacoby, B. (2015). *Service-learning essentials: Questions, answers, and lessons.* Jossey-Bass.

Jaschik, S. (2013, October 22). Pretending to be Need-Blind. *Inside Higher Education.* Retrieved from https://www.insidehighered.com/news/2013/10/22/george-washington-u-admits-it-incorrectly-told-applicants-it-was-need-blind

Kuh, G. D. (2008). *High-impact educational practices: What they are, who has access to them, and why they matter.* Washington, DC: Association of American Colleges and Universities.

Miksch, K. (2008). Widening the river: Challenging unequal schools in order to contest proposition 209. *Chicano-Latina/o Law Review, 207,* 111–147.

Michigan Community Scholars Program (n.d.) Retrieved from http://lsa.umich.edu/mcsp/about-us/mission-history-goals-highlights.html

Moraga, C., & Anzaldua, G. (1983). *This bridge called my back: Writings by radical women of color.* New York: Kitchen Table: Women of Color Press.

Musil, C. M. (2009). The civic learning spiral. In B. Jacoby and Associates (Ed.). *Civic engagement in higher education: Concepts and Practices* (pp. 61–63), San Francisco: Jossey-Bass.

National Task Force on Civic Learning and Democratic Engagement. (2012). *A crucible moment: College learning and democracy's future.* Association of American Colleges and Universities. Retrieved from https://www.aacu.org/sites/default/files/files/crucible/Crucible_508F.pdf

Organization for Economic Cooperation and Development. (2012). *Education at a glance 2012: OECD indicators, OECD Publishing, Paris.* doi: http:/dx.doi.org/10.1787/eag-2012-en. Retrieved from http://www.oecd.org/education/CN%20-%20United%20States.pdf

Posselt, J., Ozan, J., Bielby, R., & Bastedo, M. (2012). Access without equity: Longitudinal analyses of institutional stratification by race and ethnicity, 1972–2004. *American Educational Research Journal, 49*(6), 1074–1111.

Takaki, R. (1990). *Iron cages: Race and culture in 19th-century America.* New York: Oxford University Press.

Tienda, M. (2013). Diversity≠Inclusion: Promoting integration in higher education. *Educational Researcher, 42*(9), 467–475. doi: 10.3102/0013189X135161.

11 Competition and Ranking

A Comparative and International Perspective

John V. Lombardi and Diane D. Craig

The Competitive Context of Higher Education in America

An American cultural peculiarity assigns the same words to describe all American higher education (AHE) institutions. Although everyone knows the difference between a trade school, a community college, a religious sectarian institution, a private elite undergraduate college, or a major public or private research university, when Americans talk about higher education they often use the words *colleges*, *schools*, and *universities* interchangeably (Lombardi, 2013).

This device reflects the public confusion about the structure of AHE, homogenizes the complexity of the academic environment, and obscures the great American achievement of a diverse and adaptable higher education industry. At the same time, however, it reflects the core belief that higher education is about "schooling"—that is, the acquisition of formal knowledge on a range of academic subjects that will likely have practical benefits.

The National Center for Education Statistics (NCES) Digest of Education Statistics (2015) provides data on the types and characteristics of postsecondary institutions, including detailed information on their students. A total of 4,627 institutions provided postsecondary education in the 2014–2015 academic year. This number disguises the wide range of institutional types. The 1,616 2-year institutions represent 35 percent of the total, while the 3,011 four-year institutions are the majority at 65 percent (NCES, 2015).

Research Universities

Our focus in this discussion is on the 701 public and 1,584 private not-for-profit four-year colleges and universities (some 726 institutions are private for-profit), and within these, we focus on the 200 or so institutions with a substantial research commitment. These 200 universities each spend at least $25 million a year, earned from federally funded research programs.

DOI: 10.4324/9781315110523-12

This group is roughly composed of three quarters public and one-quarter private universities, and together they spend about 95 percent of the federally sponsored academic research funds distributed among more than 800 American academic institutions (MUP, 2017).

If we focus on these top 200 institutions in 2013, the range of federally sponsored research expenditures is wide. Excluding the Johns Hopkins University (at $1.9 billion dollars, whose total includes the $1.1 billion Applied Physics Lab), the next highest total belongs to the University of Washington, Seattle, with $869 million. The last on this list is Loma Linda University, with $25 million of federal research expenditures per year.

Another way to appreciate the complexity of the higher education system in America is to review the distribution of students in the traditional under-25 college age group among the various types of institutions. Public four-year universities enroll 52 percent of the nation's full-time, undergraduate students under 25 years of age while their two-year counterparts enroll another 21 percent. Four-year private institutions enroll an additional 22 percent to this group, with the remaining full-time students in for-profit institutions accounting for the final 4 percent. Students attending part-time enroll predominantly in public two-year institutions, at 68 percent, and public four-year institutions, at 25 percent, for a total of 93 percent of the part-time students in these two traditional sectors of institutions. Private four-year institutions enroll only about 5 percent of the part-time students. The remaining 3 percent of the part-time students appear in the private for-profit sector.

AHE falls into various overlapping categories. Community and technical colleges have a tremendous following. They provide remediation for college-bound but under-prepared high school students, a low-cost entry into the first two years of a baccalaureate degree program, and variable and adaptable vocational and technical education to large numbers of students. These colleges, located in and directly serving their communities, enjoy high public esteem and strong political support.

Most community and technical colleges operate in the public sector, although some proprietary for-profit and a number of private not-for-profit examples also exist. Many proprietary two-year institutions offer principally vocational training, but in recent years, the for-profit institutions have expanded into producing not only two-year academic programs but also proprietary four-year degrees. We anticipate that this trend will continue as many traditionally two-year public institutions expand their offerings into various, primarily occupationally focused, four-year programs.

Originally funded by local school districts, most public community and technical colleges have become dependent on state tax-based support and various federally sponsored programs. Almost all now also charge tuition and a variety of fees and distribute financial aid.

Community and technical colleges range in size from below 1,000 students to above 10,000. Some 12 percent are below 1,000 students and about 17 percent above 10,000, with the majority distributed in between these two extremes.

In most states, community colleges, four-year colleges, and universities compete for some of the same students and the same state dollars. Each definable sector of the AHE industry has at least one association that represents its interests in Washington, DC, and before state legislators, and that provides extensive information about that sector on its website.

Liberal arts colleges deliver a relatively standardized four-year curriculum. Characterized for the most part by relatively small size (1,000–5,000 students), and modest to nonexistent graduate education or research activity, the institutions in this category range widely. Small, private, sectarian institutions provide religious instruction along with a liberal arts curriculum and offer an intellectually safe environment with predictable social, moral, and ethical values. Prestigious and expensive liberal arts colleges serve elite constituencies in a highly secular and competitive mode. They often create innovative and experimental intellectual, academic, and cultural environments. The sectarian and most of the prestigious liberal arts colleges exist in the private sector.

In between these institutions lies a wide range of generic public, private not-for-profit, and private for-profit four-year institutions that serve primarily local or regional constituencies, although some for-profit colleges operate online on a national scale. They offer liberal arts and applied undergraduate degrees in education, business, nursing, allied health, or engineering. They enroll anywhere from 3,000 to 15,000 students or sometimes more. They may have some professionally oriented master's programs and perhaps a doctoral program or two.

These institutions enroll students at varying price points, from relatively low cost for public to high cost for private not-for-profit and for-profit institutions, and they usually have only modest, if any, participation in the national research enterprise.

Major public and private research universities in the United States follow a narrow range of organizational models. Although the internal details and relationships vary, the basic structures remain similar. They include small, elite, graduate, and undergraduate institutions of perhaps 5,000 students or even fewer and large public research universities reaching over 50,000 students or more.

Some divide the graduate and undergraduate missions into two organizational clusters, but most operate both levels of instruction with the same faculty. They have a major commitment to research and graduate education through the PhD and postdoctoral levels. They have large contract and grant revenues, and many include large enterprises in medicine and, in land-grant universities, agriculture.

Most of the criticism of American universities focuses on elite institutions (both the small elite colleges and the elite public and private research universities), not only because of their number and prestige but also because their academic values and standards apply in greater or lesser measure to all other higher education institutions in America.

Institutions must recognize their place within the different competitive niches of the national structure of higher education. Big public research universities cannot become elite liberal arts colleges, nor can liberal arts colleges offer the range of services available at large public land-grant institutions. Major private research universities cannot provide the same services to the public as public land-grant institutions.

University competition is intense, and institutions compete against similar institutions for some things and against much different institutions for others. To assume a simple model of the higher education industry obscures these distinctions and misrepresents the obstacles to and opportunities for institutional success.

Ranking

One manifestation of the confusion surrounding our definitions of "university" is the dramatic expansion of the ranking industry. Ranking of American colleges and universities has reached epidemic proportions, and the determined effort to categorize institutions has spread overseas to encompass the world.

Ranking exists because there are so many institutions of such varied character, size, and composition that most people find it difficult to sort them into comparable categories. The highly competitive university and college business encourages each institution to sell itself as being the best, advertise its remarkable qualities, and showcase its many singular accomplishments.

The most visible enterprise to identify the commercial opportunity of academic rankings has been U.S. News & World Report, whose best college rankings have become a publishing phenomenon much imitated by other magazines, such as Forbes, the Wall Street Journal, Barron's, and many other publications. The ranking business, while profitable for many commercial publications, is nonetheless highly controversial, but the intense interest has made ranking an international industry.

The key issue in rankings is methodology. In most US rankings, the goal has been to identify university or college characteristics assumed to be of interest to the public, often aimed at prospective undergraduate students and their parents. In theory, a good ranking system would produce something akin to a Consumer Reports guide for consumers of higher education. However, the data to achieve this kind of ranking are elusive because the inputs and outputs of colleges are varied and of variable importance to different constituencies.

Moreover, existing statistics do not easily identify much of what a consumer might want to know about college life, content, and results. The college rankings in the United States have, as a consequence, tended to rely primarily on reputation-based survey results combined in complicated weighting methodologies with test scores and grades of the admitted-student body, the wealth of the institution, and other identifiable statistical characteristics.

A difficulty for the commercial ranking business is that the quality of colleges and universities does not vary on an annual basis and the differences among many similar colleges are so minor as to be mostly insignificant. To resolve this dilemma, keep the rankings fresh, and sell the magazines in which they appear, many commercial publications modify their methodologies (usually recalibrating the weighting of the various elements in the ranking methodology) from year to year, thereby changing the resulting order of institutions within the rankings. They may also use significantly complex rankings schemes so that minor, indeed we might say irrelevant, annual variations will move institutions up or down on the scale.

The extensive literature on rankings of this kind often focuses on the circular nature of the process of quantifying reputation. Many of the most popular rankings use a survey of experts to provide a score that purports to reflect the national or international reputation of an institution. Then, the reputation score is used as one of the major elements in the ranking itself. If a college has the reputation of being excellent and as a result ranks highly in a major publication, then its reputation will be enhanced for the next round of reputation surveys. This results in a self-reinforcing process. If the ranking were designed to show the qualities that justify a good reputation, we would not include reputation as a component of the ranking itself.

Additionally, the validity of reputation surveys is highly questionable. The methodology presumes that the academics or other experts queried about reputation know something about the many colleges and universities referenced by the survey. In general, it is unlikely that even the best-informed academics have detailed knowledge of the internal operations of even 50 colleges, let alone the hundreds involved in these surveys. Even someone who knows details about ten colleges is not likely to know about changes that take place from year to year, as is implied in the annual questionnaires.

As a result, the reputation results are simply a word-of-mouth notion related to historical prestige and name recognition. As these rankings have value to alumni and politicians, colleges and universities work hard to show up well in them. They find ways to manipulate the data, and they advertise their colleges in periodicals read by the academic administrators who assign the reputation scores. The goal is to publicize the virtues and significance of relatively lesser-known institutions to improve name recognition and, presumably, reputation. Unfortunately, these public relations activities often distract institutions from improving their operations as they search for better buzz in the press.

Nonetheless, in America, ranking is a favorite game, and almost all universities publish good rankings results and exaggerate the significance of minor positive changes on their websites even when they know the methodology to be fatally flawed. It is better to be seen as prestigious or improving, they reason, whatever the quality or integrity of the source.

Impact of Rankings

The impact of these rankings extends beyond the beauty contest characteristics that define them. They also greatly distort institutional improvement initiatives that instead of focusing on core improvement of academic programs, often not immediately visible to the public, will invest in high profile special projects and trendy achievements. Colleges will highlight what is special and unique about their institutions rather than work to improve the long-term success of the core teaching and research enterprise. These simple ranking lists also provide trustees and legislators with the illusion that they understand the operation of the university and can set goals and standards that they expect to be reflected in the next issue of a prominent ranking. Most good things that happen in a university take time to develop, implement, and produce results, but if the incentives are to improve these spurious rankings, many university leaders can see that short term, quick fix, high visibility self-promotion is an optimal strategy for achieving trustee, legislative, and alumni satisfaction.

The constant attention to rankings tends to focus a college or university's attention on those things that influence the ranking rather than expand the focus of the institutions to consider other elements of educational delivery or performance. Nonetheless, in many contexts, while the rankings are seen to be important to some constituencies, universities remain committed to developing programs of all kinds that will have almost no impact on rankings but are designed to address other issues of relevance to the institution's constituencies. Some of these initiatives involved student-centered programming, others address the organizational structure of the academic programs, and many focus on financial issues related to affordability and access. While rankings do get headlines and often influence some university behaviors, there is often more of a publicity focus associated with the rankings conversation than a fundamental institutional organizational issue.

Ranking the Research Universities

In the special case of the American research university, the process is somewhat more complex in one sense and somewhat less arbitrary in another. Academic research is a nationally competitive business where most of the process of awarding grants, securing scholarly publications, and selecting research-related awards of one kind or another is visible to all. Identifying research institutions is less difficult than finding top undergraduate programs. The complexity of research universities, however, makes constructing a simple, single list that puts these institutions in rank order difficult. The most reliable identifier of research preeminence in America is the amount of federally awarded research expenditures of each university each year. Federal agencies award these funds based primarily on peer review, giving this indicator validity as representing one aspect of the research prowess of each institution's faculty and staff.

However, here too, differences between universities with similar research funding performance are not great, and research university quality often is best reflected by using more than one reliable indicator. By using multiple indicators (and by refusing to create a rank order by weighting and combining them into a single number) as is done in The Top American Research Universities annual reports published by the Center for Measuring University Performance (MUP, 2015), we can get a result that clusters similarly productive institutions together without attempting to create the false impression that there is a great difference between universities with similar characteristics. This process used by the MUP Center rests on the recognition that research universities have multiple products of different type, and what matters in the competition among these institutions is the overall strength of the institutions in multiple dimensions of research performance (from both federal and other sources), financial resources (principally endowment and annual giving), graduate programs (identified by number of doctoral degrees awarded), faculty quality (identified by National Academy Memberships and other significant awards), strong postdoctoral programs, and undergraduate quality. These diverse measures cannot reasonably be combined into a single metric, and instead we look for universities that fall within the top 25 and the next 25 on one to all of the measures to identify clusters of high performing institutions. We find that institutions in the top groups do not vary sufficiently, one from the other, to justify designating a rank order. Furthermore, our data demonstrate that while differential improvement among the top universities is surely possible, major changes do not occur within the span of a single year or indeed multiple years. University improvement comes from sustained focus on the key elements of excellence, not the pursuit of a mythical Number One (Lombardi, Craig, Capaldi, & Gater, 2000; Lombardi, 2010). Still, the world craves a winner, as if university performance were a seasonal competition with championship designations and league standings the desired result. So powerful is this desire to place institutions in rank order, the ranking business has become global which makes the measurement issues more complex (College and University Rankings, 2017).

International Ranking

Universities and nations believe that one of the key elements in the continued dynamism of American business and industry are the achievements of its university-based research establishment. Other countries with research universities work to improve the ones they have, and those without research universities rush to build them.

To mark the success of a national effort to improve research university performance within a global context, several international university-ranking projects have emerged. Most of these have a national origin (such as the recently presented ranking from Pakistan) and are designed to match the performance of national universities against the world market for research preeminence (ITU-QRR, 2017).

Absent the unifying structure of the United States federal research funding competition, the international projects look at a few other variables, but usually focus on publications. The notion here is that research requires publication and therefore the number of publications, primarily in scientific journals, can serve as a good comparative indicator of research productivity on an international scale.

Publication Metrics

However, the academic community does not regard all publications as being equal. Some are more important or significant than others. Not all articles in a journal publication are of equal value: some change the way we think about the world, and others fade into obscurity (Moed, Colledge, Reedijk, Moya-Anegon, Guerrero-Bote, Plume, & Amin, 2012).

To address this problem, ranking schemes use citation counts that measure the number of times authors cite another researcher's article. This is seen as a refinement in methodology over a simple count of the number of publications, but it also introduces a number of data challenges. Some are ordinary, such as the difficulty of knowing exactly who is who when authors have the same last names and first initials. Some are more complex, such as the difficulty of dealing with disciplines that have papers with many authors and those with just a few. Also, disciplines differ in how they acknowledge authorship. Some will list authors in alphabetical order while others put the primary author first or last. In some fields, the authorship will include all the participants on a project, not just the authors of the paper. These different customs for acknowledging authorship complicate the process of evaluating citations and publication productivity.

Sometimes the issue of where the citation is made becomes significant. If an article is cited many times but by authors who publish in second-tier publications, should it count as much as an article cited fewer times but by authors who publish in premier publications (Moed, 2010)? Moreover, how do we determine the premier and the secondary publications?

Some international ranking schemes use reputation surveys to enhance their publication metrics, but here too the problem of circularity appears. If we all know that Oxford is a great university, but we do not know much about the University of Queensland in Australia, how valid can our impressions of reputation be (Rauhvargers, 2011)?

The International Context for Comparative University Assessment

With the increased international interest in research university development and evaluation, reflected in a variety of ranking systems, the MUP Center (publisher of the *Top American Research Universities* annual report) was fortunate to co-sponsor with the United Nations University's International Institute for Software Technology the experimental development of the Global Research Benchmarking System (GRBS). This initiative drew on the large Scopus database of academic journal articles and other peer reviewed materials made available to this project through collaboration with Elsevier. The GRBS developed reliable measures of research productivity and quality applicable to research institutions throughout the world (Haddawy, Hassan Abbey, & Beng, 2017).

The data available for national comparisons of institutions are often not easily compared internationally. In the US, for example, a high score from the college entrance examination of the Scholastic Aptitude Test (SAT) can serve as a surrogate measure of an entering undergraduate's academic preparation for college work, and it may well also indicate the individual's socio-economic circumstances. Collegiate prestige in America depends in part on the quality of an institution's students, making the average SAT of entering students a helpful indicator of prestige. However, the sorting mechanisms that place students within various higher education institutions in other countries are quite different from those in the US, making the SAT a useful national but not international measure of comparative institutional competitiveness.

In the US, to take another national example, the federal research funding competition serves as a major determinant of university research prestige because it is primarily peer reviewed and the competition is conducted on an open nationwide basis. In other countries, national governments award research funding to institutions based on an assessment of the institution's research performance or promise. In the US the federal funds come from an individual competition among research personnel or groups of investigators proposing projects for funding. The institutional indicator of federal research support in the US, then, is the sum of the successful grants earned by individual researchers who work at the institution and it is difficult to compare with the funding grants given by national governments to institutions in support of research programs.

The International Focus on Publication

The GRBS attempted to overcome these nationally specific research measures by focusing on research publications, the most universally recognized token of research performance. Whatever else differs among countries in the development and promotion of research universities, everyone who seeks research prestige must do so by publishing results available to the world. Thanks to the advent of sophisticated bibliographic databases such as the Elsevier's *Scopus*, it was possible to approximate a universal view of the world's research publications, although these databases are much more reliable indicators of science publications than the work appearing in other fields, especially the humanities.

Within this context, the database allowed a reasonable approximation of the quantity and quality of publications by authors associated with a large and growing number of international universities within a wide range of specific fields and subfields. From these data, we could then measure the research staff's contributions and produce a more consistent indication of the relative accomplishments of research universities that serve as the basis for their reputations and international prestige.

Unfortunately, the issue of research prestige is not easily resolved. While the GRBS could count publications and associate them with individuals and the individuals with their institutions, it was difficult to distinguish precisely those publications of high significance from those of relatively modest importance. A university whose faculty consistently produce large numbers of highly significant research publications will surely deserve higher prestige than one whose staff publishes less important work.

The GRBS used a number of the available bibliometric tools developed to measure the significance of published research work. These methods recognize that a particular journal article or other published item is a major contribution to the field when other experts cite this article within their own published work. The more citations that a journal article receives from others who publish, the more significant the journal article may be (Haddawy, Hassan Abbey, & Beng, 2017).

As not all journal articles are equally important, neither are all academic journals of equal significance. If one journal publishes articles that rarely earn citations in the articles of other authors, then we can conclude that the journal is not of major importance. However, if another journal publishes articles that usually earn a significant number of citations in other articles, then we can assume that the other journal is a prestigious place to publish. This notion of prestige functions because journals can only publish a few articles out of the many they receive. The more prestigious a journal, the more submissions it will get, and thus the journal will choose only the most significant articles to publish. If it uses its scarcity well, and selects important items to publish, those items will be widely cited, increasing the journal's reputation, earning it more submissions, and allowing it to continue to be a preeminent journal. In developing its system for assessing the research strength of universities, the GRBS engaged these topics, (Hirsch,. 2005; Moed, 2010).

The MUP Center and the GRBS Approaches to University Research Performance

While the MUP Center's annual reports on the *Top American Research Universities* (MUP, 2017) continue to provide a stable and useful guide to overall American university performance within the context of the nine measures used in that study (as outlined above), the success of the GRBS in developing international bibliometric indicators for assessing research publication gave an important alternative perspective on university performance. The MUP Center focuses on a variety of measures indicative of institutional research capacity and success that address indirect evidence of research performance. Federal and total research expenditures, for example, reflect the success of institutional faculty and staff in competing for research funding but they do not measure the published results of the research. Similarly, the indicators of faculty awards, postdoctoral employees, doctorates awarded, and academy membership all touch on elements that are characteristic of high performing research universities and their faculty but again do not directly measure academic productivity. The measure of SAT scores, as mentioned above, speaks to a special circumstance of US research universities where the presence of high quality undergraduate students indicates a campus context that first rank researchers find congenial. While this may be a significant asset in recruiting and retaining highly productive faculty and staff, it does not reflect the production of academic research. Finally, resources are always important and the indicators of endowment and annual giving provide a reference to an institution's success in creating the capacity to support research.

For the purposes of the MUP Center, this approach has several advantages. Research success in America relies heavily on the organization and support of research universities, institutions with many functions only some of which are directly related to the production and publication of research results. Nonetheless, research universities in the US appear to have a set of characteristics that encourage and sustain research productivity, and the measures identified for the MUP Center's *Top American Research University* annual reports speak not only to those most indicative of research competition (federal research expenditures) but also those most indicative of a supportive institutional context.

The GRBS measured published research results directly without regard to institutional context, national research organization, or differential patterns of funding. From the MUP Center's perspective, a comparison of the American institutions that fall within the top performing categories of the GBRS data with those in the top categories of the MUP Center's annual report on American universities offered an opportunity to understand better the elements of institutional research success. The additional detail and sophistication of GBRS bibliometric data and indexes might appear to offer an easier approach to the question of aggregate academic performance by scholars associated with universities, but the added information also increases the challenge of defining high academic performance (Craig & Lombardi, 2013).

The GRBS provided measures that addressed the volume and significance of publications while continuing to develop other views of research performance, such as levels of international collaboration. The GRBS reported publications separately by academic area of specialty, allowing measurement of research success within 15 subject fields defined broadly at a top level and another 253 defined beneath these within subfields. This depth and detail recognizes that while many research institutions pursue a broad agenda competing in almost all areas of research significance, others take a more focused approach, seeking distinction in only a few fields where their resources will be sufficient to support outstanding performance.

In this essay, however, we look at the institutional level of performance across the 15 top-level subject areas, as this most closely matches the perspective of the MUP Center, *Top American Research Universities* annual report. We can anticipate that the aggregate measures of the GRBS should produce clusters of American research universities that generally match those developed by the MUP Center and published in the annual MUP Center's reports.

Comparing the MUP Center Reports and GRBS

The MUP Center's annual reports compare universities within a specific US competitive context, and it is of considerable interest to observe how the US assessment compares with the publication-driven international university assessments generated by the GRBS. Ideally, the US system that categorizes research university performance on a variety of institutional characteristics related to university support for and success in achieving research capability should reflect the publication performance evaluation of the GRBS. The purpose of research universities, whatever the national context for their operations, is to generate significant scholarly work reflected most generally through publication.

However, the MUP Center's reports capture a much wider range of institutional characteristics in identifying top research universities, many of which may not contribute to publication results. For example, federal and total research expenditures (perhaps the most directly research specific elements among the MUP indicators) include some federal and other sponsored research awarded for activities that do not lead directly to publication, for example, construction of such expensive physical objects as telescopes or the provision of experimental physics equipment. Other federal or externally funded research may be awarded for projects in the national defense, for which no publication is expected or even allowed. The federal and especially the nonfederal research awards competition can fund projects that may provide practical information that is not normally published in prestigious peer reviewed scholarly journals. Nonetheless, in general terms, the individual institutions identified as top American research universities should, however identified, also appear as stellar performers when measured on the international scale of publication quality and quantity.

US Research Funding and GRBS Publication Metrics

A final perspective on these data demonstrates the importance of understanding the purpose of MUP before presenting rating information. As indicated above, in the United States, the competition for federal research funding produces one of the key indicators of institutional research preeminence. These funds, from a variety of federal agencies, are awarded for projects in a wide range of fields using primarily peer reviewed processes. Although there are many issues with the criteria, the selection of general fields to support, and political concerns that may influence the process, the results of this competition are touchstones of American research performance. The MUP Center reports use annual federal research expenditures (reported to NSF) as a key measure among its nine indicators and reports this data element online for all institutions that receive federal support.

However, as also indicated above, federal research expenditures measure resources applied to research, not the publications produced by that research. To test the relationship between the publication data available through the GRBS and the federal research expenditures reported by the MUP Center in its annual reports, we compared the 63 institutions using a selective weighting of GRBS data with the top 63 US institutions reporting federal research expenditures. Both the GRBS list and the federal research expenditures list exclude special purpose and medical only institution. As is the usual pattern in these comparisons, a group of universities performs at the top level from both perspectives. The top 20 US institutions in federal research expenditures also appear among the top 63 within the GRBS data. An additional 22 institutions within the top 63 in federal research expenditures appear within the top 63 GRBS list. However, some 20 universities that rank within the top 63 US federal research expenditures list do not appear within the GRBS publication based list. Looked at from the publication perspective, of the 63 top institutions in the GRBS list, 21 institutions fall outside the top 63 in US federal research expenditures. Indeed, some of these institutions are well down the list based on federal research expenditures. Elsewhere we have provided a more detailed description of these results (Craig & Lombardi, 2013).

These data clearly indicate that while federal research expenditures in the US are a significant indicator of research performance leading to publication, it is not a perfect reflection of a worldwide publication view of research achievement. Moreover, the two domains, federal research expenditures and publication information collected by Elsevier's *Scopus*, capture research activity in significantly different ways as we have discussed above. Scopus captures field specific information from a defined set of worldwide, primarily journal, publications and weights this data based on criteria related to a calculation of impact and significance both of articles and the journals in which they appear. The GRBS data also reflect field and discipline characteristics of publications.

The US measure of federal research expenditures captures a key variable in the development and support of research productivity in the US, which is also an imperfect but significant indicator of an institution's total financial support for research of all types. An institution may have significant federal research funding in the US but work in fields of an applied nature with minimal publication opportunities in the prestige journals included within the GRBS data. In other cases, universities in the US may have a relatively low level of federal research funding but include faculty who receive research support from other sources (state, local, private, and medical) and publish in fields with a high presence in prestige journals (Craig & Lombardi, 2013).

Understanding University Research Performance for the Future

From these preliminary, broad brush views of GRBS results compared to the MUP Center annual reports, we can perhaps draw some conclusions with indications of future directions for public and private American research universities.

This conversation about rating institutions may frustrate because it does not provide simple answers to the complicated question of defining individual and institutional academic performance. Mostly this is the result of a lack of clarity in specifying the question. Do we want to know how well research institutions perform on a range of functions including research, graduate instruction, doctoral degree production, financial resource acquisition, and the like? If so, the MUP Center's annual reports provide, at least for the United States, a useful answer.

Or, do we want to know the relative quality of the research publications generated by the staff of an institution in very specific disciplines or fields? If so, the GRBS and other international data provide an opportunity to construct an answer. The question here, however, is too broad. If we want to know how well the publications appearing within a particular field or set of fields rank on a carefully constructed set of prestige criteria, then the GRBS and similar data offer an opportunity to answer such a carefully circumscribed question. If, however, we simply want to create a league table of great universities, the GRBS data will not give a good answer precisely because we have asked the wrong question. GRBS and similar publication data can tell us what the top 50–70 best performing research groups in the United States might be in specific fields, but it will not rank order institutions in any useful fashion because such a ranking would offer only the illusion of accuracy.

The Future

Much is likely to change over the next decade or so in the United States as concerns about institutional performance, cost, student accessibility and achievement, and regulation gain increasing attention at all levels of higher education from local and state constituencies to federal agencies. Although these concerns will gain considerable traction and some indicators of success in areas other than research continue to gain importance in some ranking schemes, the token of prestige for public and private research universities will almost surely remain published research and the resources required to support the work leading to publication.

The next decade may also show some modifications of the structure of US higher education. The elite institutions, public and private, will continue to compete aggressively in the research marketplace both for national preeminence and international recognition through rankings of one kind or another. The elite will always do well on any ranking scheme, because the elite have the resources and the large base of talent and facilities to sustain premier performance in most highly contested markets. However, the number of US elite institutions is likely to shrink as some public flagship institutions will find it harder to compete with the wealthy private research universities and the better endowed or more generously funded public research institutions.

We do not yet know the full impact of the technological revolution on higher education performance. Clearly there has been a large impact on many areas of university work from libraries to student management. The instructional innovations currently under development at many universities and colleges are likely to establish new methods of instruction, new organization of intellectual domains, and different curricular structures leading to degrees or occupationally defined certificates. These activities will continue to have an impact on how universities organize their work and deliver the quality products their many marketplaces seek. Some will influence research organization as the increasing interdisciplinary nature of research in all fields from the humanities and social sciences through all branches of science clearly indicates. These changes will challenge the stability of the current status of ranking schemes, many of which depend on stable definition of fields of study.

Public institutions in the United States will reflect these changes more dramatically than private institutions in large part because they are so dependent on public, tax-based funding. Throughout these changes, the critical element will continue to be the revenue available to support university activities. Research remains and will remain an expensive enterprise, especially scientific research in all fields. Those institutions that seek to compete at the top level of research performance will continue to require large investments in plant, equipment, and talent. Other university activities that attract significant funding from foundations, government, and donors will prosper, and institutions that successfully redesign their programs to make maximum use of available resources will clearly have an edge in any future competition.

In the future, we are likely to see the college and university marketplace divide even more clearly among the different categories of institution. Community colleges will rise in significance as they produce both degree and certificate programs that validate skills required by specific employer groups, and many will become four-year colleges offering traditional bachelor-level degrees in some fields alongside their traditional occupationally focused programs and certificates.

State colleges and universities will focus heavily on preparing students with job-related skills appropriate for employment immediately postgraduation and they will find the goal of providing completion certificates of significant importance to their public funding agencies, the federal government, and employers. They will also expand programs that transition undergraduate students into professionally focused master's level programs.

Those universities that fall in between these institutions and the premier public and private research universities will maintain some significant research capability and will also focus on the efficient and effective production of job-ready graduates. But they will also be emphasizing the preparation of college graduates who can continue their education in post-baccalaureate programs that can prepare them for careers in a wide range of professional fields.

The premier public and private research universities will participate in all of these activities to a greater or lesser degree depending on their organization and circumstances, but they will mobilize their resources to maintain their national and international competitiveness in research. Some will stay in this competition at the highest levels, but others will gradually find that the resources required are too great and while maintaining a significant research emphasis, will fall out of the top level of competition. They may find it advantageous to focus their research investment on a few fields where they can make an internationally significant impact, rather than seek overall research preeminence.

At the margins, some public institutions, too small for effective performance may, in the future, find it useful to combine with other public institutions in their states although the politics of most states makes the elimination of marginal public institutions exceedingly difficult. Some number of small private colleges will find it impossible to compete for sufficient numbers of students to sustain their operations and will consolidate with other colleges or disappear.

Still, while the rate of change reflected in the news may appear dramatic, the history of AHE indicates that while institutions change, the structure of the enterprise is more enduring than the ongoing controversies might suggest.

References

College and University Rankings (2017) University Library. University of Illinois at Urbana-Champaign. Retrieved from http://www.library.illinois.edu/sshel/specialcollections/rankings/

Craig, D. D., & Lombardi, J. V. (2013) Measuring research performance: National and international perspectives. *The top American research universities*. Tempe, AZ & Amherst, MA: The Center for Measuring University Performance, pp. 3–13.

Haddawy, P., Hassan, S., Abbey, C., & Beng, L. I. (2017) Uncovering fine-grained research excellence: The global research benchmarking system, *Journal of Informetrics*, (11), pp. 389–406.

Hirsch, J. E. (2005) An index to quantify an individual's scientific research output. *Proceedings of the National Academy of Sciences, 102*(46).

ITU-QRR (2017) *Quality research rankings of the muslim world*. Information Technology University, Lahore, Pakistan. Retrieved from http://rankings.itu.edu.pk/

Lombardi (2010) In pursuit of number one, *The top American research universities*, Tempe, AZ. Retrieved from https://mup.asu.edu/sites/default/files/mup-pdf/MUP-Publication-2010-In-Pursuit-of-Number-One.pdf

Lombardi (2013) Characteristics. *How universities work*. Baltimore: Johns Hopkins Press, 2013, pp. 33–44.

Lombardi J.V., Craig, D. D., Capaldi, E. D., & Gater, D. S. (2000) The myth of number one: Indicators of research university performance, *The top American research universities*, Gainvesville, FL. Retrieved from https://mup.asu.edu/sites/default/files/mup-pdf/MUP-Publication-2000-The-Myth-of-Number-One-Indicators-of-Research-University-Performance.pdf

Moed, H. F. (2010) Measuring contextual citation impact of scientific journals. *Journal of Informetrics*. *4*(3).

Moed, H. F., Colledge, L., Reedijk, J., Moya-Anegon, F., Guerrero-Bote, V., Plume, A., & Amin, M. (2012) Citation-based metrics are appropriate tools in journal assessment provided that they are accurate and used in an informed way. *Scientometrics 92*(2).

MUP (2017) *The center for measuring university performance*, Tempe, AZ & Amherst, MA. Retrieved from https://mup.asu.edu/

NCES (2015). Snyder, T.D., de Brey, C., & Dillow, S.A. (2016). Digest of education statistics (NCES 2016-014). National Center for Education Statistics, Institute of Education Sciences, U.S. Department of Education, Washington, DC. Retrieved from https://nces.ed.gov/pubs2016/2016014.pdf

Rauhvargers, A. (2011) Global university rankings and their impact. *European University Association (EUA) Report on Rankings*.

12 Epilogue

Creating a New Kind of Public Research University

Kateryna Kent and Andrew Furco

As influential and resilient institutions, public research universities are likely to remain a dominant force within the overall changing landscape of higher education for years to come. Yet, as the themes and topics explored in this volume reveal, even these powerful institutions are not immune from internal and external pressures to innovate and adapt to meet the new demands of a rapidly changing society. As institutions in transition, public research universities are in a constant quest to find the right balance between demonstrating sufficient responsiveness to new ways of conducting business, and remaining committed to the longstanding practices and values that have propelled these institutions to prominence. While earnest efforts are underway to re-examine and re-assess the culture, structures, and policies of these important institutions, the verdict is still out as to whether these efforts are merely tinkering with the existing system or are truly transforming it.

Public research universities are innovating and are responding to the call for renewal and change. As was discussed in Chapter 3, *the Nature of Innovation and Change*, these institutions are moving from traditional linear approaches to institutional reform in favor of more radical and innovative theories of organizational change. Such efforts will require a new kind of university leader—one who champions a culture of collaboration and who empowers positional leaders within the institution to serve as system change agents. This counter-normative, distributive leadership strategy challenges the dominant hierarchical leadership structure found at most public research universities. Yet, it holds promise for making public research universities more nimble in optimizing the application of their existing assets and resources to respond more effectively to the changing needs of society.

Public research universities are also innovating the ways in which academic work is organized and conducted. As was discussed in Chapter 5, *Public Research Universities as Engines for Economic Development and Innovation*, Chapter 8, *Interdisciplinarity and the American Public Research University*, and Chapter 9, *Research Universities in the Metro Nation*, public research

DOI: 10.4324/9781315110523-13

universities are creating transdisciplinary and interdisciplinary centers, hubs, and institutes focused on moving academic work beyond the traditional disciplinary silos. These efforts are also catalyzing new kinds of partnerships with a broad range of external entities, including corporations, local community organizations, and governmental agencies. These partnerships are increasingly operating with a more reciprocal, mutual beneficial value system and, in turn, are advancing the universities' production of new discoveries while fueling the economic growth of the partnering communities, companies, cities, and states. These innovative interdisciplinary spaces are cradles of new ideas, experiments, and designs that have a strong return on investment and keep public research universities as competitive agents in the local and global markets.

Public research universities' increased attentiveness to engagement with external entities suggests a recommitment to serving the public. As the discussions in Chapter 5, *Public Research Universities as Engines for Economic Development and Innovation,* Chapter 6: *The Iron Triangle Revisited: Re-envisioning Public Research University Financing,* and Chapter 7, *Beyond the Walls of Academic: The Role of Engagement* reveal, the refocus and recommitment to serving the public good is one that is being brought more fully into the academic core of these universities' agendas. The new engagement paradigm is one that goes beyond "outreach" (a.k.a. the third mission) and instead is one that cuts across all three parts of these universities' missions (reaching, teaching, and public service). As the authors of these chapters posit, public research universities of the future will have supportive engagement infrastructure, which will be an essential attribute of a university that is relevant, competitive, and responsive to new economic and demographic realities. Engagement will be the lens through which universities create and disseminate knowledge, develop new curricular structures, identify their grand challenges, and collaborate with their stakeholders and communities. These chapters' authors also point out that public research universities are well on their way in establishing innovative ways to collaborate with external partners, resulting in the development and delivery of new curricula that is meeting the needs of a rapidly changing workforce. They note that these innovations must continue, along with reconceptualizing academic programs to include more project-based and hands-on experiences for students, and re-envisioning faculty promotion and tenure guidelines to motivate and reward engaged teaching and research.

Public research universities are also innovating in their use of analytics to make data-based decisions about student success, expenditures, academics, and institutional performance, as was presented in Chapter 4, *The Impact of Technology: Cause and Consequence* and Chapter 10, *Diversity: An Investment in Democracy and Academic Excellence.* Public research universities of the future will depart from a single campus-based digital system whose costs are controlled and directed by their vendors in favor of interdependent digital ecosystems shared by a consortium of institutions. This new interdependent approach to digital analytics platforms is helping to lower the costs and bring empirical rigor to policy and decision making. Even though this new technology is revolutionizing the nature of work within higher education and is enhancing the efficiency of data management, the authors caution us about the dangers of relying solely on these data systems when it comes to student admissions and success. As the authors of Chapter 10 remind us, data-driven admissions perpetuate the effects of privilege and disadvantage. They strongly encourage research universities of the future to adhere more intentionally and fully to the principles of diversity and inclusion to maintain public research universities' value of accessibility of education for all.

The response to the call for renewal and change is also evident in the strategic innovations that are being put in place to enhance access to and the affordability of public research universities. While these issues are not new and are of major concern within higher education writ large, the discussions in Chapter 6: *The Iron Triangle Revisited: Re-envisioning Public Research University Financing*, Chapter 7, *Beyond the Walls of Academic: The Role of Engagement*, and Chapter 9, *Public Research Universities in the Metro Nation* bring to the fore the particular challenges that public research universities face. While in many cases, public research universities are required to accept a certain percentage of students from the state, they must do this in context of decreasing state funding and often erratic and uncertain budget scenarios. To ensure stable and adequate funding, public research universities are creating innovative ways of working with their states and other funders to secure financials commitments. They are incorporating strategic initiatives focused on responding to their respective state's needs for research and workforce development. In addition, they are developing creative ways to meet the needs of students who cannot enroll full-time to earn a degree or attend classes during regularly scheduled course times. Public research universities are finding ways to provide online programs that are cheaper than on-campus studies and that are geared towards working or non-traditional students. These programs are sometimes financed through innovative financial models that are also tied to the aforementioned new engagement agenda; these programs are built on university–industry collaborations designed to lead to a better prepared workforce. Public research universities of the future will keep expanding and improving online and cooperative education programs to adjust to the needs of changing student populations and to ensure an adequately trained workforce.

As we noted at the start of this Epilogue, while public research universities are responding to the call to innovate and change, they often struggle to calibrate the right amount of change to implement in light of their prominence as highly respected institutions of higher education. Therefore, it should be no surprise that the last chapter of this volume—Chapter 11,

Competition and Ranking: A Comparative and International Perspective—focuses on rankings. The current ranking systems do not necessarily reward institutions for their innovations or for their effectiveness in responding to societal needs. For public research universities, rankings matter. As the authors of Chapter 11 describe, the indicators used in ranking systems are often those that place high value on investments in the research enterprise and discipline-specific investigations, which in turn, tend to favor the more well-financed and well-endowed private universities and more traditional forms of research. The values of these and other traditional indicators create an uphill challenge for public research universities that face declining state support, a push to increase student access and the development new curricular models, and growing pressure to conduct interdisciplinary, community-partnered research. What might public research universities lose in terms of prestige, prominence, and influence if they shift attention away from traditional practices to innovative practices that are not necessarily valued in the ranking systems? As the authors of Chapter 11 reassure us, public research universities have little to worry about. They assert that no matter the changes that are occurring within and around public research universities, public research universities will prevail and endure as exemplary and highly revered institutions of higher education.

While this volume focuses on America's public research universities, we believe that the issues raised have resonance with other types of higher education systems, both in the United States and abroad. Across the higher education landscape, we hear calls for substantive change and reform. For public research universities, by virtue of their multi-faceted identities as research universities, state-funded universities, global institutions, and publicly accessible institutions, they face several unique challenges in responding to these calls. To be successful, America's public research universities need to find ways to effectively reconcile the pervasive tensions and dilemmas that continue to influence the ways these institutions conduct their work. This requires innovative thinking, distributed leadership, acceptance of expanded ways of knowing, the implementation of new structures and norms of practice, and a broad-based institutional self-awareness that transformation is necessary in order to remain impactful, relevant, and responsive. In essence, it requires both a re-envisioning of the roles, purposes, and potential of the public research university and the implementation of a strategic change agenda that will allow this unique and important institution to retain its influence, effectiveness, and prestige as it strives to successfully meet the challenging and competing demands of a rapidly changing world.

Index